Carthage's Other Wars

Carthaginian Warfare Outside the 'Punic Wars' Against Rome

Dexter Hoyos

Pen & Sword
MILITARY

First published in Great Britain in 2019 by
Pen & Sword Military
An imprint of
Pen & Sword Books Ltd
Yorkshire – Philadelphia

Copyright © Dexter Hoyos 2019

ISBN 978 1 78159 357 8

The right of Dexter Hoyos to be identified as Author of this work has been asserted by him in accordance with the Copyright, Designs and Patents Act 1988.

A CIP catalogue record for this book is
available from the British Library.

All rights reserved. No part of this book may be reproduced or transmitted in any form or by any means, electronic or mechanical including photocopying, recording or by any information storage and retrieval system, without permission from the Publisher in writing.

Printed and bound in the UK by TJ International Ltd, Padstow, Cornwall.

Pen & Sword Books Limited incorporates the imprints of Atlas, Archaeology, Aviation, Discovery, Family History, Fiction, History, Maritime, Military, Military Classics, Politics, Select, Transport, True Crime, Air World, Frontline Publishing, Leo Cooper, Remember When, Seaforth Publishing, The Praetorian Press, Wharncliffe Local History, Wharncliffe Transport, Wharncliffe True Crime and White Owl.

For a complete list of Pen & Sword titles please contact

PEN & SWORD BOOKS LIMITED
47 Church Street, Barnsley, South Yorkshire, S70 2AS, England
E-mail: enquiries@pen-and-sword.co.uk
Website: www.pen-and-sword.co.uk

Or
PEN AND SWORD BOOKS
1950 Lawrence Rd, Havertown, PA 19083, USA
E-mail: Uspen-and-sword@casematepublishers.com
Website: www.penandswordbooks.com

Contents

List of Plates		ix
Maps		ix
Preface and Acknowledgements		xvii
Chapter 1	Sources of knowledge	1
	1. Carthaginian remnants	1
	2. Greek and Latin records	3
Chapter 2	Carthage: city and state	7
	1. Foundation and footprint	7
	2. The Carthaginian republic	10
	3. Trade and business	13
	4. Merchants, landowners, commoners and slaves	14
	5. Friends, neighbours and potential foes	18
Chapter 3	Fleets and armies	23
	1. Carthage's navy	23
	2. The army	25
	3. The defences of Carthage	31
Chapter 4	Early Wars: Malchus to 'King' Hamilcar	33
	1. Malchus: fiction or fact?	33
	2. Malchus: victories, revenge and ruin	34
	3. The Magonids: 'empire' builders?	39
	4. The expedition of 'king' Hamilcar	46
Chapter 5	The Revenge of Hannibal the Magonid	51
	1. The aftermath of Himera	51

	2. A new Sicilian war: the first expedition of Hannibal the Magonid	55
	3. Carthage victorious, 406–05 BC	59
Chapter 6	Carthage against Dionysius and Syracuse	67
	1. Uneasy peace, 405–398	67
	2. Himilco vs Dionysius	69
	3. Mago vs Dionysius	77
	4. Mago and Himilco against Dionysius	80
	5. Last war with Dionysius	88
Chapter 7	Carthage against Timoleon	93
	1. Carthage and the turmoils of Sicily	93
	2. The arrival of Timoleon	95
	3. Sorting out sources	98
	4. The enigma of Mago	100
	5. The battle at the Crimisus	104
	6. Gisco and peace	111
Chapter 8	Carthage against Agathocles	115
	1. The advent of Agathocles	115
	2. Agathocles frustrating Carthage	118
	3. Carthage at war with Agathocles	121
	4. Africa invaded	127
	5. The destruction of Hamilcar	133
	6. The destruction of Ophellas and Bomilcar	135
	7. Agathocles fails in Africa, wins in Sicily	139
	8. The end of the war	144
Chapter 9	The Sicilian stalemate: Pyrrhus and Hiero	149
	1. The woes of post-Agathoclean Sicily	149
	2. The war with Pyrrhus	152
	3. Hiero of Syracuse	156

Chapter 10	Carthage at War in Africa and Spain	161
	1. Libya: subjects and rebels	161
	2. The Truceless War: origins and outbreak	165
	3. Horrors of the Truceless War	171
	4. Carthage's victory	176
	5. Barcid Carthage's Spanish empire	179
Conclusion		187
Abbreviations and Reading		193
Endnotes		201
Index		223

List of Plates

1. Parade armour from Ksour es Saf (near Sousse), Tunisia: bronze breastplate, 4th–3rd centuries BC. (*Wikimedia Commons*)
2. Scale-armour suit (reconstructed), found in Lake Trasimene: probably Roman, possibly from a casualty of the battle in 217 BC. (*Reproduced from* The Armour of Imperial Rome, *by H. Russell Robinson*)
3. Countryside outside Thugga (Dougga), with the Tower of Artaban (a Numidian prince, *circa* 120 BC) on hillside. (*Wikimedia Commons*)
4. View from the 'Hannibal quarter', on the southern slope of Byrsa hill; developed in 190s BC. (*Wikimedia Commons*)
5. Relief portrait of Polybius from Kleitor in the Peloponnese. (*Wikimedia Commons*)
6. View (1958) over Carthage and the headland of Megara (modern La Marsa-Gammarth). (*Wikimedia Commons*)
7. Carthaginian copper alloy coin (fourth century BC?). (*Wikimedia Commons*)
8. Syracusan silver coin, with head of Persephone and dolphins. (*Pinterest*)
9. Stele of Aristion, a Greek hoplite (infantry soldier), made by the sculptor Aristocles *circa* 510 BC. (*Pinterest*)
10. Votive stele at Carthage, dedicated to Baal Hammon and Tanit. (*Wikimedia Commons*)
11. Syracusan silver *decadrachma* (10-drachma coin), *circa* 400 BC. (*Wikimedia Commons*)
12. Supposed head of Agathocles (line-drawing by J.J. Bernouilli, 1886). (*Wikimedia Commons*)
13. Syracusan silver *decadrachma*, *circa* 317–311 BC. (*Wikimedia Commons*)

14. Syracuse, viewed from the Euryalus fortress on Epipolae. (*Wikimedia Commons*)
15. Epipolae plateau, Syracuse. (*Google Earth*)
16. Carthaginian infantrymen on the march: fourth-century BC scarab. (Author's photograph)
17. Barcid-era silver coin, *circa* 221 BC. (Author's photograph)

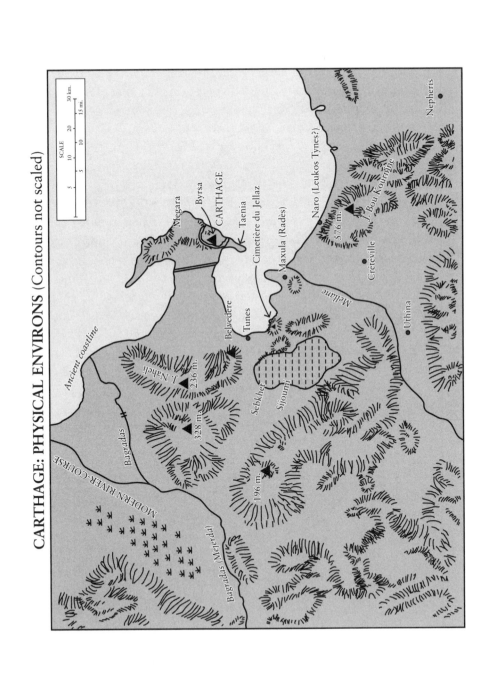
CARTHAGE: PHYSICAL ENVIRONS (Contours not scaled)

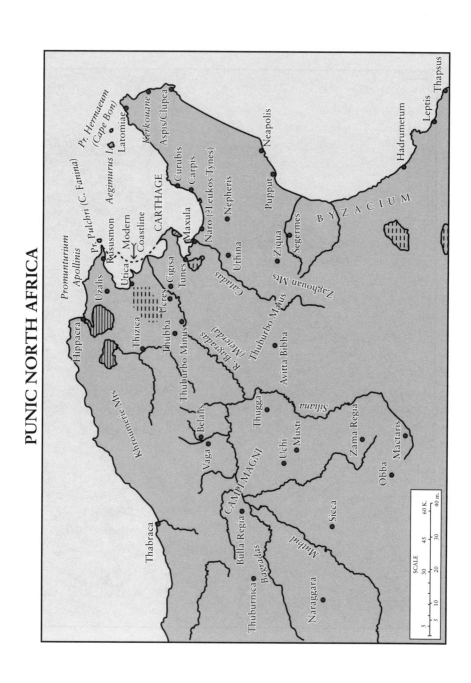

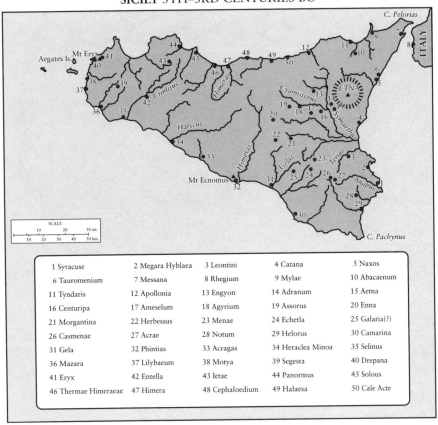

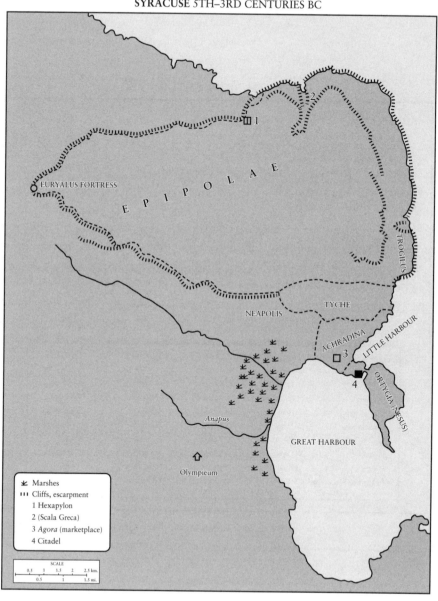

THE WESTERN MEDITERRANEAN 6TH-3RD CENTURIES BC

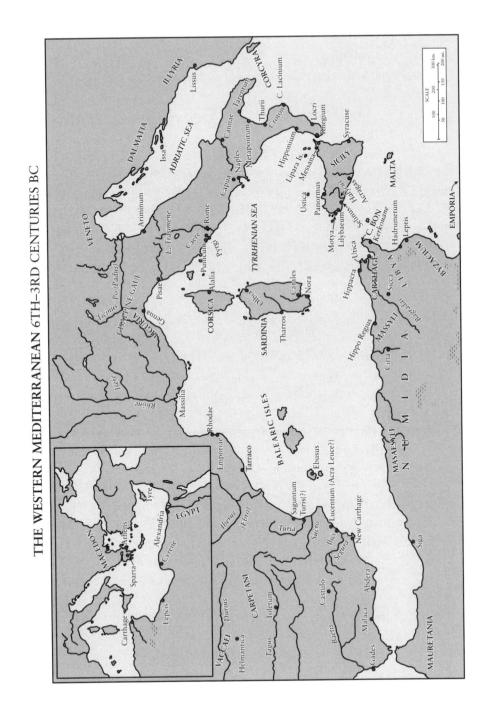

Preface and Acknowledgements

Long before the rise of its future rival Rome, the city-state of Carthage had imposed a broad dominance over many of the coastlands of the western Mediterranean and its islands, from the Gulf of Sirte in North Africa to the edge of the Atlantic and the Phoenician city of Gads in southern Spain. Founded by settlers from Phoenician Tyre not many decades before Rome, Carthage won wealth and seagoing power much earlier. By 500 BC, Carthaginian control, direct or indirect, gripped the other Phoenician-founded cities along the North African coasts, those in the western quarter of Sicily and Sardinia, and – largely through near-monopolistic trade – the Phoenician foundations in southern Spain, called Iberia by Greeks, which were linked to Carthage via small settlements on the coasts of the lands opposite then called Numidia and Mauretania. The city had close commercial and political ties to the vigorous Greek world, especially its thriving colonies in Sicily and southern Italy but also further east; and was developing relations too with other parts of Italy, like Etruria and the city on hills beside the Tiber River. In 509 (the traditional date), Carthage and Rome had made the first of a series of treaties regulating their trade and traders. The Romans called Carthaginians *Poeni* – a Latin form of 'Phoenicians', just as Greeks often used the same name for them – which has given moderns the adjective 'Punic'. This book uses both 'Carthaginian' and 'Punic'.

By 415, the Carthaginians were the wealthiest people known to Sicily's Greeks. Wealth and power did not come effortlessly, nor did keeping it. From the earliest historical records onwards, Carthage is found warring against other states both in its African hinterland, which the Greeks called Libya, and across the Mediterranean. From around 550 BC, the Carthaginians had to wage repeated wars around all their territories – above all, a 200-year duel with the rich and warlike Greek city-states of Sicily. Their neighbours the Libyans, who initially exacted a yearly ground-rent from the settlers from Phoenicia, were themselves later subjected to tribute and conscription. Some wars ended in victory, others in painful defeat, but the Carthaginians' pre-eminence and riches endured. The product of these 'other wars' was a multi-ethnic empire with a Mediterranean-wide trade network.

How that empire was achieved, what sort of people the Carthaginians really were, how they fought their wars, and who were the enemies who challenged them in the centuries before Rome came on the scene, are the themes of this work. They will reveal a Carthage significantly different in policies and achievements from its conventional image.

Acknowledgements

It is a pleasure to express my appreciation for the unwavering support of my publisher, Philip Sidnell, who has tolerated too many revised deadlines from me with gracious patience.

I am grateful, as always, to the University of Sydney for my continuing affiliation as Honorary Associate Professor in the Department of Classics and Ancient History, and to the University's Fisher Library with its impressive range of printed and online resources and its always helpful research services: without these amenities my work would not have been possible. I owe particular thanks to Dr Camilla Norman, of the Australian Archaeological Institute at Athens (AAIA), who transformed my hand-drawn maps into electronically reformed clarity.

Above all I owe special thanks and appreciation to my family for their affectionate support of a husband, father and grandfather whose attention always seems to be focused on matters very distant in space and time. And so I dedicate this book to Jann, Camilla, Anthony, Scarlett and Henry.

Chapter 1

Sources of knowledge

Written accounts of Carthage's wars come almost entirely from Greek and Roman authors: not because the Carthaginians failed to keep records, but because very little of what they wrote remains. Archaeological finds and Punic-language inscriptions throw light on the city and its people, but only a little on its wars or politics: for instance the fragmentary text of a 406 BC treaty with Athens. As a result we depend on reports, often brief or allusive, by ancient authors from Herodotus onwards when their subject-matter deals with the Carthaginians involving themselves in Sicilian or Roman affairs. Most wrote much later on, drawing on previous (and now lost) sources.

1. Carthaginian remnants

The longest Carthaginian text we have is the three-page *Periplus* (sea-voyage) of 'Hanno, king of the Carthaginians', which began as an inscription in one of the city's great temples. In a Greek translation, probably condensed, it records a large expedition through the Strait of Gibraltar and down the west coast of Africa, settling colonists at various sites and then exploring further south. The voyage probably took place between 500 and 450 BC, when Carthage was extending its reach westwards. Who 'Hanno the king' was, why his expedition was sent out, where his colonies were placed and how much further south the fleet sailed are questions perennially debated.[1]

A still shorter Greek text, on a damaged papyrus, supplies a fragment from a history of the Hannibalic war by one of that general's close friends, Sosylus of Sparta. Narrating a sea-battle – a joint Roman and Massilian fleet versus a Carthaginian one – Sosylus makes the only mention we have of the Carthaginians' supposedly favourite naval manoeuvre, called the *diekplous* in Greek. Massilia (Massalia in Greek, Marseilles today) was a flourishing Greek city long in alliance with Rome. Sosylus reports the Massilian squadron countering the *diekplous*, but the fragment does not record where the battle took place or anything of its numbers or commanders.

2 Carthage's Other Wars

Two surviving inscriptions in Punic, the Carthaginians' language, mention historical events – subject to plenty of debate as Punic is not fully understood despite being a descendant of Phoenician. One, very incomplete, commemorates the military expedition to Sicily in 406 BC which captured the major Greek city of Acragas; the other is largely preserved and records how a street, apparently a sizeable one, was built from central Carthage to a 'new gate' by several named officials, seemingly in the fourth or third century.

A few surviving Greek inscriptions supply useful information too. A damaged one of 406 BC records Carthage and Athens striking an alliance (clearly a *pro forma* bond). Another, by contrast, shows the Athenians, only a dozen years later, throwing hopeful flattery on Carthage's foe Dionysius of Syracuse. A lengthy third-century BC chronological table called the Parian Marble, two large parts of which survive, lists selected events in the Greek world between 400 and 298; a few of them concern Sicily. Brief though the information in all these documents is, they have major value as contemporary, or near contemporary, sources, while almost all our other written evidence comes from later informants.[2]

Little of Punic Carthage remains on the ground. Though the Roman sack of the city in 146 BC did leave temples alone amid the ruins (which, incidentally, were not salted), the new Roman city founded by Julius Caesar and Augustus almost entirely replaced the old remnants, over time, with new structures such as the sizeable Antonine Baths complex beside the shore. The great temple of Eshmun, whom the Romans identified with Aesculapius, that had stood on the citadel-hill of Byrsa, was removed – along with the entire top surface of Byrsa – in favour of a temple of Rome and Augustus; this in 1890 became the Cathedral of St Louis (now the Acropolium).

Modern archaeological work at available sites has, however, uncovered some notable features of the Punic city, above all the much-debated children's cemetery (conventionally termed the *tophet*, an Old Testament word), the nearby enclosed harbours – one rectangular, one circular – that were described by the Greek historian Appian, and a sector on the southern slope of Byrsa which was developed as an up-to-date residential and business quarter around 200–190 BC. This and the harbours date to the Punic Wars period, while the *tophet* finds are largely undatable. Material evidence from the age of Carthage's earlier wars consists mainly of objects for religious, commercial or everyday use, along with coins struck from the fourth century on to pay its armies in Sicily. Most surviving Punic texts are on votive items once deposited in cemeteries or temples, naming the deceased person or persons and usually their occupations in life if they had been adults (priest, priestess, carpenter, bow-maker, chariot-maker). While not closely datable, they throw light on Carthage's social and economic makeup over centuries. Military information, though, is thin. For the story of Carthage's other wars and their impact on Carthaginian life and politics, we rely mostly on written and non-Punic sources.[3]

2. Greek and Latin records

The earliest Greek historian, Pericles' contemporary Herodotus of Halicarnassus, had much to say about Carthage's sixth- and fifth-century doings, including Atlantic sea-voyages (though not Hanno's expedition) and, above all, Carthage's first great clash with the Sicilian Greeks in the same year that Xerxes invaded Greece. Herodotus travelled widely in the eastern Mediterranean to gather materials for his seven scroll-books of *Histories*, written in the 440s – the first work to bear that name, Greek for 'inquiries' – and Carthaginians were among his informants. He found Carthage interesting and, implicitly, not too different from Greek states as a trading and military power.

A century after Herodotus, the philosopher Aristotle brought Carthage's political structures into his *Politics*, the sole non-Greek state in the work. Its various comments amount to not much more than an impressionistic sketch: 'kings' (*basileis*) selected, in a way not stated, from eminent families; a 'senate' (*gerousia*) of equally unstated provenance; 'boards of five' (*pentarchiai*) wielding very extensive powers and – puzzlingly – exercising these even before holding office and after it; a high council of 'One Hundred and Four' whose functions are opaque; and the people (*demos*), sometimes consulted and sometimes not. Yet the *Politics* gives more information about how Carthage was governed than all other sources combined.

What we know of its wars before 264 is thanks mainly to Diodorus of Sicily's *Historical Library*, written around the time of Julius Caesar. Of this history of the Mediterranean world down to Diodorus' lifetime (so far as that world was known to Greeks), only Books 1–5 and 11–20 survive complete, though excerpts from the *Library* made in Byzantine times preserve some content from lost books. Diodorus' main interests were wars in Greece and Sicily. Their chequered histories between 480 and 301 are told in Books 11–20 (with intermittent mentions of Rome), and his historical method was to consult and compress a small number of earlier histories – sometimes just one – for a given period and region. He only occasionally favoured his readers with the name of a source he was using.

Diodorus' chief authorities for Carthage's relations with Sicily were Greek: the fourth-century Ephorus, whose very large history of Greece down to his own time included accounts of the Greeks of Sicily (the Siceliots) and Italy, and the long-lived Sicilian Timaeus' ambitious history of that island and its dealings with other lands and peoples, the Carthaginians among them. Ephorus and Timaeus must themselves have drawn on earlier writers, like Antiochus of Syracuse (probably Sicily's and Italy's first historian, around 420 BC) and Philistus – ally, later ex-friend of Dionysius the elder, tyrant (that is, dictator) of Syracuse from 405 to 367 – who in exile wrote a history of Sicily and especially of Dionysius' part in it.

Diodorus reported western events unevenly. He wrote in detail of Carthage's invasion of Sicily in 480, its later campaigns there from 409 and the first half of Dionysius' long rule (down to 387), then its mid-fourth century Sicilian wars (350s to 330s) and above all the spectacular, murderous and paradoxical upheavals of Sicily and North Africa in the era of Agathocles of Syracuse (spanning the 320s to 306). Contrastingly, most of fifth-century Sicilian history he recorded thinly, and so too Dionysius' final decades; perhaps the exiled Philistus lost some of his interest. Since Book 20 is the last full book to survive, later Sicilian and Carthaginian events crop up only in the extracts made 1,000 years later in Byzantine times.

A friend of Cicero's, Cornelius Nepos, composed sketchy biographies of twenty-two 'illustrious foreign generals' including Dion, Syracuse's liberator from the son and successor of Dionysius in the 350s, and Timoleon of Corinth who, twenty years after Dion, liberated Greek Sicily from all its various tyrants and from Carthaginian domination. Very brief (*Dion* takes 10 paragraphs, *Timoleon* five) and necessarily simplified, the sketches do not add much to the fuller records by Diodorus and the Greek philosopher-essayist Plutarch. Even shorter (three paragraphs) is his résumé of Carthage's third-century empire-builder Hamilcar Barca, father of her most famous general Hannibal.

Another of Diodorus' contemporaries, Pompeius Trogus, a learned Roman from southern Gaul, wrote a quasi-world history of his own in forty-four books called *Philippic Histories*. This survived Roman times only in a later abbreviated version by one Justin and in a separate, short contents list called *Prologues*. Justin's *Epitome* of Trogus became one of the Middle Ages' most popular Latin books. Unusual in giving Rome meagre attention, Trogus focused on Greek, Macedonian and Hellenistic affairs, and he also supplied a noteworthy account of Carthage's origins. Like Diodorus, he then mentioned Carthage mainly when narrating Sicily's endemic wars. At the same time, he (or else his epitomator) could make odd mistakes: at one point the *Epitome* proffers a 'Leonidas, brother of the king of the Spartans', in command of Sicilian Greek resistance to Carthage around 490, a plain impossibility (see Chapter 4 below). Justin must therefore be used with care.

Around AD 100, the Greek philosopher-essayist Plutarch contributed to what we know of Carthage's involvement in Sicily between 360 and 270 BC with three biographies in his *Parallel Lives* series. One deals with Dion, another with Timoleon and the third with Pyrrhus, whose tumultuous life (spent largely outside his kingdom of Epirus) included an expedition in 278–76 to lead the Siceliots against Carthaginian assaults. Plutarch's focus being Greek and Roman, events are rarely seen from Carthage's viewpoint. But he followed contemporary or near-contemporary sources such as letters to Dion from Plato, a history by a Syracusan friend of Dion's named Athanis or Athanas, and Ephorus and Timaeus (all of them, typically, he mentions only now and again).

Other writers occasionally had things to say about Carthage before its Roman wars. Plato's letters to Dion (*Epistles* 7 and 8) are probably genuine, discussing mainly Sicilian politics and philosophic principles. Polybius, the second-century BC Greek observer, participant and historian of Mediterranean events during Rome's rise to dominance, included translated texts of Carthage's earliest treaties with Rome – generally dated to 509, 348 (or 306) and 279/78 – which among other topics dealt with trade in Carthage's western Sicilian territories. He also wrote a concisely riveting account of the 'Truceless War' of 241–37, when Carthage came near to ruin at the hands of its rebel mercenaries and Libyan subjects (his narrative indirectly inspired Gustave Flaubert's famous novel *Salammbô*). Polybius recorded this war, one of the few fought by Carthage that did not involve Greek Sicily or Rome, partly to remind his Hellenistic Greek readers how dangerous it was to employ and then not pay professional troops, partly too to illustrate the moral differences between how civilized states like Carthage and uncivilized hordes like the rebels behaved under extreme stress, and partly to help explain why Carthage twenty years later found itself entering a second war with Rome.

Scattered items of information and misinformation occur in other Greek and Latin works. Plautus' comedy *Poenulus*, 'the little Carthaginian' – a non-rancorous farce featuring a bumbling Punic merchant – was staged less than a decade after Hannibal's War ended. How Carthage and its wealthy Greek neighbour Cyrene fixed their shared boundary sometime in the sixth century was told (in a semi-legendary version) by Sallust, Julius Caesar's first governor of newly annexed Numidia. A fairly short overview of pre-Roman Carthage and its territories in Libya (today the northern half of Tunisia) was given by the Augustan Greek Strabo in his *Geography*. Something is known of Punic farming and estate managment because an admired twenty-eight-book encyclopaedia on agriculture by one Mago was among the sources used by the Roman agronomist Columella writing around AD 60.[4]

Anecdotes from Carthaginian history – not always plausible – were included by authors relaying tales of past famous personalities or military stratagems, such as Valerius Maximus' early-first-century AD collection of *Famous Deeds and Sayings* in nine books (another medieval favourite) and the compilations of military *Stratagems* written by the Roman Frontinus around AD 100 and the Greek Polyaenus sixty years later. Scattered, and not always accurate, items about Carthage apart from its Roman wars are to be found in plenty of other authors, like Polyaenus' contemporary Appian of Alexandria, the third-century AD historian Cassius Dio and his Byzantine epitomator Zonaras, and even St Augustine's friend Orosius in his history of pre-Christian world calamities.

Classical writers did not hold a uniform, still less a uniformly hostile, view of Carthage. Plautus' 'little Carthaginian' Hanno is an unthreateningly hapless elderly merchant trying to find his kidnapped daughters, and *Poenulus*' love-struck hero is a handsome young Carthaginian (though with a Greek name). More seriously, Carthage's alleged rites of child sacrifice were mentioned by various authors, sometimes with vivid details and suitable disgust (notably Diodorus and Plutarch – but not Herodotus, Aristotle, Polybius, Strabo or Appian). Plutarch, too, wrote an acrid and much-quoted censure of the Carthaginians of old in one of his philosophical essays: 'they are bitter, sullen and subservient to their magistrates', he wrote, making a direct contrast with his image of the virtuous and cheerful men of Athens.

Yet the items and the disgust do not permeate broader ancient accounts of Carthaginian events, society and personalities. Herodotus was intrigued by Punic maritime ventures and impressed by Hamilcar, leader of the expedition into Sicily in 480; he also tells us that Hamilcar's mother was a lady from Syracuse and that Gelon, the Syracusan leader who defeated him, had a wife very well-disposed to Carthage. Aristotle put the Carthaginians' political system on a par with those of many Greek states. Cato the Censor admired Hamilcar Barca (the famous Hannibal's father) as much as he did Pericles and Themistocles. They all knew that there was more to Carthage and its people than the notion, still popular, of a dark and money-grubbing oriental society.[5]

Chapter 2

Carthage: city and state

1. Foundation and footprint

Carthage was a city made for trade. Sited on a small peninsula in the Gulf of Tunis, guarded on its northern side by the broad headland called Megara and watched from across the gulf by the much greater peninsula of Cape Bon, the city lay almost exactly halfway along the long maritime route between the ancestral motherland Phoenicia and the Strait of Gibraltar. Though not the oldest colony founded by Phoenicians (Gades in south-west Spain claimed that honour), Carthage became the richest and most populous of all their colonies within a couple of centuries, with commercial and religious links crossing the entire Mediterranean. This inevitably meant coming to blows with neighbours and rivals.

The Sicilian Greek historian Timaeus dated the foundation to 'the thirty-eighth year before the first Olympiad' – thus 814/13 – according to the Augustan-era author Dionysius of Halicarnassus: not a date to be taken simply on trust, for Timaeus also dated Rome to the same year (six decades earlier than anyone else). However, archaeological finds have brought Carthage's founding to the latter part of the ninth century, against supposed later dates. The city's traditional foundation-tale is famous: when Dido, a princess of Tyre, fled to North Africa to escape her murderous royal brother Pygmalion the local Libyans permitted her and her followers to found a settlement on the peninsula's Byrsa hill which they called New City, *Qart-Hadascht*. Dido later slew herself rather than be forced to wed and therefore become the vassal of the neighbouring Libyan king – or in Virgil's chronologically mixed retelling, after being seduced and abandoned by the wandering Trojan prince Aeneas, ancestor of Rome's founders Romulus and Remus.

Though generally taken to be mere myth, the tale's core brings us a woman founder – a very rare item in ancient foundation stories – fleeing from a Tyrian king named Pygmalion, first to Cyprus for succour and then on to North Africa. 'Dido' was an epithet bestowed on her again by Timaeus: her alternative name in the stories is Elissa, most likely the Phoenician Elishat, 'woman of Cyprus' (that island's Phoenician name was

Alashiya). Pygmalion of Tyre was real. He ruled his city from 831–785 – or 820–774 by another reckoning – and a gold pendant found close to Byrsa hill apparently names him: in ninth-century Phoenician lettering, its legend hails the goddess Astarte and also Pygmalion, and its owner Yadomilk, son of Pidiya, declares that Pygmalion (*Pgmlyn*) 'armed him' or 'rescued him'. This does not show that Pygmalion was Carthage's true founder. Elissa/Dido was accompanied by many leading Tyrians (among them, Livy wrote in a lost book, the admiral 'Bitias', in Phoenician Pidiya); and a solid gold ornament was something to be prized – and bequeathed to descendants – even if its owner had deserted his old ruler for a new one.[1]

'New City' was a functional name. There were others among Phoenician Mediterranean settlements – one in Cyprus, another in Sardinia and even one 80km south-west of Carthage: Greeks and Romans called it Neapolis, which means the same (modern Nabeul on the gulf of Hammamet). When in 228 BC the famous Hannibal's brother-in-law Hasdrubal founded his own city in southern Spain, he would give it exactly that name, even if for clarity the Romans came to call it New Carthage (today, Cartagena).

Elissa's city began quite small. From Byrsa eastward to the shore is only half a kilometre; from the citadel hill northward, an arc of other low hills, rising gradually to the high and broad plateau of Megara (now La Marsa and Gammarth), was used for numerous burial-grounds. Much of Megara itself later became a lovingly cultivated expanse of gardens, orchards and comfortable country villas; the city's walled defences were extended to it only centuries later.

South of Byrsa, flat marshy terrain spread down to the edge of what is now called the lake of Tunis, a broad inlet with a narrow entrance from the Gulf outside. A channel running up from the lake to the southern side of Carthage was dug, probably in the fourth century, to let merchant ships row up to docks to deliver and take on goods – a testimony to the expansive wealth and trade of the city by then. Carthage's famous hidden harbours, still visible just beside the eastern shoreline, came still later. As prosperity and population grew, so did Carthage's size and amenities. The eastern shoreline gained massive fortifications during the fifth century, large warehouses and residences filled the urban area and Megara developed its villas and orchards.

Byrsa held a great temple dedicated to the god Eshmun, whom Greeks and Romans equated with their healing god Asclepius/Aesculapius. Reached by a broad staircase of sixty steps, strongly fortified, it will have been visible from afar like its current successor the Acropolium. Below it and near the sea walls stood the temple of Reshef, a Phoenician-Punic god identified with Apollo. This came to be covered entirely with sheets of gold – Appian reported how Roman soldiers sacking Carthage in 146 BC hacked so avidly at these that some even lost a hand in the frenzy. Other Carthaginian deities, especially Baal Hamon, Tanit his consort (called 'Tanit Face-of-Baal' on many inscriptions), Tyre's Melqart and Astarte and Egypt's Isis will also have had temples. In 396, Greek Sicily's patron goddesses Demeter and Kore-Persephone also received a shrine in the city to avert a plague brought back from Sicily. Everything would be obliterated by the Romans, either in the sack or later. As mentioned earlier, when Augustus refounded the city as a Roman colony he even had the entire top of Byrsa shaved off to accommodate a new temple for Roman gods.

Carthaginian culture from early times was equally open to foreign influences. Grave goods and other site-finds include statuettes, reliefs on stone, miniature shrines and temples, ornaments and sculptures based on Egyptian and Greek models. When coins began to be struck, late in the fifth century, they borrowed motifs – and perhaps mint-masters – from Greek Sicily and the eastern Greek world. One of the most splendid finds from pre-Roman North Africa is a two-piece set of bronze armour, probably third-century in date: one armourplate for the chest and one for the back, plus accompanying shoulder straps, all intricately embossed with the heads of Gorgons and animals and floral motifs. Found in the countryside near Hadrumetum (Sousse) and surely meant for ceremonial use, not battle, by a wealthy officer, it gaudily reflects southern Italian Greek art styles, and recalls too the hauls of gorgeous Carthaginian equipment which in 341 took Timoleon's troops two days to collect after their crushing victory at Sicily's River Crimisus.[2]

Though Elissa/Dido and her followers were Phoenicians from Tyre and the Carthaginians always kept close links with their mother-city, the common notion that they remained a profoundly Near Eastern people and culture is flawed. When Dionysius, tyrant of Syracuse, planned war against Carthage in 398, he made preparations on a huge scale because, Diodorus' source noteworthily affirmed, he knew that 'he was entering a struggle with the most powerful people of Europe' – not of Asia or Africa. To Greeks, Carthage was a far from alien (even if not closely akin) culture, which by then was widely influenced by theirs.

On at least one occasion, around 362, we find a delegation of Carthaginians travelling to Delphi to consult the Pythian oracle there. Nor could the city-state have grown in population simply through a constant stream of

Phoenician migrants over centuries (there is no evidence of these). Sources both inscriptional and literary reveal Carthaginians with links to the outside world and immigrants from there to Carthage. It was mentioned above that Hamilcar, the grim commander of the Sicilian expedition of 480, had a Syracusan mother, and the Syracusan Dion who liberated his city from tyranny in 357 had a Carthaginian guest-friend, 'Synalus' – Greek for Eshmunhalos – who helped him at a crucial early stage of his venture. Dion actually had plentiful contacts at Carthage, which eventually got him into trouble. Later, two enterprising Punic officers busy in Sicily around 212–11 were grandsons of a Syracusan soldier who had settled in Carthage and even bore Greek names, Hippocrates and Epicydes.[3]

That Carthaginians could legally marry spouses from other Phoenician colonies is attested by Diodorus. That they married wives or husbands from Libyan communities too – legally or not – can scarcely be doubted. They certainly formed marriage links with peoples further west, as Hamilcar Barca's family illustrates from 240 on. He gave, or promised to give, a daughter to the regional Numidian lord Naravas as a reward for the latter's armed support; one of his granddaughters later married two of Naravas' royal kinsmen in turn. In the 220s, both Hamilcar's son-in-law and his famous son, Hannibal, wedded Spanish wives. More famously, Naravas' kinsman Masinissa briefly wedded the beautiful young Carthaginian aristocrat Sophoniba in 203 – snatching her from his fallen rival Syphax – before liquidating her at the behest of his new patron Scipio Africanus. In a sharp historical irony, one of Carthage's most resolute generals in its final war with Rome was the grandson, through his mother, of its relentless enemy, the same Masinissa.

2. The Carthaginian republic

This resourcefully multicultural city-state was, at least during its later centuries, a republic. It probably began as a monarchy if the story of Elissa/Dido is more than mere myth; but its fifth-century 'king' Hamilcar was actually an elected official: according to Justin he had held eleven terms as 'dictator' by 480, which suggests not kingship but a limited though powerful magistracy. Hanno, 'king of the Carthaginians', the protagonist of the fifth-century *Periplus* mentioned earlier, can be seen as another such magistrate. He may have belonged to Carthage's then politically dominant family the Magonids. In the same way the later Magonid leaders Hannibal and then Himilco, each described by Diodorus as 'king under the laws', are each termed *rab* – 'leader' or 'head' – on the inscription that Himilco set up to mark their deeds: not as *malik*, 'king'. They all, in fact, can be seen as sufetes – a magistracy which down to the mid-fourth century probably also exercised military power.

Its proper Punic title was *shophet*, 'judge' (*špṭ* when transliterated), a long-established title in the ancient Near East, most famously borne by Israel's 'judges' in the Old Testament. It was Latinized as *sufes*, plural *sufetes*, by Livy and several Punic-descended cities in Roman North Africa – though this did not deter some other ancient authors from calling the sufete a 'king' (in Greek *basileus*, Latin *rex*). Normally, in later centuries anyway, two were elected each year, like the consuls at Rome (with whom *sufetes* were sometimes compared).

A Punic votive inscription of the early fifth century seems to date itself to 'the twentieth', or even 'the one hundred and twentieth', year of 'the rule of *sufetes*' – the text is unfortunately damaged. Then Aristotle, sketching the Carthaginian political system a century-and-a-half later, termed the chief magistrates 'kings' but made it clear that they were elected for a fixed term. Not many decades after Aristotle, in 279, a Carthaginian named 'Iomilkos' – that is, Himilco – in a dedication on the sacred Aegean island of Delos called himself 'king' (*basileus*): he again must have meant the chief magistracy.

Both Aristotle and later Polybius saw virtues in Carthage's republican system. Political office required personal merit and distinguished ancestry, and was unsalaried. Officials were regularly elected by the citizens; a council of elders (the *adirim* or 'great men') advised the *sufetes* and could direct affairs in collaboration with them. After about the mid-fourth century, warfare was entrusted to separately elected generals holding command until victory or failure. In turn the powerful judiciary called the One Hundred and Four – Carthage's 'highest authority', according to Aristotle – supervised both these generals (often crucifying the ones who failed) and probably also the other state executives. Ordinary adult male citizens, meeting in their formal assembly, the *ham* ('the people'), had a role both limited and broad. When the *sufetes* and senate agreed on an action, the *ham* was bypassed; but if a proposal did come to it, the citizens had total freedom to discuss and decide.

Less admirable to Aristotle was that to hold office a Carthaginian had to possess wealth no less than merit, and that it was common to hold more than one office simultaneously. To Polybius it was deplorable that by Hannibal's time ordinary Carthaginians had too much say in affairs: 'the common people had become the dominant political force' (though neither he nor other sources recorded any example of this excess). Both writers were uneasy at Carthaginians' cheerful unconcern about using office to make more money. For Polybius, it was an unseemly contrast with puritanical Roman abstemiousness.

Day-to-day administration (according to Aristotle) was run by five-man boards, but his description of these 'pentarchies' is fuzzy. How many of them existed is not stated, nor who qualified to be a member. Members were not elected: vacancies were filled by co-opting new members. By some process the pentarchies – whether some or all is unclear – appointed the judges in the court of One Hundred and Four. Still more remarkably flexible, pentarchies also judged lawsuits (presumably ones not dealt with by the highest court) and – most opaquely of all – 'they are in power after they have gone out of office and before they have actually entered upon it.' This dictum must refer to individual pentarchy members, but is no clearer for that. In reality, Carthaginian inscriptions mention administrative bureaus of ten, twenty or thirty, but none of five. These bureaus may have been subdivided for various tasks or, at least as likely, Aristotle not only compressed what he had been told but garbled it.

The head of a bureau is called a *rab* in inscriptions, an all-purpose title (plural *rabim*). The chief priest of Carthage was the *rab kohanim*, 'chief of the priests' (the vowels are approximate; Punic, like Phoenician and Hebrew, did not write them), the head of finance was the *rab mehashbim* (chief of the accountants) and a 'general' was suitably *rab mahanet*, 'chief of the soldiers'. The unique military inscription of the generals Hannibal and Himilco, commemorating the capture of Acragas in Sicily in 406, terms them *rabim*. *Rab* may have been used still more widely as an honorific term (by senators, for example), given the many epitaphs and dedications by Carthaginians who put it after their names. The same inscription, for example, calls each general's father a *rab* too.

In spite of the limitations he himself noted, Aristotle gave Carthage's constitution the highest accolade: unlike some others, it cultivated not only wealth and virtue but also the good of its people – for him the definition of an 'aristocratic' polity, one governed by the best men, the *aristoi*. He was not the only Greek offering praise. His contemporary, the Athenian writer Isocrates, put Carthage (for rather different reasons) on a par with authoritarian Sparta as the best-governed state in the world. Polybius would make a similar comparison for the Carthage of pre-Hannibalic times. It was an enthusiasm all the more remarkable in view of the many centuries of Carthaginian warfare against their fellow-Greeks in Sicily.[4]

3. Trade and business

Carthage's wealth came reputedly from seaborne trade. Hanno's *Periplus* illustrated the city's ambitious reach into the Atlantic, and Herodotus attested how Carthaginian merchants bartered goods for gold on the West African coast. They would set their goods out on a particular beach and return to their ships; the locals would come, put down an amount of gold, and withdraw; and if the traders judged the gold a fair payment, they would take it. If not, they waited aboard ship for more to be put down, and so on until both sides were satisfied – neither seeking to defraud the other, Herodotus stressed.[5]

Carthaginian traders also ventured northward from the Strait of Gibraltar, especially seeking tin from the lands at the north-western edge of Europe. The first to visit these was a mariner named Himilco, dated by Pliny the Elder to the same generation as Hanno the seafarer. Himilco's voyage (real or supposed) along Europe's Atlantic coasts survives, rather bizarrely, only in mentions by a fourth-century AD Latin poet, one Avienus. The trip took Himilco as far as the Cassiterides islands, called Oestrymnides by Greeks, generally thought to be the Scillies off Cornwall. The dwellers there traded tin and lead for salt and other goods, a trade so valued by the Gaditanes and Carthaginians, Strabo claimed, that they did everything they could to keep other merchants from finding the route.

To ease westward voyages, the Phoenicians and then Carthaginians dotted Africa's western Mediterranean coastlands with small harbour towns like Chullu, now Collo in Algeria, Tipasa (Tefased), Icosium (Algiers), and further west Rusaddir (Melilla) and Tingi (Tangiers). Spain's southern coasts had plenty of long-established Phoenician settlements, Malaca and Gades especially, which enjoyed flourishing relations with Carthage. At some early date, the small island of Ebusus (Ibiza) off south-eastern Spain fell under Carthage's own rule to become another prosperous centre. Despite the efforts at deterring foreign competitors, Greek merchants had busy and productive relations with southern Spain from early on: Herodotus recorded sixth-century traders from Samos and Phocaea in the Aegean earning impressive profits from Tartessus, the silver-mining culture north of Gades.

Equally or more important to Carthage were the great islands to its north: Sardinia, Corsica and Sicily. Carthage's Phoenician forebears had planted settlements in Sardinia such as Carales (Cagliari), Nora and Tharros, traded with the Corsicans, and in western Sicily colonised the island stronghold of Motya just north of modern Marsala, the port of Panormus (Palermo) – its Phoenician name was Sys – and Solous nearby. These and the areas around them came under Carthage's dominance during the sixth century, the product of its first overseas wars. In the same era, but rather less forcibly, Carthage made itself mistress of the coastlands – some fertile, some desolate – of the Gulf of Sirte to the east, up to the territory of the Greek colony of Cyrene.

Foreign peoples and states in North Africa and beyond were busy trading partners as well. Carthage's imported Egyptian artworks and architectural borrowings indicate regular contacts, just as it always kept commercial and religious links with Tyre in the motherland. The Sicilian Greeks were not only repeated opponents in war but also regular collaborators and competitors in commerce. There was friction between Syracuse and Carthage over 'ports', unspecified, as early as the 490s, while throughout the fifth century the city imported massive quantities of olives from Acragas.

Carthage also had trading and diplomatic ties further north and east. The Carthaginians teamed up with Etruscan states against troublesome Greek colonists in Corsica in the 540s, and as already mentioned made commercial treaties with Rome, usually dated to around 509 and 348. These set out regulations that mostly bound Roman merchants: for example listing territories and coasts they could and could not approach, laying down rules for them when doing business with Carthaginians and guaranteeing that Carthage would not attack Italian coastal cities allied to Rome. From early times too Rome itself had a street or sector called the Vicus Africus, the 'African quarter', as it did a Vicus Tuscus (the 'Etruscan quarter'), probably streets where traders and visitors from such places lodged. Aristotle noted that the Carthaginians, Etruscans and other peoples had standard agreements with one another to regulate business and military relationships. Indeed, a Greek inscription set up around 360, though now lost, heaped praise and privileges on a Carthaginian named 'Nobas' – his actual name was probably Hannibal – for his benefactions to Boeotia, the federation north of Athens.[6]

4. Merchants, landowners, commoners and slaves

The standard image of the city as a merchant oligarchy, like medieval Venice or later the Dutch Republic, is nevertheless mistaken. Every Carthaginian leader whose background or connections are known was a landed aristocrat first and foremost, like the failed coup-maker Hanno in

Aristotle's time, whose last refuge was a strongpoint manned by thousands of his slaves, and Rome's ex-enemy Hannibal, who had a coastal estate near Thapsus just south of today's Monastir. Hannibal's father, Hamilcar Barca, had few maritime interests either. He spent most of his adult life as a military commander, developed Carthage's land empire in Spain and, like his successors in command, paid so little attention to its naval power that the start of the second war with Rome found the navy damagingly enfeebled. It is not very likely that, like Venice and the Dutch, a Punic merchant aristocracy left warfare to landowners. For long periods the republic itself was run by powerful military families: almost certainly, therefore, its landed magnates dominated affairs, if with merchant kinsmen in support. Carthage became famous for its territories' prosperity – the admiration that these excited in Greek invaders in 310 and Roman invaders in 256 is on record – and then for Mago's detailed encyclopedia on farming.

As we shall see, it was not until the fifth century that the city acquired much territory in Libya itself, but from then on its reach expanded. By 240, Carthage dominated the lands westward to about the line of today's northern Tunisian-Algerian border. Of these, the city directly annexed only its immediate hinterland and the fertile Cape Bon peninsula, enough (Polybius wrote) to produce the food and goods needed by Carthage itself. The once-independent Libyan communities in the lands watered by the region's rivers – the Bagradas, Muthul, Siliana and Catadas – and in the uplands between them kept their autonomy but paid tribute, often onerous, to Carthage and had to supply manpower for its wars.

According to Aristotle, Carthage's oligarchy every so often chose to soothe discontent at home by sending out Carthaginians, no doubt needy ones, 'to the cities' to enrich them. We are not told how often this was done, nor which cities found themselves hosting needy newcomers, or how these became rich. If the policy was as successful as is implied, the Libyan hinterland (not to mention Utica, Hippou Acra, Hadrumetum and other sister-colonies under Punic hegemony) must in time have become closely linked to Carthage's own population, society and culture. Yet even so, Carthage's hegemony was often oppressive and the Libyans repeatedly rose in revolt against it.

Inscriptions over the centuries commemorated Carthaginians' varied callings and professions: bowmakers, chariot-makers, carpenters, fullers, butchers and other working-class men; and at higher social levels, merchants, goldsmiths, urban engineers, priests and priestesses (like Hannabaal, priestess of Kore the Greek goddess), not to mention generals and *sufetes*.

How mobile or rigid social relations were among Carthaginians is hard to pin down. Aristocrats were proud of their heritage: on some surviving inscriptions, dedicants list their fathers and paternal ancestors over four, six or even more generations. The Barcid Hannibal claimed descent from Elissa/Dido's own brother, or so the Roman poet Silius Italicus claimed in his epic on Hannibal's war.

Carthaginians' reported money-making ardour and widening territorial expansion would no doubt have opened the way for some new men, merchants as well as landowners, to climb the social hierarchy and join older-established aristocratic families. Inevitably, some of these in turn would lose members over time, via impoverishment or extinction (as happened for instance to the early Roman Republic's patrician houses, over much the same era). The powerful family of the Magonids, for instance, dominated Carthage's affairs for a century-and-a-half but disappeared from the historical record after 396.

For lesser folk, there are only intriguing glimpses on inscriptions of status changes: for instance, a cloth-worker named Gry (Garay or Guray), who termed himself the slave, or employee, of one Hanno but could also afford his own tomb; and one Hannobaal, who returned to work for his old master 'of his own free will' – using his personal seal to register the new agreement. Though both men were probably ex-slaves, their relationship to their old masters was obviously more than just passive dependence. For one thing, it looks as though they were now Carthaginian citizens, and they had also become men of some means, even if moderate by the standards of a *rab* or a Magonid.

As in every ancient society, slaves were plentiful. The traitor Hanno, around 350 BC, had some thousands – even if Justin's '20,000' must be an exaggeration – and a century later the Romans invading Carthage's home territories liberated the same number of enslaved war-captives working in the fields. Supposedly they rescued others, especially Roman and Italian PoWs, on their return in 204. The Carthaginians acquired slaves through purchase as well as war, though the only direct mention is Appian's unsupported claim that, at the last gasp of the Second Punic War, they bought 5,000 as oarsmen for the fleet (which was playing little part in operations by then, all the same). When Rome forced a new war on Carthage in 149, there were enough slaves in the city to make freeing them worthwhile and so strengthen the available manpower. A freed slave could (it seems) become a citizen, probably if some conditions were met, even if, as usual, details are thin. Certainly Gry the cloth-worker, Hannobaal and their ilk bore Punic names, wrote in Punic, and had a degree of independence: all of which suggests that, even if they had been slaves, they could become Carthaginians at some stage.

How big Carthage's population was in any period is far from clear. The city covered some 140 acres (57 hectares) in the sixth century, and perhaps three times that by the time the wars with Rome started in the mid-third century. Strabo the geographer reported that in 149 there were '700,000 people in the city' – a physical impossibility, but his figure (whether Strabo realised it or not) may well have referred to city and territory together, and to both men and women. Even so, it may be an exaggerated estimate, like his added claim that Carthage was still ruling 300 Libyan cities in 149. Both estimates would more plausibly fit the start of the First or Second Punic War, times when the whole of Rome's territory in Italy had 250,000–300,000 male citizens and therefore a total Roman population (men and women) roughly the same as Strabo's figure. What the population of Carthage's allied and subject territories was around 300 BC – in Libya, western Sicily and Sardinia – remains unknown, but between three and five times its own size would be a passable estimate.

Carthaginian names merit a mention. Punic inscriptions record several hundred, all of them – men's and women's – of religious import. Down the centuries, nonetheless, the ruling elite were content with a dozen or so: Hannibal (probably meaning 'Baal's grace') is the most famous example, and others in their Greek forms – the standard ancient and modern usage – were Adherbal ('mighty is Baal'), Bomilcar (Bodmilqart, 'servant of Melqart'), Carthalo (Qarthalos, 'Melqart has saved me'), Hanno ('divine grace'), Hamilcar (Abdmilqart, 'servant of Melqart'), Hasdrubal ('my help is Baal') and Himilco ('my brother is Melqart'). Sophoniba, one of Carthage's few famous women, was in fact Saponbaal, usually translated as 'Baal has judged' but more likely 'my refuge is Baal'.

With the names of *sufetes*, generals and other aristocrats very largely limited to this dozen or so – the enigmatic 'Malchus' in the sixth century BC is a rare exception – the Carthaginians themselves attached nicknames to some to specify them. The recorded examples are nearly all from the third and second centuries, with Hamilcar Barca, the famous Hannibal's father, being the best-known (the Punic Baraq apparently meant 'thunderbolt' or 'lightning-flash'). In telling the story of Carthage, its wars and its leaders, modern writers do at times have to make slightly repetitive clarifications.[7]

5. Friends, neighbours and potential foes

During its long history Carthage went to war with every one of its non-Phoenician neighbours, with the sole exception of Egypt. The neighbours varied in language, social and economic practices, religion and techniques of war. Carthage's Phoenician sister-colonies along the north and east coasts of Libya, like Hippou Acra (today's Bizerte), Utica, Hadrumetum (Sousse) and Leptis (Lamta), shared the same language, religion and no doubt social forms as their hegemon, and held a special relationship with Carthage, including the right of intermarriage. Their occasional collective name in Greek and Roman sources, Libyphoenicians, suggests that they too intermarried with their Libyan neighbours – but as the name was never applied to Carthaginians it has a slight hint of disdain, and the only Libyphoenician known to history, a Hannibalic War cavalry general called Muttines, was so disdainfully treated by his less competent Carthaginian superior in Sicily that he eventually joined the Romans.

The native Libyans were the most easterly of the peoples who extended across the North African lands now called the Maghreb, between the Mediterranean and the edge of the Sahara desert. Farmers and small traders who lived in or around villages and a few larger towns, once subdued by Carthage they underwent regular taxation, often heavy during Carthage's wars (see Chapter 10), and had to provide fighting men for their hegemon's armies. When Strabo claimed that in 149 BC Punic-ruled Libya – a region by then much smaller than a century before – still consisted of 300 'cities', he must have included villages and hamlets, but Libya was certainly populous in Carthage's time, as well as under later Roman rule.[8]

Numidia lay further west, its hills, mountains and valleys more or less matching today's northern Algeria, and its language the forerunner of modern Tamazigh, spoken by the Numidians' descendants the Berbers. Thinly spread across their broad country, Numidians were a blend of settled farmers and more mobile pastoralists: it was the latter who prompted the Greek name for the entire people, *nomades*, meaning 'pasturers'. Until larger political units formed during the third century BC, the Numidians were a profusion of small communities with few (if any) towns. Their later capital, Cirta, on its fortress-like site in the east (Constantine today), and Siga, near modern Oran on the coast 900km to the west, both earn first mention only in Hannibal's time, while the little trading ports along its coasts were Phoenician or Carthaginian. Numidia was especially valuable to Carthage for its small and tough horses and their skilled riders, recruited as the best cavalry in Carthaginian armies, and the elephants captured in its forests. On the other hand, the Numidians sometimes gave trouble, raiding Punic territory for plunder or resisting Punic efforts to force greater control over them. The dichotomy persisted through all of Carthage's history.

Outside Africa, Carthage's most important, intransigent and ingenious neighbours were the Sicilian Greeks. Settlers from the Greek homeland began to arrive there in the eighth century (well after the Phoenicians), part of the Mediterranean-wide diaspora that between about 750 and 500 BC planted Greeks on coastlands from the north-western Mediterranean to Asia Minor and the Crimea. Most colonising expeditions were despatched not from city-states later dominant in Greece such as Athens, Sparta, Thebes or Argos – Corinth was the exception – but from other seagoing cities like Chalcis and Eretria on the island of Euboea, Corinth's neighbour Megara, Naxos and Rhodes in the Aegean, and Miletus and Phocaea in Ionia on the western shore of Asia Minor. In Sicily, starting with Naxos' foundation of a colony with the same name on the east coast in 734, one settlement after another followed: notably Syracuse, founded by Corinth in 733, and Leontini and Catana soon after by the founders of Naxos. Messana (originally called Zancle), on the tip of the island opposite the toe of Italy, was founded by Greeks already established in Italy, while settlers from Rhodes and Crete established Gela on the south coast.

These colonies prospered – so much so that within a few decades some were themselves able to found new cities. Camarina was created by the Syracusans not far from Gela; Messana established both Mylae, on the neighbouring Milazzo peninsula, and, much further west, Himera on the coast close to Phoenician Panormus. Megara Hyblaea, placed by its Greek namesake north of Syracuse in about 729, sent out citizens a century later in 628 to found Selinus, a bold 300km away on the south-western coast, again close to the Phoenician-settled quarter of the island. Selinus in turn afterwards created a daughter-colony of its own, Minoa (later called Heraclea Minoa), 60km down the same coast to the south-east. By far the most memorable of these further colonies, though, was Acragas, sited in 582 or so by its Geloan settlers halfway between Selinus and Gela, on heights 4km inland.

Syracuse, Gela, Messana and Acragas quickly grew in size, population and wealth to become Sicily's leading Greek city-states. In the sixth century, Himera and Selinus were not far behind. They and their fellow-Siceliots shared the island not only with the Phoenician colonies in its west, but also with a range of older native communities: Siculi, Sicani and Elymians.

These, by 600 BC, dwelt mostly in the island's central regions. Siculan Enna and Agyrium (the future historian Diodorus was Agyrian), Elymian Segesta – often spelled Egesta and Aegesta by Greeks – and the Elymian mountain strongholds of Entella and Eryx were their chief sites.

The political norm in all Sicilian states, as at Carthage, was oligarchy, sometimes tempered by democracy. Syracuse, the best-known example, was ruled by its landed elite the *gamoroi* (the name means simply 'landowners') until a democratic revolution in the 460s. Repeatedly, rivalries within elites or between elites and lesser citizens brought successful faction-leaders to power as dictators, termed *tyrannoi* (a word actually non-Greek). Perhaps the earliest, and certainly one of the most notorious, was Phalaris of Acragas, whose rule from about 570–54 was defaced by the hollow brazen bull in which he roasted his opponents. Tyrants' regimes seldom lasted more than a few decades, however, before more flexible politics returned.

The prosperous and populous Siceliot cities were also fiercely – at times lethally – competitive among themselves. This started long before Carthage began to play its own part in the island. Syracuse fell out with its daughter-city Camarina in the 550s, just a few decades after founding it, and subdued it. Then around 500, Gela, under a series of able tyrants, grew strong enough to defeat Syracuse, and so soundly that in 485 Gelon of Gela took power there too, restoring its temporarily dispossessed *gamoroi* and presiding over a hegemony that commanded most of eastern Sicily. Selinus in the far west was often at odds with pro-Carthaginian Segesta to its north – a rivalry which would also influence Carthage's Sicilian policy – while around 490, Messana fell from Gela's temporary dominance into that of the Italian Greek city of Rhegium across the straits. It was the tyrant of Rhegium, Anaxilaus, who changed its name from Zancle to Messana. Ten years later, Anaxilaus and Himera's ejected tyrant Terillus became allies of Carthage against their fellow-Greeks in Acragas and Syracuse, so helping to launch the first of Carthage's great Sicilian wars.

Slightly smaller than Sicily, Sardinia is an island of plentiful mountains and fertile plains, and its peoples practised agriculture, stock-raising and metalworking, and mined gold, silver and lead. Their communities were lordships centred around imposing dry-stone towers now called *nuraghi* (7,000–8,000 still stand). Relations with the Phoenicians and Carthaginians varied. Archaeological finds show that some Sardinian aristocrats were able to settle in colonies like Tharros, while there is also evidence of settlers pushing out locals to take over their land. From the fifth century on, if not earlier, Sardinian soldiers were also recruited by Carthage as mercenaries for service abroad, although their propensity for warfare equally made them difficult subjects, a trait that later would bedevil the Romans too.

Greek colonists largely steered clear of Sardinia, though sometime between the sixth and fourth centuries they did found a city in the northeast, still called Olbia today. They were equally chary about Corsica: Phocaeans from the Aegean coast of Asia Minor did settle on its east coast around 565 and more came twenty years later, but their colony Alalia (Aléria today) caused so much trouble – as we shall see – that they soon abandoned it to the Etruscans.

Southern Italy was, like Sicily, a mixture of coastal plains and inland heights. The Greek diaspora from the eighth century to the sixth began with Cyme (Cumae in Latin) on the Campanian coast, and would include such notable colonies as nearby Naples, Paestum (initally named Poseidonia) – both of them offshoots of colonies such as Cyme and Sybaris – Rhegium opposite Sicily, Sybaris (destroyed by its fellow-Greeks of Croton in 510) and Tarentum. The rest of the peninsula presented a variegated pattern of city-states and rural communities, most of them bound together in ethnic confederations or alliances: for instance the Samnites of the mountainous interior east of Campania, the Latin League dominated by Rome, and the Etruscan cities to Rome's north.

As in so many other regions, Italian peoples and groupings regularly fought their neighbours. The Bruttians and Lucanians of the southern interior envied and assailed the coastal Greek cities, and sometimes each other. The Samnites clashed with their Campanian kinfolk and Greek colonies like Naples. Rome and its Latin allies spent the fifth and fourth centuries progressively combating all the peoples surrounding them; and during the fourth and third centuries, the whole of Italy was periodically terrorised by marauding armies of Gauls who had settled in the plains around the River Po but liked to range further for plunder. One army famously sacked Rome itself around 390.

Even so, over the same time-span, the Carthaginians could watch how Rome and its allies gradually spread their military dominance – in practice, Rome's dominance – across the peninsula. By 272, even the rich and powerful Greek states of the south had became more or less obedient Roman allies. The Carthaginians probably judged it fortunate that their republic and Rome continued to enjoy friendly relations and productive trade, as they had done for centuries.

Chapter 3

Fleets and armies

1. Carthage's navy

Carthage's naval might started small. Its earliest known fleet, which joined an equal Etruscan force to fight the Phocaean Greeks of Corsica in 540, was only sixty penteconters strong. A penteconter ('fifty-oarer') was the normal war-vessel of the time, rowed by twenty-five oarsmen on each side. Battles were invariably fought close to shore (warships could not stay out on the open sea for long stretches); their simple but stressful tactics aimed at piercing enemy ships with the penteconters' bronze underwater rams or else shearing off one side of an opponent's oars. The victors would be able to capture or kill survivors in the water or after pursuing them ashore, unless their own losses hampered them.

By the start of the fifth century, penteconters, though still used, were replaced as first-line warships by the trireme. This was a long, sleek and – with trained crews – highly manoeuvrable craft, rowed by oarsmen sitting in three banks, one above the other, each man wielding his own oar. Athenian triremes, the only ones known in any detail, each carried 170 rowers and a few (under twenty) soldiers and archers. The trireme was an eastern Mediterranean development: they were in use in Pharaoh Necho's fleet in 600 BC, and by 525 formed part of the powerful navy of Samos, then allied with Persia. The Carthaginians probably adopted them some years after 540. Philippus, an aristocratic Italian Greek follower of the Spartan adventurer Dorieus, sailed to join him in Sicily in 510 with his own trireme and crew, which suggests that it was now in common use.

Carthage's 200 warships for the invasion of Sicily in 480 were no doubt triremes, for Syracuse's navy was just as large and the Syracusans had triremes. This warship remained standard, Mediterranean-wide, throughout the fifth century and well into the fourth. As in penteconters, the main tactic was to use the heavy bronze ram fixed to the bow below the waterline to smash into an opposing hull or its oars. This manoeuvre could be developed (it took skill and boldness) into what Greeks called the *diekplous*, the 'passage', whereby a fleet sailing line abreast sought to pass straight through the enemy line, then swing round so that each trireme could attack an opponent from the rear.

The next developments in warships were quadriremes ('four-oarers') and quinqueremes ('fives'). Each kept three levels of seats for the oarsmen, but had four and five of these respectively. Diodorus credited the Syracusan tyrant Dionysius with being the first to build them, around 398, but they came into regular use only late in the fourth century. They then relegated triremes to secondary status: quinqueremes became the capital ships. Their layout is not certain in detail, as literary and archaeological details are thin, but each was fitted as usual with a massive bronze ram beneath the prow and most probably still had three banks of oars like the trireme. Two Carthaginian rams have been found (so far), along with over a dozen Roman ones, on the seabed just off Sicily's west coast, relics of the decisive naval battle of the Aegates Islands fought in 241. Every bronze ram projects three horizontally layered ridges or flanges, powerful enough to crash through a thick wooden hull if driven at speed; practised oarsmen could then pull their ship back to let the victim founder.[1]

The quinquereme's much larger size apparently accommodated two men per oar on both the top and middle levels, while one rower on the lowest bench-level pulled one oar, but details are debated because no clear evidence survives. Its rowing complement numbered about 300, while the on-board soldiery would be several dozen strong. Thus a fleet of 100 quinqueremes could in principle carry as many as 40,000 men, not counting those on lesser companion ships. Quinqueremes were also big enough to embark war machines like catapults, themselves a fourth-century development. Manoeuvrability must have been more cumbersome than in trireme battles. Sosylus' fragmentary account of a Hannibalic-war clash does attest that its Carthaginian ships were still using the *diekplous*, but it does not give numbers, ship-types or a location, and it is possible that those combatants were triremes.

In wartime, Carthage's citizens went into the navy, along with some contributions (of unknown size) from coastal allies like Utica and Hippou Acra. As its population and wealth grew, so did its forces. The pentaconter fleet in Corsican waters in 540 can at most have had 3,000 sailors. Sixty years later, the Sicilian expedition's armada would have some 34,000 – if Diodorus' figure for warships can be believed – and the crews of the supposedly 3,000-strong transport fleet would be still more numerous. Many of these crews were probably Carthaginians too. Between 100 and 200 remained the usual strength of a Punic fleet, when numbers are mentioned, before the first war with Rome. This suggests that until then, Carthage could normally put 17,000–34,000 trireme oarsmen to sea, accompanied by a few thousand shipboard troops who might be Carthaginians or Libyans and mercenaries.

Crew numbers must have gone up dramatically after 264, for according to Polybius and other sources, the Carthaginians launched fleets of more than 100 quinqueremes, and occasionally more than twice as many, to combat the Romans. Citizen numbers alone may not have been enough to man all these. If so, extra personnel were probably levied from the Libyphoenicians and Libyans. The manpower for smaller naval vessels and transports was an added need in all periods, with crews again probably not limited to Carthaginians.

For most of their history, the Carthaginians kept their navy in dockyards (*neoria* in Greek), which must have been sited on the city's eastern shore or in the shipping channel dug from the lake of Tunis up to the city's edge just below Byrsa. In 368, the *neoria* were ravaged by a fire severe enough to make Dionysius of Syracuse reckon that no Punic fleet survived, but he soon (and painfully) learned otherwise. In peacetime, existing warships were kept in ship-sheds, like those excavated in the circular enclosed harbour that was built in the third or second century. They could be launched swiftly when needed, so long as crews were available (and trained) and the necessary equipment ready.

Whether the state maintained skeleton professional crews between wars, and whether Carthaginian warships carried out peacetime naval exercises to keep them in trim, we are not told, but Sosylus' remark about the skill of the Punic *diekplous* does suggest regular practice. We also know that early in the great mercenary and Libyan rebellion against Carthage, around 241–40, merchants from Italy doing trade with the rebels were intercepted by Punic naval patrols (which kindled a serious though brief diplomatic crisis with Rome). This happened soon after Carthage's first Roman war had ended in a disastrous naval defeat, but plainly warships were still available for watching home waters.

2. The army

Some ancient writers sweepingly depicted the Carthaginians as serving only on warships and leaving land warfare to mercenaries and conscripts levied from their subjects. As often with generalizations, the claim was inexact. Early Carthage, lacking possessions in Libya or abroad, must have fielded small and mostly citizen forces, although these would not have to fight any enemies beyond occasionally troublesome neighbours. According to Aristotle, Carthaginians wore armlets matching the number of campaigns in which they had served. Citizen soldiers are certainly reported from time to time in later armies, and of course most senior army officers were Carthaginians.

The first army we learn of did consist of citizens – the army which, as Justin told it, returned from Sardinia around 550 with its general 'Malchus', as he is conventionally called, to purge the sentence of exile that the city had inflicted on it after a defeat (see Chapter 4). Like Greek and Roman armies of the same era, Carthage probably fielded a citizen militia, consisting of able-bodied Carthaginians of fighting age who normally would be enrolled for a specific campaign and return to civil life after it. Justin's account, however, implies that Malchus' campaigns ran for lengthy periods and his men became devoted to him: this should mean that at least some served for several years.

On one interpretation, Carthaginian leaders of the time relied on bodies of personal armed followers or retainers, whereas armies levied and maintained by the state developed later. Perhaps that might explain why Malchus' army stayed loyal to him even against their home city – but if so, his political foes in Carthage should have had retainer forces of their own and could have fought back. Instead they capitulated. When he later fell, Justin's account makes no mention of a loyal personal army rallying to help him. By the 550s or 540s, then, it is more likely that armies like his were authorized and maintained by the republic, using such revenues as it had available (customs dues, money levies, loans – the sort of funds administered by the *mehashbim*) and looking to booty and exactions from defeated lands to recoup costs. But as in Carthage's later ages, a powerful leader would get what he wanted from the state to pursue military policies dear to him. If he then failed, he could be brought down by resurgent political foes.

At some date Carthaginian armies added foreign soldiers for hire – in other words, mercenaries. If Malchus had any of them in Sardinia, he left them behind. Later in the same century, things started to change. In 480, with Carthage's wealth and outreach now well established, Hamilcar the Magonid's expeditionary army to Sicily recruited men not only from the city but from much of the western Mediterranean: Libya, Iberia, Liguria, Sardinia, Corsica and maybe Gaul. These and a few other places like Numidia, Campania in Italy and the Balearic islands, became regular suppliers of Punic mercenary manpower. To these, especially from the fourth century on, were added Greek professionals, generally viewed as the best in the world. That many of Carthage's greatest wars were fought against Greek states was rarely a problem: for professional troops, war was business.[2]

As just shown, even before Carthage brought its Libyan neighbours under its rule, it could obtain Libyan recruits for wars. These must have been volunteers serving for pay, but later the Libyan communities under Punic dominance were required to supply levies. They received pay too, but the terms of service for non-Carthaginian soldiers – pay, length of enlistment, booty entitlements, conditions of discharge – are not known. Probably enough different contingents had different pay and conditions, and cavalry were always more highly paid than infantry. As so often in armies ancient and modern, however, pay could be irregular, inadequate or both. These were among the long-standing grievances that provoked the great rebellion of Carthage's Libyan and mercenary soldiery in 241, just after the long and unprofitable First Punic War ended.

In the fifth century and after, large citizen forces did also march out from time to time. To wreak havoc and vengeance on Sicily in 406, the Punic generals recruited not only Libyphoenician, Libyan and foreign soldiers, but also 'the strongest of their fellow-citizens' (their number is unstated). They were, not surprisingly, well equipped and even pampered – perhaps the first appearance of the 'Sacred Corps' known from fourth-century wars. At any rate we read that at a crisis in the siege of Acragas, the commander Himilco averted a mutiny of his foreign soldiers by giving them 'the goblets belonging to the troops from Carthage'. Again, after the Battle of the River Crimisus in 341, the Carthaginian camp yielded a profusion of silver and gold drinking cups to its Greek captors. In that century, the elite Sacred Corps (or Sacred Band, *hieros lochos* in Greek) – 2,500–3,000 Carthaginian citizen troops – is recorded taking the field on a few known occasions. Even if sacred, it may have been more dazzling than successful: recruited from rich military families, equipped with splendid weapons and armour, its men fought bravely, but their recorded fate was to be virtually annihilated each time. The unit is not heard of after Agathocles' invasion, and the detailed inventory that Rome's enemy, Hannibal, compiled of the forces fielded by Carthage in 218 mentioned no Carthaginian units at all.

Other citizen forces are attested on occasion. To confront Timoleon's Greeks, along with the Sacred Corps marched 10,000 other Carthaginians, all handsomely equipped and identifiable with their white shields. Three decades later, no fewer than 40,000 citizens were called up in a general levy to confront Agathocles' invading army, probably the largest single citizen army in Carthage's history. By contrast, when Hamilcar Barca took over operational command against rebel mercenaries and Libyans in 240, his muster of citizen soldiers, fresh mercenaries and ex-rebel deserters gave him a mere 10,000 men to lead out from the city. No doubt he had to leave at least as many again to garrison Carthage, while his discredited colleague Hanno was somewhere in the countryside with another small army.[3]

Two magnificent pieces of bronze parade armour of late fourth or third-century date, found near Hadrumetum (modern Sousse) and now in the Bardo Museum in Tunis, give an idea of what Carthaginian officers will have worn. One is a breastplate, the other its matching backplate. On each, two shield-bosses in high relief surmount a helmeted head – probably a deity, one female and the other male, with distinctive features – while an intricately wrought palm-tree and other motifs weave over the flat surfaces between. Bronze shoulder-straps engraved with a palm tree and a moon circle are attached, and to the side edges of the backplate a pair of small oblong plates with the same motifs. The first-class workmanship is thought to be southern Italian, but could equally well have been wrought at Carthage, a city constantly receptive to foreign influences and equally ready to adapt them to Punic themes; the palm tree, for instance, is a regular motif on coins. It is not hard to visualize equipment like this being worn, at least for parades and ceremonies, by the men of the Sacred Corps in the age of Timoleon and Agathocles.

Carthaginian and other heavy infantry, including Libyan troops and Campanian and Greek mercenaries, were equipped with pike, sword and shield for weapons, and for protection a plain leather cuirass or one – much costlier – sewn with metal scales or chainmail, a leather or metal helmet and, if the soldier could afford them, greaves for the shins. Some surviving items give an idea of what ordinary infantrymen might look like. A fourth-century carved scarab seal found at Kerkouane, a Punic town on the Cape Bon peninsula destroyed around 256, depicts a four-man marching file armed with shields, heavy pikes and plumed helmets. A scale-sewn sleeved cuirass of third-century date, recovered from Lake Trasimene in Italy, is probably Roman but gives a clear idea of the armour which better-off, or state-subsidised, soldiers might wear. The seabed finds from the Battle of the Aegates include several bowl-shaped metal helmets topped by decorative knobs, probably again Roman but no doubt typical of their time.[4]

For combat, the pike was the main weapon, the sword largely for defence. Pike-fighting required a closely packed formation, for if pikemen spread out they became highly vulnerable. Hannibal, in Italy in 217, did equip his troops with captured Roman weaponry, which would have enabled them to fight using swords, but this was unusual if not unique even in that war. The complex and malleable formations of Roman infantry – much admired by Polybius – were rare elsewhere in the Mediterranean.

Some other formations were more individually equipped. Numidian cavalrymen on their agile small horses wore little or no armour while carrying a light round shield and some javelins. Tirelessly tough, they were used not for direct frontal attacks but to harass enemy forces and relentlessly pursue them once they broke and fled. Numidian infantry (much less celebrated) seem to have been light-armed skirmishers. Ordinary Gallic soldiers wore no armour – some foot-soldiers no clothing at all, berserker-style – though their chiefs bore chainmail armour and high pointed helmets. All fought with a long slashing sword, oval wooden shield and also sometimes a long lance; Gallic cavalry was similarly outfitted.

Iberian fighters, both horse and foot, wielded a machete-like sword (moderns term it a *falcata*) with a J–shaped hilt and one edge of the blade forged in a wave-like shape, or else used a short two-edged blade with pointed tip, so efficient for slashing and also stabbing that the Romans adopted it, perhaps in the early third century, as their standard legionary weapon. Vase paintings and archaeological finds show that Iberians might also wield spears. Protective armament varied, probably according to warriors' means: over the chest a mailed or leather cuirass, or else a circular bronze plate (or no armour at all), a round shield called a *caetra* and one type or other of helmet, either of metal, leather or animal sinew. A quite different class of professionals were the slingers recruited from the Balearic islands: unarmoured fighters wielding animal-skin or rope-rush slings to hurl stone or lead slugs with enough force and accuracy, even from a distance, to smash armour. Each slinger carried three slings for hurling shots of differing sizes, winding them round the head or body. Though never numerous in any army, Baleares were prized specialists.

The size of Carthage's armies varied, and (unsurprisingly) ancient sources could offer imaginatively inflated figures, or guesses. The 300,000 supposedly sent to Sicily in 480 BC and 120,000 (or 300,000, according to Ephorus) sent there in 406 might well need to be divided by three, four or even six in reality, but the 40,000 assembled in western Sicily in 310 and the same number for the levies against Agathocles in 307 are more believable. To supply such forces with food, horses, packhorses or mules, spare garments, weapons and armour – and with pay – took effort and organization. Diodorus claimed 3,000 supply ships were used in 480 and 1,500 in 409, though these figures too may be exaggerated. On campaign, armies could gather some munitions like food and animals locally, from providers willing or forced, but adequate amounts could never be guaranteed. Either the troops went hungry and wore down equipment, or fresh stocks had to be pushed forward from Carthaginian strongholds or transported from Africa.

When successful, wars brought quantities of plunder – human as well as inanimate – to the city. Diodorus' history paints a pathetic picture of the suffering women and children of Selinus in 409, harshly treated when their wealthy city fell to the Carthaginians and now facing lifelong slavery in Libya. The physical spoils displayed at Carthage from many wars were more than plentiful. After Scipio Aemilianus sacked the city in 146, he allowed the cities of Sicily to reclaim sacred objects and artworks looted from them in past eras: Acragas, for instance, got back Phalaris' bronze bull after 260 years. While enslaved war prisoners are mentioned only in Punic wars' narratives, it can be assumed that in earlier centuries PoWs came from many other lands and peoples, including Numidians, Sardinians, Iberians and Greeks.

Booty could be won by ordinary soldiers too, even if arrangements for sharing it out were possibly less efficient than Rome's tightly organized system. Pay, though, was the key incentive for men to take up mercenary service – or, for conscripts, not to desert – for fighting could not guarantee regular victories or plunder. Evidence for rates of pay is thin apart from Rome. In the late fifth century, a Greek soldier could be paid one drachma per day (and another for his servant), but a wealthy employer might offer more: the rebel Persian prince Cyrus promised his Greek mercenaries one and a half daily drachmas, a good rate, in 401. Two hundred years later, a mercenary expected eight obols a day as a rule (there were six obols to a drachma), but again actual rates would depend on circumstances. It was common to provide rations like corn and oil as an extra form of pay, or the men might receive money to buy their rations.

Cavalrymen, who had to look after their horses as well, were naturally paid higher amounts, twice or three times as much in both salary and rations, as a couple of early Hellenistic inscriptions indicate. Light-armed fighters, on the other hand, were paid less – perhaps half the regular infantryman's rate. Carthage was willing to pay well for experienced mercenaries: its rates were famously competitive with what the endlessly warring states of the eastern Mediterranean offered, even the great post-Alexander monarchies.

Even so, one endemic problem for mercenaries in every age was that often their wages were not paid for long periods (or not at all). States might go to war for political or military goals, then run short of the funds needed to fight the war. That would leave generals in a quandary: unpaid soldiers (and not just mercenaries) might mutiny or desert. One wily Carthaginian general in the fourth century prevented this, according to Diodorus, by enticing his 6,000 restive mercenaries onto a small island (possibly Ustica north of Sicily) and sailing away. Much the same trick was performed by a First Punic War general on some of his unpaid mercenaries, or so the later Roman historian Cassius Dio claimed. After that war, it was the grievances of both mercenaries and Libyan conscripts over long-unpaid arrears of regular wages and ration-money that led to one of the most harrowing of all Carthage's conflicts, in its own homeland of Libya (see Chapter 10).[5]

3. The defences of Carthage

Carthage began as a fairly restricted settlement on the Byrsa hill and down to the Mediterranean shore. Like every coastal Mediterranean city, it must have built walled defences from early on, since its Libyan neighbours were invariably not well-disposed. By the late fifth century BC, as archaeological explorations have shown, massive defensive walls lined its eastern shore. The other sides of the city must have been at least as well guarded, especially its western perimeter which faced the flat isthmus leading to the small town of Tunes (ancestor of today's Tunis) at the far end of the lake named after it.

The only detailed description of Carthage's fortifications is late: Appian's account of the final war with Rome, based probably on Polybius' first-hand narrative. When these latest defences were created is not known, but some time in the fourth century is likely, amid the constant wars with Syracuse – especially perhaps during or after Agathocles' invasion in 310–07 which menaced the city's actual existence.

Appian's description is circumstantial. While a single wall protected Carthage on its seaward sides, the 5km-wide isthmus was barricaded north to south by a triple line of walls 45ft high (nearly 14 metres), overlooked by towers 200ft (61 metres) apart. Some traces of these defences were found in military excavations after the Second World War. The towers held four storeys, each of the three walls two. Within the triple walls, the Carthaginians could maintain stables and supplies for 300 elephants and 4,000 horses, plus barracks for 20,000 soldiers. By then there were also fortifications around the perimeter of the entire peninsula, including the heights of Megara to the north.

The whole enclosed area was ten or more times larger than Carthage's urban zone and thinly inhabited. Megara was a district of gardens, orchards and country houses, while its southern slopes and the hills between these and Byrsa were burial grounds. Between the built-up city and the triple walls to its west lay 3km or more of flat and mostly open country (some of it still open today), no doubt with farms and villas. This might seem the hardest sector to defend, but Appian instead stressed that the defences running eastward alongside the lake of Tunis, over to the inner harbour, were the weakest point: there it was a single wall again. A sandy tongue of land, called the Taenia, jutted southward beyond it (vastly extended and built up today), marking the division between the sea to its east and the lake to its west.[6]

These formidable defences defied centuries of attacks. Even the Taenia sector was breached only once – by the Romans in 146, after a three-year siege and when the defenders were weak from hunger and desertions. If threatened by land, as by Agathocles in 310–07, the rebel mercenaries and Libyans in the 'Truceless War' of 241–37 and even during the first years of the Third Punic War, the Carthaginians could bring in munitions by sea and also fresh forces to strengthen the defenders. The only time that a total blockade by sea and land was imposed was in 147–46 by Scipio Aemilianus, and that marked the beginning of Carthage's end.

Chapter 4

Early Wars: Malchus to 'King' Hamilcar

1. Malchus: fiction or fact?

Malchus was the first known individual in Carthage's history after Elissa/Dido and her entourage. Malchus was not his real name, though for convenience it is used here. Justin's manuscripts, all medieval, vary between Mazeus, Maceus and Maleus; the Christian author Orosius, copying Justin, wrote 'Mazeus' too; and they are our only sources. Seventeeth-century Dutch scholar Isaac Vossius proposed 'Malchus', a Latin form of Phoenician *mlk* meaning 'king', but no ancient evidence supports this. Even various Carthaginians called 'king' by Greek and Roman authors bore actual Punic names, like 'king' Hanno of the *Periplus* and 'king' Hamilcar who led the expedition into Sicily in 480. Malchus' actual existence is debated: partly because his reported wars – in North Africa, Sicily and Sardinia – seem repeated as wars waged in these same lands by his military successors at Carthage; partly too because of Justin's melodramatic story about how he and his army returned from defeat in Sardinia to restore him to power and crush his enemies, only for Malchus himself to be tried and put to death soon after.[1]

For both Malchus and a later generation of Punic generals to campaign in the same territories is no more peculiar than for a succession of Roman generals half a millennium later – Caesar, Augustus' stepsons Drusus and Tiberius, and Drusus' son Germanicus – to wage wars in Germany, with success as varied as the Carthaginians'. Justin's account of Malchus and his son Carthalo (whom he crucifies for disobedience) is certainly overblown and rhetorical, but rejecting it as pure fiction does not automatically follow. It cannot serve as an origin-myth explaining the (alleged) Carthaginian ritual of child-sacrifice, as sometimes suggested – Carthalo is not a child but a chief priest – nor as a symbolic fable of a king (a *mlk*) clashing with aristocratic opponents, since this depends on Vossius' manuscript change.

Malchus' and his army's rebellion, return and revenge do resemble the Roman consul Sulla's military seizures of Rome in 88 and again in 82 – each time after suffering political checkmate from his enemies – just enough to cause suspicion that Pompeius Trogus invented Malchus with Sulla as his inspiration. On the other hand, for a thwarted and ambitious commander to rally his loyal soldiery to offset political defeat is a widespread historical phenomenon (in France as recently as 1815). Nor did any priest figure in Sulla's reprisals, and he himself never suffered either defeat in battle, as Malchus does in the story, or trial and execution later. If Malchus is a fiction, then Trogus was both imaginative and inventive. It is quite likely that the basics of Malchus' career and confrontations remained in Carthaginian tradition, even in historical records, though literary narrators could afterwards choose to embroider them with rhetoric and drama.

2. Malchus: victories, revenge and ruin

Malchus, like other known Carthaginian leaders, will have been a member of the aristocracy. His son was priest of Melqart, one of Carthage's principal gods, with a close bond to mother-city Tyre. To be chosen as war-leader (Justin used the Roman word *dux*) and command in a series of wars in Africa and abroad, Malchus must have headed a strong faction. Inevitably they also faced bitter enemies among the city's elite. Enhancing Carthage's fighting strength and so projecting its power further afield were probably the policies that he and his faction developed. While all went well, their opponents had to acquiesce.

Malchus (Orosius reported from a source other than Justin) was active in the time of Cyrus the Great, founder of the Persian Empire, who reigned from around 559–30 BC. Justin, in his one-paragraph account of the Carthaginian, placed him two generations before Carthage's Sicilian expedition of 480. Both items point to the period around 550–30, which may tie Malchus in one way or other, too, to the Carthaginian and Etruscan alliance against the piratical Phocaean Greeks of Alalia in Corsica (see below).

Malchus' wars in Justin are listed as, first, against 'the Africans', then in Sicily and finally (but unsuccessfully for him) in Sardinia. The Africans can only be Carthage's Libyan neighbours, especially those in the fertile hinterlands to the west and south between the lower Bagradas river and the Zaghouan mountains – all within a week's march from the coast. In the city's first centuries, Carthage lived in a slightly uneasy coexistence with them: as mentioned earlier, it had to pay them rent for the land that the city stood on. If true, it means that in early days the neighbours were strong enough – if they joined forces – to exact the payment. It would follow that other Phoenician colonies like Utica and Hippou Acra, smaller than Carthage, had to pay too. They would not be the only coastal cities that had to satisfy sometimes predatory locals: Greek Massilia (Marseille) was often harassed by Ligurians on the coast and inland-dwelling Vocontii, while at the other end of the known world, Tomi and Olbia (Greek cities on the north-western coasts of the Black Sea) suffered predatory attentions from the Scythian peoples around them, enough to trouble the poet Ovid when he was exiled to Tomi by Augustus.[2]

Malchus did 'great deeds against the Africans', according to Justin. This might be doubted on the grounds that Justin himself later reported the Libyans forcing Carthage to pay them their rent, sometime before 480. This report all the same plainly states that the Libyans then were 'seeking back' the payments 'of many years': in other words, they had not been paid for a long while, conceivably not for decades. Malchus' 'great deeds' against them would amount to successfully rejecting their demands for payment, using Carthage's growing military resources to resist unfriendly pressures. Not that the Libyans were brought under Punic rule: that lay far in their future. But Malchus' success would strengthen his political position at Carthage and ready the city for its first known military intervention outside Africa – in Sicily.

Sicily was a long-established focus of Phoenician trade and settlement. Panormus and its neighbour Solous, and Motya on its offshore island in the north-west, were prosperous and suffered few tensions with other Sicilian peoples or Greek settlements. The exception was Selinus, the ambitious Greek colony on the south coast. Its unfriendly Elymian rival to the north, Segesta, had the Phoenician colonies' support when clashes came – as in 580 or so when an Aegean Greek named Pentathlus settled with his followers in the district around Mount Eryx, close to the east coast (Erice today), and took Selinus' side. With Phoenician help, the Segestans won the day. Pentathlus was among the battle-dead and his surviving followers gave up the attempt, moving instead to the island of Lipara, north of the Strait of Messina.

Whether Carthage itself sent any help to Segesta is not known. Diodorus' reference to 'the Phoenicians' leaves it open: his history sometimes applies the term to the homeland Phoenicians, sometimes to those in Sicily and occasionally to the Carthaginians. Early in the sixth century, the Carthaginians were certainly adopting more ambitious overseas habits. Their occupation of Ebusus near Spain, though dated by Diodorus to the much earlier 654 BC, in fact according to archaeological evidence occurred some while after

600. Intervening in Sicily around the middle of the sixth century is no great surprise; the obvious question is why it happened.

The Carthaginians' widening activity in the western Mediterranean could be seen as a reaction to Tyre's lessening role in trade there, as the mother-city suffered growing stress from acquisitive Near Eastern empires – first Babylon in the age of Nebuchadnezzar, then Persia under the mighty Cyrus. Still, it may equally or more have been due to Carthage's own growing wealth, population and resulting self-confidence. Unprotected trading at overseas centres had to endure competition from locals and foreigners, but setting up a military or naval presence – even if small or periodic – could tilt matters in the sender's interest, still more if it then encouraged trade partners into friendly and favourable agreements. By the 550s, Carthage had a navy and a citizen army, perhaps beefed up with recruits from allied cities and some mercenaries. On this interpretation, Malchus and his supporters could opt to start projecting Punic influence more vigorously than before.

The Greek historian Thucydides, writing around 400 BC, seems to have known of a still-earlier venture, and a bold one at that. Listing powerful early Greek naval states, he wrote that 'the Phocaeans when founding Massalia defeated the Carthaginians in a sea battle'. Phocaeans from the Aegean had founded Massilia around 600. Though sometimes read as a mistake for the sea-battle of Alalia, fought in about 540, Thucydides' item scarcely fits that context: Alalia was in Corsica, the Phocaean colonists who won that fight were not a major naval power and had no known help from Massilia, and not only Carthaginian naval forces were involved against them (see below).

Attempting to block the earlier Phocaeans matches other colonial Phoenicians' unease at the steady tide of Greek migration. Newcomers meant competition over sites, resources and trade – Thucydides stated that the Greek arrivals in Sicily pushed everyone else further and further westward. Hence the firm local reaction against Pentathlus' Eryx settlement around 580, and late in the same century Carthage's equally robust rebuffs to the Spartan leader Dorieus' colonising moves in both North Africa and Sicily (see below). In 600, probably not just the Carthaginians but other western Phoenicians were worried about Greeks making an appearance in the north-west Mediterranean. But the move against them failed, leaving Massilia to prosper and before long send out its own colonists to found Antipolis and Nicaea nearby (Antibes and Nice) and Emporion (whose name, significantly, meant 'the market') in north-eastern Spain at the site now called Ampurias.

The Carthaginians chose to focus on nearer territories, beginning with Sicily. Another motive for activity there was quite likely political. Malchus no doubt had supportive friends at home, but he had enemies too (as the sequel shows). The prestige of defying the Libyans over tribute could not last forever, but it could certainly make him and Carthage more confident about sending forces overseas to Sicily. A third motive was, conceivably, the vigour of the new Sicilian Greek city of Acragas.

In about 570, barely a dozen years after being founded, that city fell under the rule of Phalaris, Sicily's earliest known 'tyrant' (homeland Greece was already well acquainted with the breed). Not just proverbially and pathologically vicious – the poet Pindar, less than a century later, mentioned his habit of roasting victims in his brazen bull – Phalaris energetically pushed Acragas' dominance over surrounding territory almost as far east as its mother-city Gela, and may have had designs too on Himera beside the north coast. He made no recorded moves against the Elymian or Phoenician cities and was assassinated around 554, but those neighbours had no way of telling whether a new burst of Acragantine expansionism might yet follow.[3]

As mentioned earlier, a modern view of Malchus and after him the Magonid clan is that they were personal warlords leading private armies against foreign peoples for their own profit and renown. This view extends to the large-scale military expedition of 480, under the Magonid leader Hamilcar 'the king' (as Herodotus called him): a family response to the plight of the ousted Terillus of Himera and the persuasion of Terillus' father-in-law Anaxilaus of Rhegium. Yet Hamilcar's armaments were sizeable, varied and elaborate enough – even though the numbers given to him by Herodotus and Diodorus are grossly overblown – to mean that if he really was pursuing personal (or clan) goals, he was extraordinarily able to marshal massive public resources for it. That public resources were heavily drawn on for the war of 480 (even if the Magonid clan also contributed from private sources) is equally clear from the devastating aftermath, as we shall see.

According to Justin, Malchus and his army campaigned long and successfully in Sicily and subdued part of it, but we have no details. As with the 'great deeds' in Libya, this flattering claim should be slimmed down, for there is no sign later on that Carthage actually ruled – meaning taxed, administered and imposed laws and courts on – any Sicilian region. Malchus would have aimed instead at impressing Sicily's western peoples with Carthage's strength, encouraging them into agreements that favoured Carthage's interests (the first treaty between Carthage and Rome, made in 509, did something similar), clashing with places disinclined to comply, and gathering booty and gifts to take home. Malchus, or else one of his successors, even put a stop to Selinus' and Segesta's rivalry, for in 480 Selinus was Carthage's sole Greek ally against the major Greek states. All these proceedings could readily be puffed up, then and later, into a claim of outright conquest.

At some stage afterwards, Malchus and his supporters decided that similar action was called for in Sardinia. The stimulus could have been a demand from Sulcis, Tharros or other Phoenician centres for help against their native Sardinian neighbours; or Malchus needed fresh military successes and booty; or both. If he acted around 540, that was the time too when Carthage made a war-alliance with the Etruscans to deal with the piratical Phocaeans in Corsica, who for years had been attacking Carthaginian and Etruscan merchants plying Corsican waters. It would be hard to leave Malchus out of that planning too.

At the same time the Sardinian expedition was opposed by many at Carthage: so events soon showed. Nor did it end well. There was real fighting, and finally Malchus' army was badly beaten – he lost more than half his men. The Alalia effort fared little better. The Phocaeans who had founded that colony in 565 had been reinforced twenty years later by others fleeing their homeland when the Persians took it over. Confidence in their new numbers prompted piracy (obviously more congenial than farming), but five ensuing years of harassment pushed Carthage and its Etruscan friends, particularly the then wealthy city of Caere, into sending out sixty ships apiece against them. The Phocaeans had only sixty themselves but won the battle – a 'Cadmean' victory in Herodotus' phrase (we would say Pyrrhic), for they lost forty ships and their crews. Before long they abandoned Alalia to the Etruscans and moved to southern Italy. Most of the captured crews were taken to Italy by the Caeritans and stoned to death, although those assigned to the Carthaginians probably met the slightly less gruesome fate of enslavement.[4]

If Malchus was associated with the Alalia defeat it cannot have enhanced his esteem at home. But in Justin's telling, he and his surviving men were punished by Carthage for their Sardinian disaster with a decree ordering them 'to live in exile', in effect banning them from coming home. Defeat had compounded the weakening effect of long absence from the political centre; plainly the opposing faction or factions had gained the upper hand. The army and general sent an appeal for pardon but, when rejected, sailed back to Africa to blockade Carthage itself by sea and land. That (we are told) was when his priest-son Carthalo, back in the city from a ritual visit to Tyre, briefly refused his father's summons because he had rites to perform, and then suffered crucifixion as punishment when finally he obeyed.

The city eventually gave in, allowing Malchus to retake control and – very mildly in Justin's view – have only his ten principal opponents executed. Even so, he did not keep power for long. Soon he was charged with 'grasping at kingship' – and with illicitly killing Carthalo – and he 'paid the penalty'.

Justin used Roman political language for these actions: the reinstated Malchus first justified himself to 'the people' at a *contio* (a formal gathering), his ten victims were 'senators' and 'grasping at kingship' (*regnum*) was an accusation fairly often flung at radical or high-handed leaders in the later Roman Republic. The language, though, hardly makes the actions unbelievable. The aristocratic council of elders, the *adirim*, surely existed by the sixth century and even earlier, though its powers and tasks may have varied from earlier to later times. Equally conceivable for the period is a general gathering of the people (the *ham*), not to legislate or elect, but to be harangued by an official, as in fact Justin's term *contio* means. 'Grasping at kingship', meaning tyranny in the Greek sense, was a danger to which ancient republics were fully alive, and recent or living examples around 540 or 530 were not only those in Greece and the Aegean (like the flamboyant Peisistratus of Athens and Polycrates of Samos) but Acragas' Phalaris.

Why Malchus, triumphant at last, then voluntarily 'restored the city to its laws' cannot be answered, but again that does not prove it a fiction. Ill-health or age, or even familial and religious distress over executing his son the priest, could push him into stepping down – perhaps with a further push from the man Justin called his successor: Mago, another experienced soldier. Aristotle, in the *Politics*, mentioned Carthage as a case of a state changing from tyranny to aristocratic rule. He may or may not have had Malchus' fall in mind, although Malchus' 'tyranny' was very brief (at least in Justin's account). But certainly the next stage of Carthage's political life was the return of an aristocratic, meaning oligarchic, regime. This time, and much more lastingly, it was dominated by Mago, his family and their powerful faction.[5]

3. The Magonids: 'empire' builders?

Mago and his sons figure in the opening sections of Justin's next book in his *Epitome*. It poses problems. Mago reforms the army and revitalises the state, then is succeeded by two sons: Adherbal, who is later mortally wounded in Sardinia, and next Hamilcar, whose 'eleven dictatorships and four triumphs' are achievements so glittering that his death in battle brings universal grief to Carthage. These two may actually have been grandsons of Mago, for Herodotus calls Hamilcar's father Hanno. This detail could have escaped Justin as he epitomised. If correct, that Hanno made no mark on events; it is possible he predeceased Mago. The two brothers had three sons each: Hannibal, Hasdrubal and Saphon for Hasdrubal, and Himilco, Hanno and Gisco for Hamilcar.

Closer dates for the Magonids can only be estimated. Malchus' chequered career had covered, it seems, roughly the decades from 550–30. Hamilcar's triumphs and sufeteships in turn should span twenty years or so; there is no indication that his eleven sufeteships were over successive years. His predecessors Mago and Adherbal would then date, roughly, to the period 530–500. It is likely that they all held the sufeteship from time to time to maintain their dominance, and each may have also held important priesthoods. Such offices would be important supports for political leadership: Malchus' son Carthalo, as priest of Melqart, would have played that role until he made the mistake of defying his parent. In 480, Hamilcar the Magonid met his end in camp at Himera conducting a huge ceremony with animal sacrifices, in the hope that 'Poseidon' (perhaps Baal Saphon, or even Melqart) would send omens favourable to the battle that was raging. Notably too, despite his defeat and death, his countrymen commemorated him from then on with sacrifices and statues.

The narrative of Magonid doings in Justin has strangely varied contents. It includes the unflattering report of how, in their time, Carthage's Libyan neighbours forced the city to pay up its arrears of ground-rent – and, implicitly, to keep paying rent from then on. This item, because unflattering, can be believed. Not so the surprising claim that follows: after Hamilcar's death, the Sicilian Greeks, 'because of incessant wrongdoings by the Carthaginians', enlisted 'Leonidas brother of the king of the Spartans' as their leader in a long and fluctuating war. Not much more believable is a further report that, 'amid these events', Darius, king of Persia, sent orders to the Carthaginians to stop sacrificing humans and eating dog-flesh, and a request for help in his invasion of Greece; the Carthaginians supposedly declined the request but obeyed the commands.

These fantasies are not believable. Pompeius Trogus had perhaps used an alternative source blessed with a strong imagination, or the errors may be due to Justin's erratic memory or misplaced and garbled excerpts (the real Leonidas is recorded much earlier in his *Epitome*). 'Leonidas' warring in Sicily is a clumsy confusion with that famous Spartan's older half-brother Dorieus, who had indeed come to Sicily around 510 with hopes – soon dashed – of refounding Pentathlus' colony near Eryx. As for Darius' message, that is partly a mangled recall of the story (probably just as fictitious) that his son Xerxes later ordered the Carthaginians to conquer Sicily while he conquered Greece. It may also be partly fake propaganda about Punic religious peculiarities. In the late fourth century, the learned polymath Theophrastus, Aristotle's most eminent student, credited the same human-sacrifice ban to Gelon of Syracuse's peace treaty of 480 with Carthage. It was one of the notions, alluringly repellent even if bogus, that Greeks cherished about the Carthaginians.

Another misplaced item in Justin comes a little later. The dead Hamilcar is replaced in Sicilian command by one Himilco, whose picturesquely disastrous fate is then told. But Hamilcar's defeat and death occurred in 480, whereas the picturesquely fated Himilco warred some ninety years later, as we know from Diodorus (see Chapter 6). Since one of the dead Hamilcar's sons was an earlier Himilco – and as we have seen, Carthaginian aristocrats used a very narrow range of personal names – Justin, if not Trogus himself, pretty certainly mismanaged the choice and arrangement of materials on the Magonids (not to mention the crass mistake about Leonidas).[6]

With caution, on the other hand, Justin's information about the Magonid trio themselves is believable. It is not an uncritical paean; in the very middle of lavishly praising their sterling moral and leadership qualities, it tells of Carthage's humiliation by the Libyans. This may have befallen the city early in the period after Malchus' fall, for instance while Mago and other leaders were competing for political dominance, or else at another time, when the city and its leadership had been weakened in some way or had chosen to focus their energies elsewhere. Certainly on other fronts the outward thrust initiated by Malchus was renewed.

Around 515, Dorieus the Spartan, frustrated at not being chosen one of his city's two kings, sailed with a company of intending colonists to the River Cinyps in North Africa, very near the Phoenician colony of Lepcis Magna ('Magna' was a Roman addition). This famous city stands on the coast of modern (not ancient) Libya some 140km east of Tripoli. Well watered and fertile, the region had never been settled by Greeks, and neither the locals nor Carthage were prepared to let them start now. An alliance between a native African people called the Macae, the Carthaginians and 'the Libyans' – so called by Herodotus, but he may mean the Lepcitans – threw Dorieus out after two years.

This was Carthage's first known political and military venture east of Libya. What forces it contributed to evicting the Spartans can only be surmised, but a naval squadron and a body of Mago's improved citizen troops seems a reasonable surmise. In the same period, Justin's reported fresh warfare in Sardinia and Sicily, each with ups and downs, can fit what we know from elsewhere.

In or near 509, Carthage made a friendship treaty with the just-installed Roman Republic, a fledging regime threatened on every side by enemies – including Etruscans – after the expulsion of Rome's last king. Already a busy commercial centre, Rome no doubt welcomed being confirmed as friends with a premier naval state, and especially one on good terms with the Etruscans.

Preserved in Greek translation by Polybius, the treaty throws vivid but contested light on Magonid Carthage's overseas interests. Very much *de haut en bas*, it laid down rules for merchants of either state plying their business in regions of interest to the other – most of the rules being imposed on Rome. Romans must not sail beyond the 'Fair Cape' (either Cape Farina, the western point of the Gulf of Tunis, or Cape Bon, the eastern point), while 'in Libya and Sardinia' they must trade under the supervising eye of a local official. A trader driven by bad weather beyond the Fair Cape had five days, maximum, to repair and replenish craft and crew. But in 'Sicily which the Carthaginians rule', a Roman 'shall be on entirely equal terms'.

Carthage's merchants were under no similar trading rules in Italy. Its only promises were negative: not to attack Rome's allies in Latium (the region where Rome itself stood), to hand over to Rome any non-Roman Latin city if Carthage took it and not to establish themselves in that region. The treaty said nothing of Roman attacks on North African cities, for the good reason that no Roman navy (or naval policy) existed before the late fourth century.

How much of this friendship treaty was realistic and how much of it bravado? Neither before 509 BC, nor even before 262, did Carthage attack any Latin (or other Italian) city, far less capture one or land troops in Latium. Even if the newly republican Romans – perhaps mindful of the Alalia episode – worried that Carthage might do any of these things, marauding Magonid ventures along the Italian coasts were hardly a serious prospect. The promises may well have been put in as a fine-sounding sop to Carthage's new friends. Again, implying (on paper) that in Sardinia a Roman merchant would find Punic or pro-Punic bureaucrats, at any port of call, was just bombast. The merchant might find some in Libyan harbours, most of them belonging to Phoenician colonies or their offshoots, but all Sardinia was not under Carthage's control in 509 – or even later. Roman merchants and senators would be fully aware of this obvious fact. Equally, the phrase 'Sicily which the Carthaginians rule' would again be blatant bravado: the island's Greek cities owed no obedience to the Carthaginians. We might wonder why these wanted to put it in, unless again for propaganda.

Probably the aim was as much to impress the Romans, and others who learned of the treaty, with Carthage's supposed wide-ranging power as it was to impose real control of commerce, even where it did now have a hegemony. In Libyan and Phoenician Sardinian ports, it need have changed matters very little. Local officials there must already have existed anyway (the treaty did not create them) and any bureaucratic apparatus for collecting merchants' details – still less for forwarding these to Carthage or for Carthaginian scrutineers to come out to inspect them – would be minimal. For Punic-dominated Sicily, the terms imply that details were not recorded at all, even though sixth-century (and later) Rome did more business with Sicily than with Sardinia or even Africa.[7]

Friendly Carthaginian contacts with other Mediterranean states did exist too, as the naval alliance with the Etruscans against Alalia illustrates. Aristotle would later note how the Etruscans and Carthaginians, and other states, 'have import agreements, treaties about not doing injustice, and formal documents of alliance'. None of these instruments was novel in his time, and indeed his words could almost describe the 509 treaty. Sixth-century Punic trade with Etruria flourished, according to archaeological finds, and how close Punic-Etruscan contacts were is vividly shown by three carefully inscribed gold sheets, two in Etruscan, the third in Punic, found in 1964 at Pyrgi, one of nearby Caere's two ports on the Etruscan coast (now Santa Severa). They commemorate how, around 500 BC, the Caeritan king Thefarie Velianas dedicated a shrine to the Phoenician-Punic goddess Astarte, equated with Etruria's chief goddess Uni (who in turn was Rome's Juno). Whether the Carthaginians correspondingly put up any Etruscan deities in their city is not at present known.

Mago's own family forged important links with Sicily and Italy. His putative son Hanno, or else Mago himself if there was no Hanno, married a Syracusan lady. Their son Hamilcar, as mentioned already, enjoyed guest-friendship with Himera's tyrant Terillus – Himera in that era was one of the island's most prosperous Greek cities – and was also on warm terms with Anaxilaus, who ruled Rhegium from 494–76 and annexed Messana. Selinus was another loyal Greek ally.[8]

Even so, as with Malchus, Mago's and his successors' achievements need not all be accepted at Justin's valuation. That Mago 'regulated military training' is credible: for one thing, he had to restore discipline among the citizen soldiers who had followed Malchus (and afterwards abandoned him to his fate). He may have widened the range of citizens eligible to serve under arms, perhaps also improved their weaponry and armour and made recruiting mercenaries a more systematic practice, but in the absence of records these are guesses. That he was 'the first to create the Carthaginians' empire' reads less convincingly, unless Justin used Latin *imperium* in its abstract sense, power or might, to laud Mago's reforms as the measures that enabled his successors to build Punic power.

Punic influence over southern and south-western Sardinia did advance around 500, and not merely by peaceful methods if the late sixth-century damage or destruction found at various archaeological sites came from warfare, as widely believed. Well-established old Phoenician sites, in the south-west at Monte Sirai and east of Cagliari at Cuccureddus di Villasimius (their modern names), declined or vanished. Athenian black-figure pottery started to predominate – meaning larger imports from Greece – and over the century-and-a-half from about 525, much denser settlement patterns developed in Sardinia's south and centre. Two places were refounded or else hugely developed over the next century: Carales (Cagliari) and Neapolis – its Phoenician-Punic name would be *Qart–hadasht*, like so many other 'new cities' – on the west coast near Tharros.[9]

In Sicily, by contrast, there is no evidence of late sixth-century havoc. Panormus and Motya, especially, flourished. Military measures by Carthaginian forces probably were intermittent: whether against Elymians and other locals unfriendly to the Phoenician cities and to Carthage aiding these, or against these Phoenicians themselves to compel them to comply with Carthage's commercial or political demands. Without details of the campaigns, apart from that against Dorieus, the Magonids' actions cannot be analyzed. Hamilcar's four 'triumphs' – some sort of victory celebration – in the course of his eleven 'dictatorships' (probably sufeteships as suggested above) do point to strenuous campaigning.

What happened to Dorieus gives a glimpse of late sixth-century Sicilian strife. When the restless prince, undeterred by his earlier discomfiture in Africa, arrived in 510 to set up his colony of Heraclea near Eryx, he was swiftly attacked and slain with most of his followers, and his colony razed. In Herodotus' account seventy years later, this was done by 'the Phoenicians and Segestans'; in Diodorus, by 'the Carthaginians'; while the second-century

AD travel writer Pausanias named only 'the Segestans'. As 'Phoenicians' in Greek authors can also cover Carthaginians, and as both Carthage and its west Sicilian sister-cities continued to see any new Greek colonisers as intruders, the forces arrayed against the hapless Spartan and his settlers likely involved military elements from all three parties.[10]

Dorieus' ill-fortunes illustrate the nature of Carthage's position in the regions open to it in this period. It may well have taken some years, shows of military strength and even real fighting – Justin's 'four triumphs' for Hamilcar come to mind – to confirm Punic hegemony over the region. Treaties or other types of agreement are likely: for example, treaties about regulating imports, not doing injustices to one another (to use Aristotle's terminology) and setting up formal alliances. Diodorus' *History* regularly calls Carthage's hegemonial area in Sicily its *epikrateia*, though the term first appears in it only from 406.

It was not an imperial possession like a Roman province – no administrators sent out by the ruling state, taxes paid to it and courts under judges answering to the governor. Instead, Carthage's *epikrateia* more resembled the Roman Republic's dominance over its neighbours, first in Latium and later over all of peninsular Italy, and was probably like Carthage's own relationship with its Libyphoenician neighbours. They governed themselves but furnished troops and supplies when instructed. Western Sicily's Phoenician cities, and allies like Elymian Segesta and (in the fifth century) Greek Selinus, paid Carthage no regular taxes in money or in kind, though requisitions in wartime were perhaps a different matter. Late in the fifth century, they would issue their own coinage while Carthage issued its.

Regular tribute was certainly later exacted from Greek cities subdued by Carthage, like those left under its hegemony by the peace of 405 with Syracuse. Like the rest of the *epikrateia*, though, these continued to be self-governing. In a speech given by Diodorus to a political foe of the unscrupulous Syracusan tyrant Dionysius, drawn from a knowledgeable earlier source, the speaker Theodorus takes such tribute and autonomy for granted: in contrast to the tyrant's violence and lawlessness, 'even if the Carthaginians conquer us in war they will collect a fixed tribute, but will not prevent us from governing our city with our ancestral laws'. This was much like how Carthage ruled its Libyan subjects.

The west Sicilians had their own soldiery which a Carthaginian commander could call on, although these never formed the bulk of a Carthaginian army operating in the island (and are never heard of serving outside Sicily). In 480, Hamilcar expected his Greek ally Selinus to send a cavalry contingent to him, and when Dionysius of Syracuse periodically invaded the *epikrateia* a century later he found its cities strongly defended.

From 409 onwards, it was apparently normal for Carthage to station regular troops there too (most would be mercenaries), no doubt because wars flared up every so often with Syracuse and its allies. A stray item in Plutarch suggests that these would be under a Carthaginian officer (see Chapter 7, §1). Sooner or later in each war, all the same, Carthage would need to recruit, equip and despatch more powerful armaments, both military and naval, from Africa and elsewhere.[11]

4. The expedition of 'king' Hamilcar

Loose but acknowledged hegemony in western Sicily seems to have suited early Magonid Carthage. There were no confrontations with the Greek city-states or the native Sicilians; trade and peace went on as before. But the situation changed around 490.

After 510, some survivors of Dorieus' disaster went on to take over Heraclea Minoa, on the coast east of Selinus, and overthrow Selinus' current tyrant. Yet Selinus soon reverted to its friendship with Carthage. Punic diplomacy over this was probably seconded by Selinuntine anxiety at the revived strength of Acragas. That city reached a new height under a tyrant named Theron, who seized power in 488 and, five or six years later, expelled Terillus from Himera – the guest-friend of Hamilcar the Magonid – and took over that city. Small but wealthy, on Sicily's north coast 100km from Acragas over plains and mountains, and only 40km short of Panormus, Himera completed Theron's mastery of a broad middle swathe of the island.

Even so, this was outdone by the eastern dominion created by his fellow-tyrant – and son-in-law – Gelon, ruler of both Gela (from 491) and Syracuse, which became his with its aristocrats' support in 485. Gelon's lordship extended from the south-east coast up to the lower reaches of Mount Etna, so that the two tyrants between them dominated much of Sicily's eastern half and most of its Greek cities. This bloc plainly troubled the Carthaginians no less than it did the sole remaining independent Greek dynast, Anaxilaus, and the Greeks of Selinus. Though Anaxilaus had recently won control of Messana, that city had earlier been mastered (briefly) by Gelon's predecessor at Gela, Hippocrates. Not only Anaxilaus might suspect that Gelon would be keen to win it back.

Frictions between Carthage and the bloc grew from around 490. One reason was a dispute – or actual contest – over control of unnamed trading ports. When envoys from Greece came to Gelon in 481, asking for Syracusan aid against Xerxes, he countered that the homeland Greeks had earlier refused to aid him against a Carthaginian army and 'to take part in freeing the trading ports from which you have gained great advantages and profits' or in avenging Dorieus. Herodotus' rhetorical presentation shows that Gelon was pitching his reply at a propaganda level, but the specific mentions of a Punic army and contested ports are believable. Herodotus did not try to explain them and may not have known the details.

The ports, Gelon implied, were in Carthage's power, extremely profitable and in need of freedom. Phoenician cities like Panormus and Motya could not be seen by a Syracusan as needing liberation, so the likely candidates are Himera – wealthy, Greek, but until recently allied to Carthage through Terillus – and Selinus, also wealthy and Greek. Gelon's complaint also implies that an effort to 'free' them had been made despite no help from Greece, and his hearers could recall that Himera had just been won over (Gelon might say 'freed') by his father-in-law. In Herodotus' telling, it was Terillus' ousting and Anaxilaus' anger at this that prompted Hamilcar to act. Although no Carthaginian army took the field in Sicily before 480, plans for a major military intervention had already begun: Diodorus wrote that planning took three years. It could scarcely be kept secret from Syracuse and Acragas.

It was beyond Carthage's means, or needs, to subdue all of Sicily. Greek writers' insistence that Carthage acted under orders from Xerxes has nothing to support it. Almost certainly it was a Greek fancy, influenced by the notion that the battles of Himera and Salamis, disastrous for both invaders, were fought on the same day – a notion that Herodotus gathered from his Carthaginian informants. The real point of a military expedition must have been to wreak major damage on the Acragas-Syracuse bloc. Retaking Himera for its ousted tyrant would be a start, but defeating Theron to safeguard a restored Terillus and force Acragas under Punic dominance would surely be further aims. Acragas could not be crushed, of course, without defeating Syracuse too. Hence the scale of the planned expedition, unprecedented in Carthage's history.[12]

Hamilcar formed his army with 'Phoenicians' (Herodotus surely meant Carthaginians and other western Phoenicians) and contingents from Libya, Iberia, Liguria, Sardinia and Corsica. Diodorus added Gauls to the list. Even though his and Herodotus' claimed 300,000 soldiers is as unbelievable as Xerxes' supposed 1.7 million marching to Greece, the

Punic forces had to be sizeable if they were to fight the numbers that Theron and Gelon could muster from their citizens and allies. Between 50,000 and 60,000 is at least a reasonable surmise.

There were also the personnel of his large fleet of transports and warships. According to Diodorus, Hamilcar had 200 warships (most or all would be triremes) and 3,000 transports – soon reduced in numbers en route from Africa to Panormus by a massive storm that cost him his cavalry horses (perhaps only some of them in reality) and war-chariots. Two hundred warships may be right, for Syracuse alone had a fleet that strong: Gelon's speech to the envoys boasted that he could send that number to Greece, if they made him commander-in-chief. Such a fleet would need 30,000 or so crewmen. Three thousand transports, however, are a hopeless exaggeration. It is the same figure that Herodotus reported for Xerxes' fleet alongside the Persians' 1,207 triremes. Herodotus' figures (3,000 transports for 300,000 soldiers) would average one ship for every 100 soldiers. If Hamilcar's army actually numbered 50,000–60,000, the same average gives a more believable 500–600 transports.

The warships were mainly there to guard these transports, although Hamilcar also had to reckon that the Syracusan fleet (and any Acragantine warships if they existed) might attack. In fact the Greeks kept their ships at home. As triremes could not ride at anchor for long in open waters, the Carthaginian fleet had to be brought ashore and protected with a ditch and palisade, except for twenty ships that Hamilcar used for communications. In effect, he ruled the fleet out of any active involvement in what followed.

The campaign of 480 was short. The first Carthaginian objective was Himera, which soon had the invading army encamped outside its walls and the fleet on the shore alongside. It would be interesting to know if Terillus had accompanied his friend and champion, but he disappears from the record after appealing to Carthage for restoration. Theron of Acragas in turn arrived with his army, and he too sat down outside Himera. Despite repelling a sortie by the Himeraeans, Hamilcar chose not to attack either the well-fortified city or the nearby Acragantines. Since he now unloaded his transport fleet and sent the ships off to bring further supplies from Carthage and Sardinia, it seems his plan was to blockade Himera while holding off Theron. He was also awaiting reinforcements, including cavalry from Selinus 150km away.

This gave Gelon time to march across the island with the army of Syracuse, supposedly 55,000 strong including 5,000 cavalry, but probably smaller in reality. The year before, Gelon had boasted to the Greek envoys that he could send not only 200 warships but 20,000 infantry (the Greek term was hoplites), 2,000 cavalry and 6,000 archers and light-armed fighters to aid against Xerxes – all this on the unspoken proviso that there would be no war with Carthage. If the boast reflected reality it should offer an idea of Syracuse's military potential. In addition he had hired several thousand mercenary troops (he later gave citizenship to over 10,000), so that his and Theron's combined forces could now have amounted to over 50,000.[13]

Hamilcar, notwithstanding his past 'triumphs' and 'dictatorships', showed very little generalship. Greek tradition afterwards claimed that he was chiefly occupied with readying a huge sacrificial ceremony to win the gods' favour. The Greek cavalry swept up numbers of soldiers whom he incautiously sent out on plundering missions without trying to protect them (losing so many horses at sea probably hampered this). Then Gelon intercepted a Selinuntine letter meant for the Carthaginian, confirming that the promised cavalry would arrive on the required day. As a result, the Greek cavalrymen who rode up to the ships' encampment at sunrise on that day were Syracusans pretending to be the horsemen from Selinus. As soon as they were let in they created havoc. They set the warships on fire and looked for Hamilcar – Gelon had found out, no doubt from prisoners, that he was there by the ships and not in the army camp. Hamilcar, obsessively sacrificing whole animal victims on a huge pyre, was killed in the melee or else, so Herodotus' Carthaginian informants told him, leapt into the huge blaze himself.

During this chaos by the shore, the Carthaginian and Greek armies clashed outside Himera in a long struggle that ended only towards sunset. Hamilcar, intent on religion, must have delegated command of the Carthaginian army to a deputy – or deputies, according to Diodorus – but none is named. The death of their leader and the spectacular conflagration of the fleet, and maybe also the disparate make-up of the multinational army now without its overall commander, wore down resistance. At last it broke up amid massive slaughter, and fleeing survivors were soon trapped on a waterless hill and forced to surrender. Hundreds of others boarded the twenty warships that had not been beached, but the overburdened vessels went down in a gale as they fled. Fugitive soldiers wandering inland were all rounded up by Acragantine troops.

Diodorus preposterously claimed that 150,000 of Hamilcar's men were slain. The figure perhaps arose from the victors' estimate that half the Punic army died. The prisoner haul was as great. They were distributed among all the allied states, Syracuse and Acragas of course taking the lion's share.

Diodorus took pleasure in detailing the many building projects that Acragas' new slaves were put to – temples, underground water channels, a vast basin for fish – and mentioned that some (obviously important) Acragantines were given as many as 500 of them. Enormous quantities of booty were also captured and shared out.

Gelon returned in triumphant glory to Syracuse to be hailed as saviour and, Diodorus added, as 'king' (if so, purely an honorific accolade). Carthage and its Magonid leaders, by contrast, would have to face the realities of defeat. In the end, however, they would emerge stronger than before.[14]

Chapter 5

The Revenge of Hannibal the Magonid

1. The aftermath of Himera

The Carthaginians had expected, maybe not a walkover in Sicily, but at any rate a striking victory in line with their great armament and all the treasure spent on it. Instead, the first news to reach the city was brought by a handful of survivors in a small skiff: 'Everyone who crossed over to Sicily has perished.' The terror that gripped the city must have been very like the terror at Athens in 405 after the Battle of Aegospotami which effectively ended the Peloponnesian War or Spain's shock and horror after the catastrophe of the Armada. Losses of citizen soldiers were severe, with Diodorus painting an affecting picture of all the children now left orphaned and all the lamentations throughout the city. Expecting that at any moment Gelon and his forces would land in Africa, the Carthaginians sent off envoys with full powers to make peace.

Yet neither Gelon nor Theron had any intention of leaving Sicily, and neither did they care to wage a long-running war in the island. The peace terms that Gelon dictated extracted an indemnity of 2,000 talents (equivalent to 12 million Athenian drachmas) to cover the war's costs, and required the Carthaginians to build two temples in their city to store copies of the treaty. However, the victors made no move against western Sicily – not even against Selinus, which apparently made its peace with them on unknown terms, as did Anaxilaus, who died in his bed in 476.

Carthage even had a friendly voice at Gelon's dynastic court: none other than his wife, Theron's daughter Damarete. She received a thank-you gift of a gold wreath (*stephanos*) worth no less than 100 talents. It is relevant too that the dead Hamilcar was half-Syracusan. Members of his mother's family very likely dwelt in Syracuse and, along with Damarete, could agree to use influence if the envoys appealed to them. In any case, the scale of Hamilcar's disaster was such that Gelon and Theron plainly felt no concern about a Carthaginian revanche for the foreseeable future. Gelon even demobilized his 10,000 mercenaries to make them Syracusan citizens, rather to the annoyance of some native Syracusans.

The debacle of Himera arguably should have ended the Magonids' dominance at home, yet it did not. One reason could be that enough aristocrats had been killed in the battle to deprive the family's political opponents of strong leadership at this critical moment. Another was that the six sons of Hasdrubal and Hamilcar survived and, in Justin's words, 'through these men the affairs of Carthage were governed in that period'. This point (as often with Justin) has to be modified, for Diodorus elsewhere recorded that one son, Gisco, died at Selinus, exiled from Carthage 'due to his father's defeat'. This may have been a political excuse, instigated years later, as we shall see.

As noted earlier, the dead Hamilcar, far from being reviled for the defeat in Sicily, received cult honours at home, and not just there but in Carthage's sister-colonies too, even in Sicily. An intriguing theory is that a famous and beautiful Greek (or Greek-modelled) statue of a young man in exquisitely chiselled robes, found at Motya in 1979 and datable to the early fifth century BC, portrays Hamilcar (or on another interpretation, Gelon). If he died not only as general and *sufete* but also as high priest of one of the city's great gods, his self-sacrifice, real or claimed, could redeem his reputation and serve the interests of his sons and nephews. There were enough of them in any case to keep the family linked to much of the rest of the city's surviving aristocracy through kinsmen and marriages. Even after 480, critics and enemies may therefore have found it hard to undermine the Magonids, although they did not give up and were to win an important success nearer home, one which probably affected Gisco.[1]

Himera disabused the Carthaginians, for seventy years anyway, of thoughts about intervening in Greek Sicily. The hegemony over the island's western quarter continued, but there too the unusually long – and surely welcome – peace was rarely disturbed. Another clash between Segesta and (it seems) Selinus did flare up in 454, with the Selinuntines victorious (it also seems), but Carthage took no part and nothing came of it.

The dynasties of Gelon and Theron did not last much beyond their immediate successors, Gelon's brother Hieron ruling in splendour from 478–67 and Theron's vicious son being ejected from Acragas in 471. Hieron had no quarrel with Sicily's Phoenician or native cities or their Punic protectress, nor did Carthage play any part in a war he fought against the Etruscans. Hieron won a great naval victory in 474 off Cumae near the Bay of Naples in Italy, commemorating it with a bronze Etruscan helmet which he dedicated to Apollo at Delphi. Pindar's flattering odes in Hieron's honour included the hope that Carthaginians and Etruscans together had been taught to keep the peace. The hope was certainly fulfilled, though not from fear of fresh Greek lessons.

Once the tyrannies were overthrown, the broad hegemonies of Syracuse and Acragas across Sicily collapsed and various forms of aristocratic and even democratic regimes took over. The Siceliots even indulged in a rare event, a general congress of city-states in 461 which settled interstate affairs for over a decade. Their main headache in the mid-fifth century was a revival of the eastern native Sicilian communities, the Sicels, under a charismatic leader named Ducetius. He cooperated with, or defied, the Greeks as it suited him, built up a pan-Sicel league across much of central Sicily and founded a new colony at Cale Acte, 'Fair Cape', on the mid-north coast (it would be the birthplace of one of the famous Hannibal's personal historians). At one point he even brought Syracuse and Acragas into conflict: Acragas supported him but they lost, and his success was long gone before he died around 440.

The Carthaginians could have chosen to buy into these frictions to weaken the Sicilian Greeks and bring the Sicels, and their more obscure neighbours the Sicans, under Punic influence like the Elymians. Instead, they let Greeks and Sicels play out their differences untroubled by any prodding. The Magonids surely calculated that such rivalries guaranteed Greek non-interference in the *epikrateia*, which was entirely suitable. Magonid Carthage had plenty of preoccupations elsewhere.[2]

Once supposed to have suffered almost crippling economic damage and loss of trade thanks to Himera, the republic in fact rebounded over the rest of the century. Archaeological investigations show that the physical city expanded to well over 60 hectares (150 acres), perhaps not far below 100 by the end of the fifth century. New residential areas grew up between Byrsa hill and the shore, and below the western side of Byrsa. Some at least of the houses were well-built, even luxurious: wall paintings and internal peristyles began to appear. New walls were put up to protect the extended city, not to mention other features of heightened resources and sensibility: improved rubbish-disposal for instance (pits for garbage, common earlier, almost disappeared) and toilet facilities in the larger houses.

This growth in amenities and population was due, in part at least, to strong and indeed widening trade, particularly with the Greek world. Archaeological remains of trade goods, such as tableware pottery and oil and wine amphorae, point to busy trading with most of the Mediterranean, from Spain and Massilia to Corinth and cities around the Aegean. Greek Sicily was a prime business partner. In a welcome if slightly censorious description of fifth-century Acragas' riches and prosperity, Diodorus stressed how most of its territory was planted with olive trees 'from which they gathered an abundant harvest and sold it to Carthage', one of the sources of 'fortunes of unbelievable size' (which, regrettably, made Acragantines effete). Wealth also accrued to Carthage, greatly impressing the Greek world. In 415, a Syracusan leader, Hermocrates, described Carthage as owning 'very much gold and silver', and so worth cultivating against Athens, which had designs on Sicily.[3]

Carthage's fifth-century wellbeing will partly also have stemmed from profitable new assertiveness in Africa. To be sure, Justin's claim of wars against 'Mauri' (the peoples of Mauretania) and Numidians must be treated sceptically, and we do not know who the Hanno was who – according to the separate *Prologues* to Trogus' history – campaigned in fifth-century Africa (see Chapter 10). Nevertheless, Carthage's own citizen territory (its *chora* in Greek) extended to all of the Cape Bon peninsula by 400 BC, no doubt also over the coastlands between there and the city, and probably beyond Tunes to the west. It also now ruled, taxed and exploited much of inland Libya, harshly enough to provoke seething bitterness and, in 396, a major war with the city's new subjects. But before then Carthage built up the resources to launch new expeditions into Sicily, win stunning victories and suffer dramatic reverses, all these under Magonid leaders.

Like Malchus before them, the later Magonids did not have things wholly their own way. Intermittent setbacks and even the glory of success in Libya provoked political resistance at home. According to Justin, a time came during the fifth century when Magonid dominance ('a family of generals' who 'directed and judged everything themselves') was seen as a threat to civic freedom and so was curbed by a new court of 100 'senators', set up to scrutinize and if necessary punish a general's misdeeds. This report needs correction. Justin fairly certainly confused two separate developments: political attacks on the Magonids in the mid-fifth century and the creation of the famous council or court of One Hundred and Four, probably some time after 396.

Justin wrote that Himilco, one of Hamilcar's three sons, replaced him in Sicily and won victories, but in the end brought down disaster on Carthage and shame on himself. In reality, this disastrous Himilco is quite plainly the much later Magonid whose many victories in Sicily were cancelled by catastrophe in 396 and who killed himself not long after (see Chapter 6).

Justin cut out all details of Carthage's Sicilian wars between 409 and 396, yet we know that Trogus narrated the essentials: they are stated in the

Prologues. His epitomator, by contrast, preferred lavishing rhetoric and imagination on how the Carthaginians bewailed the later Himilco's disaster and how miserably he ended. In doing this, he fatuously mistook that Himilco to be Hamilcar's son, and almost certainly too he dragged the creation of the One Hundred and Four back two or three generations into the fifth century. In reality, neither Justin's account nor the longer one in Diodorus report the later Himilco being prosecuted by the One Hundred and Four: what condemned him was the contempt of his fellow-citizens and his own sense of guilt. The court was probably, therefore, set up after 396, maybe as a reaction to his mishandling of the recent war with Syracuse, in which he had not only shown military and naval incompetence but had committed sacrilege against Greek temples and tombs.

The exile of Gisco, another of Hamilcar's sons, was more likely (though not certainly) by judgement of the *adirim*, the Carthaginian senate – whether or not on the vengeful charge stated by Diodorus. Gisco's was the sole known Magonid scalp, but their enemies' success blunted his kinsmen's potency. Even though his son Hannibal stayed and later reached high office, the family could not have the exile recalled. Gisco chose, moreover, to live and die in Selinus, whose pro-Carthaginian attitude was cooling over time because of its virulent enmity to Segesta. The choice (rather than, say, Panormus) suggests both disenchantment with his fellow-citizens and fear that he would still be vulnerable if he remained within Carthage's *epikrateia*. It would take the victories in 409 and 406–05 of his son Hannibal and nephew, the later Himilco, to restore Magonid primacy, at least for a time.[4]

2. A new Sicilian war: the first expedition of Hannibal the Magonid

Carthage watched but did not involve itself when a fresh general conflict erupted in the Greek world from 431 – the notorious Peloponnesian War between the Athenian and Spartan alliances, which lasted until 404. Carthage stayed so aloof that in 433 or 432, Leontini, north of Syracuse, and Rhegium in Italy sought alliances with Athens to protect them against bullying Syracuse. These alliances brought Athenian naval forces into Sicilian waters a few years later, inducing unsavoury notions at Athens about involving itself more deeply.

Whether the Magonids were still in exclusive charge or now shared power with others, the Carthaginian leadership was probably content enough to see Syracuse, freshly ambitious under a democratic constitution, being distracted by enemies from the eastern Greek world. It meant continuing security for Punic-dominated western Sicily. This attitude held even when, probably in 418 or 417, Segesta and its smaller Elymian neighbour Halicyae gained Athens as a treaty ally too, as fragmentary inscriptions show. They acted not from fear of Syracuse but through enmity with Selinus. Athenian intervention in that quarrel, the Carthaginians could reckon, was impossible with Syracuse and Acragas in the way.[5]

The situation changed with the great and disastrous Athenian expedition against Syracuse in 415–13. Its pretext was aiding Segesta against Selinus: but in reality its goals were Syracuse and – at least in the eyes of would-be Athenian imperialists like Socrates' friend, the charismatic Alcibiades – mastery over Sicily. Alcibiades even spoke of crushing Carthage, which did not deter Athens from making overtures to it in 415, with predictable lack of success. The Athenian fleet and army that then sailed to Sicily went nowhere near the west of the island, instead bogging down in a hopeless siege of Syracuse. Their final destruction – 40,000 soldiers and sailors, Athenians and allies – was as total as Hamilcar's at Himera. Even the commanders did not survive, and in Greece and the Aegean, Athens' sixty-year-old maritime empire began to collapse.

Syracuse's triumph set the Carthaginians thinking. Their reasoning, though, was not straightforward. The revival of Syracusan power, with Himera, Gela and Camarina as allies, was the obvious potential destabilizer in Sicily: Syracuse was therefore the obvious target for intervention. Acragas and Messana had stayed neutral in Syracuse's recent life-and-death struggle, so might be seen as natural allies for Carthage, but they were not approached. Hannibal son of Gisco proved to have quite other plans.

When in 410 the Segestans appealed to Carthage for help in their latest war with Selinus, Hannibal pressed his countrymen to act. Now quite elderly, he was, in Diodorus' words, Carthage's 'leading citizen' and 'holding the kingship under law' (as well as being, we are told, a hereditary hater of Greeks). The description must mean that he was one of the *sufetes* that year and implies, too, that the Magonid family had regained its domestic primacy, although they had to argue their case when proposing new policies.

Hannibal's actions as general of the resulting expedition to Sicily in 409 would show a new face of Carthaginian and Magonid policy: two large and rich Siceliot cities captured, sacked, depopulated and razed, mass slaughter of captives and force combined with terror the watchword. These methods would be applied all over again, on a still more fearful level, when Carthage struck into Sicily a second time three years later.[6]

When Segesta appealed, the Carthaginians – all the while making military preparations – made a diplomatic gesture: Carthage and Segesta together advised Syracuse that they would accept its arbitration over the quarrel with Selinus. That city rejected the idea as (supposedly) Hannibal knew it would, and his calculation that this would keep Syracuse neutral paid off. He could now launch operations. The opening move was to despatch to Segesta a Libyan force of 5,000, plus 800 mercenaries from Campania in Italy – the first appearance of these tough and often unscrupulous Italic professionals in Punic service. The Segestans and these reinforcements badly defeated Selinus' forces, giving Hannibal time to embark his own army for Sicily.

Like his grandfather, he had made thorough preparations. An army, which Diodorus' sources Ephorus and Timaeus grandly estimated at 200,000 and 100,000 respectively, was recruited during 410, drawn like his grandfather's again from varied parts of the western Mediterranean: Iberians, Campanians, Libyans and Carthage itself. Hannibal's contemporary, the Athenian general and author Xenophon, also gave him 100,000, so Timaeus' figure might be correct. On the other hand, Punic strength after the fall of Selinus was only 40,000, again according to Diodorus – this before Hannibal was supposedly reinforced by 20,000 Sicans and Sicels, the native inland peoples. That number looks like another propaganda piece (or a guess), but 40,000 for Hannibal's own army, after losses at Selinus and desertions, would fit. It could reflect a realistic account that Hannibal later gave to his home authorities or put into a commemorative inscription, like the one set up by his colleague Himilco narrating their later expedition.

Diodorus gave the Carthaginian army 80,000 men during the ensuing siege of Himera, again a likely exaggeration. A clue to Hannibal's original strength may be estimated from Ephorus' figure for the cavalry – 4,000 men – which looks plausible in itself. On a common though not invariable ratio of ten infantrymen per cavalryman (like Gelon's army in 480), it would suggest infantry 40,000–50,000 strong. As for the naval forces, Diodorus asserted sixty warships and 1,500 transports, again a mix of the plausible and implausible. While the warship total looks reasonable, the figure for transports (half the total claimed for Hamilcar's transports – and Xerxes' – seventy years before) is surely an overblown guess; 400–500 would be a better surmise. On these reckonings, apart from the transports, Carthage sent some 54,000–64,000 combatants to Sicily in 409 BC.

Hannibal conducted his campaign more sagely than his ancestor. As well as a powerful conventional army, he brought six ironclad battering rams and – their first mention in western Mediterranean warfare – six huge siege towers, called *helepoleis* in Greek. Landing at the site of the later city of Lilybaeum (Marsala) and beaching his ships in Motya's nearby lagoon, he was now joined by Segestan and other allied troops. Who these latter were is not stated, but it seems they included some Greeks – perhaps pro-Carthaginian exiles from Siceliot cities. Reinforced, the Carthaginian army marched to Selinus, put it under siege, and after nine days of fierce Selinuntine resistance – but crucially before a relief force of Acragantines, Syracusans and others could arrive – broke into the city. Pillage, massacre, enslavements and physical destruction ensued. The slaughtered citizens – men, women and children – numbered 16,000, wrote Diodorus; 5,000 others were captured. Only 2,600 defenders escaped to Acragas.

This exercise in terror, against a city which had been Carthage's and Hamilcar's sole Greek ally in 480, was deliberate. A harsher exercise followed. Hannibal quit the burnt-out corpse of Selinus to march north against Himera, joined en route by the reportedly 20,000-strong Sicels and Sicans. The 6,000 Himeraean defenders had been reinforced by 4,000 Syracusans, Acragantines and other Greeks, but the attackers' ferocious onslaught could not be stalled for long. A skilful Punic-inspired rumour reached the defenders that the enemy fleet was setting out to attack Syracuse. The Syracusan troops promptly left for home, starting a mass flight from Himera: women and children on some triremes sent from Syracuse, the Syracusan and other allied fighters overland and with them a large body of civilians – apparently with no pursuit from the Carthaginians. Those who had to stay behind could not be saved by the returning triremes, for Hannibal's army burst into Himera first.

An orgy of slaughter left perhaps half these Himeraeans dead. After a systematic sack of the city, Hannibal had it razed to the ground, temples and all. Of the captives, the women and children were enslaved, but Hannibal ordered the 3,000 male prisoners to be taken down to the shore, where Hamilcar had died. There he tortured and then killed them.

The massacre and Himera's utter destruction were symbolic vengeance for his grandfather's death, but were also illogical. Hamilcar had been slain by Gelon's Syracusans, if not by his own hand. No doubt Hannibal also meant to intimidate the rest of Greek Sicily, but he swiftly undercut any impact from it. The campaign had lasted just three months. After rewarding the army with plunder, assigning some forces – not large, to judge by the sequel – to garrison duty in the *epikrateia* and dismissing the Sicilian allies and Campanian mercenaries, he sailed with the rest of his men back to Carthage to a predictably rapturous welcome.[7]

3. Carthage victorious, 406–05 BC

Although Hannibal's expedition in 409 has sometimes been judged a private Magonid revenge-crusade, that is no more likely than his grandfather's. To be sure, the eradication of Himera and liquidation of its captured menfolk symbolically appeased Hamilcar's ghost, but the even greater bloodletting at Selinus – Carthage's one-time friend and never a foe – came out of the blue. If the agony of Selinus had any aim besides plundering one of the richest cities in Sicily, it must have been to spread shock and awe through the rest, and not just those outside the *epikrateia*. The measures at Himera will have had the same aims, while added to them was the ritual purging of Carthage's seventy-year-old humiliation. Not only Hannibal felt that humiliation: as his grandfather enjoyed cult honours in the Punic world, avenging him would be pleasing to the gods and their worshippers.

Yet the victors of 409 gave only limited thought to the major reverberations that their war could arouse. Apart from the garrisons in the west, Selinus was given back to the citizens who had escaped (they had to pay a tax to Carthage) and plans were made to replace Himera with a new colony of settlers from North Africa. This was duly founded in 407 at a site with hot springs (*thermae*) 12km further west, and named Thermae Himeraeae. Later, it seems, some survivors of the shattered city were also allowed to return. By then the clouds were already gathering for a new military intervention in the island by Carthage.

This may have been prompted by a Greek act of revanche in 408 by a Syracusan exile, that city's one-time leader Hermocrates. Forced out by his political foes and eager to earn recall by damaging the western Phoenicians, he seized Selinus with a small mercenary force, gathered Selinuntine and other survivors, and with a still small army of 6,000 attacked Motya and Panormus, defeating troops from those cities (no doubt including the garrisons left by Hannibal) and garnering plentiful plunder. At Himera he gave proper burial to the Syracusan soldiers who had died in combat. None of these acts led to his recall, and when he tried force in 407 he lost his life. One survivor of the failed putsch at Syracuse was a badly wounded but gifted young officer named Dionysius.

The quixotic campaign in western Sicily galvanized Carthage. It did not help matters that in 407 a Syracusan embassy arrived 'to blame them [the Carthaginians] for the war and demand an end to the quarrel'. Why was it sent, assuming that Diodorus' dating is right? By then, blame for ongoing hostilities lay really with Hermocrates and his invasion of the *epikrateia*. If the

Syracusans meant Hannibal's campaign two years earlier, the blaming came very late. Either way, it would serve only to feed the Carthaginians' irritation. They were in fact already planning a second expedition, as Syracuse knew (wide-ranging mercenary recruitment and large-scale military and naval preparations could not be covered up), so such an embassy would look more like a challenge to fight rather than an even semi-serious call for peace.[8]

The new expedition was again carefully planned, with Hannibal reappointed to command – overriding his own objection that he was now too old. Instead of retiring him, the Carthaginians gave him an equal colleague, his kinsman Himilco son of Hanno. Their recruitment hunt ranged even more widely than in 410, bringing in Iberians, Balearic islanders, Libyans, 'Phoenicians' (meaning Libyphoenicians; maybe men too from Phoenician Sardinia), Campanians, Mauretanians, Numidians and warriors from the Lepcis-Cyrene region (among them no doubt Macae, whose ancestors had collaborated in ejecting Dorieus). Predictably, the total was imaginatively bloated by Ephorus, who alleged no fewer than 300,000 men, while both the contemporary Xenophon and later Timaeus gave him 120,000. This time Timaeus' figure may be near the mark, for it is clear that the Carthaginians had determined to teach the Sicilian Greeks an unforgettable lesson in blood, fire and ruin. On the sea, the Carthaginians launched 120 triremes and supposedly 1,000 transports.

An odd piece of international diplomacy also featured in 406. Carthage, amid its war-efforts against the Siceliots, and Athens – struggling to avoid disaster in the closing stages of the Peloponnesian War – struck a treaty making them 'friends and allies'. No ancient source noted it, but a very damaged inscription at Athens supplies the barest outline: heralds were sent from Carthage to Athens, then heralds from Athens 'to Sicily' to the generals Hannibal and Himilco, to confirm the treaty. What practical meaning it could have had is not obvious, but, at the time, Athens' naval foes in the Aegean included a Syracusan squadron, so any trouble that Carthage could bring down on Syracuse would be welcome. Carthage in turn might wish to show that it had no quarrel with Greeks across the sea or even perhaps in southern Italy. But the treaty was not publicised, and in any case the Greeks in Italy continued to see Carthage as a menace.[9]

Diodorus and others were to claim that the Carthaginians' ultimate goal was to make the whole of Sicily subject. It may be true, to judge from the scorched-earth destruction wrought from the edge of the *epikrateia* up to the walls of Syracuse. Only Sicily's north east escaped attention – and that only because circumstances would turn at a crucial moment. Even so, the campaigns of the Magonid generals in 406–05 ended with Carthage's greatest success in the long history of its wars in Sicily.

The Siceliots knew they were menaced. By contrast with the piecemeal reactions to Hannibal's expedition three years before, Syracuse, Acragas and many others readied forces of their own and agreed to cooperate. Apprehensive Italian Greek states contributed to those of Syracuse and its allies, while Acragas boosted its army with 1,500 mercenaries under a Spartan officer named Dexippus, and also with Hannibal's former 800 Campanians (these had deserted him, dissatisfied about pay). Syracuse readied its fleet too.

The Carthaginian operations started badly. A naval advance force of forty triremes, sailing probably for Panormus, was intercepted by a similarly sized Syracusan squadron off the Eryx coast and soundly beaten. But the Greek victory was not followed up, though the allies could (for instance) have stationed a strong fleet near Selinus, Heraclea Minoa or Acragas to fall on the main Punic armada as it made for Motya or Panormus.

In summer 406, the generals disembarked their huge army without opposition, marched unopposed across hills, mountains and valleys to Acragas (130km by the shortest route from Panormus, longer if via the new colony of Thermae, or from Motya a good 140km), and put the second-largest city of Sicily under close siege as soon as a *pro forma* demand for it to be friendly or neutral was rejected. They had enough troops for two siege camps, one directly outside Acragas and the other on nearby hills.[10]

Hannibal and Himilco ran their siege poorly and suffered for it. Their opening assaults were beaten back, siege towers and all. Then after (it seems) just a few days, a serious plague epidemic broke out in their army. The men blamed Hannibal's impious destruction of tombs and other sacred monuments outside the city, done so as to gain better access to its walls, but the sickness had probably been picked up on the march or brought by one of the army's contingents. Not only ordinary soldiers died, but so too did Hannibal son of Gisco, paying a mortal price for his countrymen's trust in him.

Himilco, left in sole command, was at any rate energetic and undeterred, even if his situation was far from easy. One way – a rare one, to judge from our sources – of dealing with his men's superstitious fears was to sacrifice a young boy, probably a slave or captive, to Carthage's chief god Baal Hamon ('Cronus' in Diodorus' account), and throw cattle overboard from one or more transports as offerings to 'Poseidon', perhaps Baal Saphon (the same god who had failed to help his ancestor). The gods were at first no greater help than in 480. To confront a powerful Syracusan and allied army of 30,000 foot and 5,000 horse under a general named Daphnaeus, Himilco despatched the Iberians and others from the hilltop camp, only for them to be overwhelmed near the River Himeras halfway between Gela and Acragas, and be chased all the way back to his remaining camp while the Greeks seized the other. In these actions, incidentally, one of Daphnaeus' most vigorous subordinates was Hermocrates' supporter Dionysius. The besiegers were now blockaded.[11]

With his numbers cut back by plague and losses, Himilco may now have had only about as many men as the Greeks, and could do no more than hold his position for weeks while the enemy controlled the countryside. As a result, provisions ran short and his troops became restive to the point of mutiny, especially the current Campanian contingent. This was the moment when he had to placate them with his Carthaginian soldiers' no doubt luxurious goblets (see Chapter 2 §3). However, the opportunity abruptly came to turn the situation around – with notable help from his foes.

Punic military intelligence outclassed that of their opponents, for when he learned of a large Syracusan provision fleet sailing for Acragas he had time to summon forty triremes from Panormus and Motya, sally out to sea, defeat the escorting warships and capture the fleet, with its lavish stocks of food. Even before this, fissures and factions had begun to appear among the Greeks. For failing to attack the remaining Punic camp directly after the victory at the Himeras River, four of the five Acragantine generals had been murdered by the combined Greek army and the Spartan Dexippus was accused – maybe rightly – of treachery. The loss of the provision fleet and the exhaustion of supplies in Acragas now led to an utter collapse of morale.

The Campanian deserters, for a reported bribe of 15 talents, re-deserted back to the Carthaginian army and compatriots there. The allied army from the east, prodded by Dexippus (himself supposedly bribed by Himilco with 15 talents), decided that Acragas could not be held or the campaign be continued. It meant that the city had to be completely abandoned. Tens of thousands of its people took the road eastward to Gela under the protection of the retreating Greek army. It was late December 406, seven to eight months since the start of the siege. Himilco let them go, then at dawn the next day took over the city of Phalaris and Theron. One of the jewels of fifth-century western Greek urban culture, it was systematically ransacked, everyone still remaining was killed, and the temples and shrines destroyed. After spending winter and spring there, readying his troops and manufacturing new war-machines, he had the empty city razed flat and marched for Gela.

Over the same winter, bitterness, suspicion and betrayals wracked his foes. The disheartened Italian Greeks left for home. At Syracuse, the returning generals were denounced for supposed treachery, first by Acragantine refugees and then by Dionysius. Quickly elected one of the new generals and playing on everyone's fear of a looming Carthaginian onslaught, this charismatic young man – he was only 25 – skilfully garnered support from all sides: the mercenaries in Syracuse's employ (promising them double pay), Gela's garrison and citizens, those at Leontini and most though not all of his fellow-citizens. He based much of his popular appeal on attacking Syracuse's rich elite as parasites and unpatriotic – yet two of his chief backers were rich aristocrats themselves, Philistus (whom he would one day exile) and Hipparinus, who became one of the other generals and later his father-in-law.

When Himilco sent a herald, probably in the spring of 405, to discuss ransoming prisoners (the Carthaginians must have captured some Syracusan aristocrats), Dionysius claimed that the real purpose was to corrupt the other generals – Hipparinus no doubt excepted. Amid mounting hysteria, he denounced the generals as traitors and was appointed 'general with supreme powers' (*strategos autokrator*) along with a 1,000-strong personal bodyguard corps. Dexippus was sent away, and after that it was no problem to have the still dangerous Daphnaeus executed. These were standard tactics for an intending Greek tyrant, so much so that most or all Syracusans surely realized where things were heading. But fear of Carthage and distrust of factional leaders paralysed the city's democracy.

Greek political quarrels gave Himilco plenty of time to ready his forces and march from Acragas to Gela in early summer. Dionysius' promises of help were not matched by speed, leaving the desperate Geloans to defend their city by themselves for some days. He did eventually arrive with a claimed 30,000 or more Syracusan, allied and mercenary infantry and 1,000 cavalry, while fifty triremes sailed up via Cape Pachynus (modern Passaro) in support. But his complex and poorly coordinated attack by land and sea on the Carthaginian camp fell apart. A scene ensued balefully reminiscent of Acragas the year before. The tyrant determined that saving Gela was impossible, forced its entire population to evacuate – this time to Syracuse, 150km away by road – and did the same to Camarina. As at Acragas, Himilco was able to enter a deserted Gela and thoroughly sack it.

Himilco now had an opportunity to strike a decisive blow against Syracuse while a furious uprising there of embittered citizens confronted their new tyrant. It took all of Dionysius' daring and ruthlessness to force his way into the city and smash them, but he achieved it without Punic interference. Himilco's army had been struck again by plague and his campaign stopped. Where he was we do not know, as a paragraph or so is lost from Diodorus' text. He had probably advanced to the now-abandoned Camarina, possibly even up to Syracuse itself, only to be immobilized with his fever-wracked army. It was thus in Carthage's interest as well as Dionysius' to end hostilities. Himilco offered peace talks.

Dionysius' enemies at the time accused him of colluding with Himilco to secure his power, and they were very likely right. The shaken tyrant was left with minimum room for manoeuvre. The treaty of 405 stipulated that Carthage should have the Elymians and Sicans, 'together with the original colonists' (the Sicilian Phoenicians), and should allow people from Selinus, Acragas, Himera, Gela and Camarina to return home, but they must not refortify their cities and must pay a tax to Carthage. Leontini, Messana and the Sicels were to be independent, leaving Dionysius solely Syracuse and its territory to rule. A final proviso required prisoners of war and captured ships to be returned by either side. This was a hopeful rather than practical demand, for it can hardly have been applied to the thousands of Greeks (including women and children) who had been sold off into slavery, many abroad, over the past two years.[12]

Carthage was finally ascendant in Sicily, at great human cost. According to Diodorus, more than half of its army had died from the plague alone, and of course the massacres, enslavements, lootings and city depopulations were a further human toll. From 405, the Carthaginians dominated half or more of the island. The shrunken hulks of once-great Greek cities – Selinus, Acragas, Gela and Camarina – were satellites, and Syracuse was stripped of all the areas that Gelon and Hieron had mastered.

When Himilco came home, he dedicated an offering in the children's cemetery below Byrsa to commemorate his and Hannibal's deeds, with the inscription mentioned earlier (see Chapter 1). Only damaged fragments survive and varied translations have been tried. It seems to date its year by two magistrates (surely *sufetes*), 'Ešmunamos son of Adnibaal the *rab* and Hanno son of Bod'astart son of Hanno the *rab*'. According to the surviving text, 'the *rabim* Adnibaal son of Gescon the *rab* and Himilco son of Hanno the *rab*' acted against – or went to – a person or entity called *'Iš*, then 'seized Agragant and pacified it' (or, in a different interpretation, 'seized Agragant and established peace with the citizens of Naxos'). Old Hannibal son of Gisco had died before the capture of Acragas, but Himilco still honoured him as partner in the victory. If the small city of Naxos on the east coast did earn his mention, maybe it had made overtures to him and Hannibal in 406 – like Athens – and opted out of the war. That did not save it from Dionysius' vengeance a few years later: Naxos had backed Athens against Syracuse in 415.[13]

The Carthaginian triumph was tainted. The army brought back not only glory and plunder but the plague, which began to ravage the city and the rest of Libya. The hegemony that Himilco had imposed on two-thirds of Sicily was precarious, won at the cost of enduring Greek resentment. And in recognizing Dionysius as master of Syracuse, Carthage ensured four more decades of see-saw Sicilian warfare.

Chapter 6

Carthage against Dionysius and Syracuse

1. Uneasy peace, 405–398

Dionysius of Syracuse was resourceful, cunning and cultured, and ruthless to the point of savagery. Defeat by Carthage freed him over the next few years to focus on consolidating his position at home and expanding Syracuse's power outside the Carthaginian *epikrateia*. In spite of strenuous, but poorly led, efforts by his fellow-Syracusans to get rid of him, he turned Ortygia island, the oldest sector of Syracuse, into a fortified stronghold for himself, his closest supporters and the mercenaries who maintained his regime. To make Syracuse almost impregnable, he built a 27km wall to enclose the plateau on the city's northern and western sides, with a powerful fortress called Euryalus – still visible today – at its westernmost point 10km from Ortygia. According to Diodorus, 60,000 workers, the tyrant himself among them, completed the mammoth project in just twenty days.

That done, Dionysius turned his eyes to Syracuse's neighbours. He seized the east-coast cities of Naxos and Catana, selling their citizens – all Greeks – into slavery, gave Catana to Campanian mercenaries who had rescued him from his own citizens' attack, forced the residents of Leontini 50km north of Syracuse to migrate to swell the population in his own city, seized the small Sicel city of Aetna on the southern edge of that mountain and later settled discharged Campanian mercenaries there. He made war on the inland Sicel cities of Enna, Herbita and Herbessus as he strove to bring central Sicily under his control. Rhegium and Messana made warlike noises – they had historic ties with the depopulated Naxos and Catana – but soon accepted coexistence.

Peace with Carthage had started reviving Syracusan trade and economic life. Businessmen from Carthage, and no doubt other Libyphoenician cities, returned in some numbers to Siceliot cities, especially Syracuse itself, where by 398 they owned fine houses and its harbours were packed with Punic cargo ships. More troubling to Dionysius (so at least Diodorus claimed), the continued fighting and population displacements in Greek Sicily were encouraging too many Siceliots to migrate over to the Punic quarter, where they were welcomed by its cities with grants of their citizenship and land. If Diodorus was right both about this migration and in stating that the Greek cities under Punic rule were eager to be freed, the migrants must have gone to places like Motya, Panormus and Thermae Himeraeae; especially Thermae, where a Greek population soon became significant. Migrants of a different and less attractive type were a body of other Campanian mercenaries paid off by Dionysius. After making their way back to Sicily's west, they were welcomed at Entella, a mountaintop city near Segesta (they had perhaps been stationed there earlier, when in Carthaginian service), but then slaughtered its male citizenry overnight, married the widows and took over the city for themselves.[1]

Peace and reviving prosperity would seem exactly what Sicily, and particularly Syracuse, needed. Dionysius, however, was a military dynast needing military successes and mercenary forces to keep himself in power – two factors that depended each on the other. Moreover, he had wider ambitions than merely recreating Gelon's old hegemony over the eastern half of the island. Once this hegemony was achieved, or even sooner, he launched a massive naval and military build-up, with Carthage's *epikrateia* the obvious target.

Specialist and well-paid craftsmen were brought in from elsewhere – even from the *epikrateia*, apparently without the Carthaginians trying to prevent it – to construct warships in the dockyards in Ortygia, fashion weapons and armour, and build new siege engines and a new device, the catapult. Dionysius would be credited with inventing this powerful machine, which fired steel-tipped missiles that struck terror into the Carthaginians first exposed to them. The forests of Mount Etna and southern Italy supplied the huge quantities of timber needed, enabling the Syracusan navy to leap from 110 ships to 310.

Diodorus was to claim that Dionysius devised two new warship types, the quadrireme and quinquereme; but according to Aristotle, the quadrireme was a Carthaginian invention. Whatever the case, neither type earns much mention in ensuing events: Dionysius used his very first quinquereme to fetch a bride from Locri in Italy in 399, and a few years later was aboard one in a sea-fight with Italian Greek foes – perhaps the same one, used as his flagship. Otherwise, the only warships mentioned in his wars were triremes. It may be that his naval defeats in 397 and 396 persuaded him to stick chiefly with the tried and true trireme after all. The big ships came into their own, the quinquereme especially, only much later in the century.[2]

His land forces were the most imposing ever seen in Greek Sicily. Recruits came not only from Syracuse itself, whose citizens actually welcomed the supposed crusade to free Greek Sicily, but from other Siceliot states, even those reviving under Carthage's rule – notably Camarina, Acragas and Selinus – all of them enthused by the call to arms. Dionysius also hired at least 10,000 mercenary troops, and once the campaign opened in 397 BC, his army was joined by further contingents en route, to reach Motya with 80,000 infantry and more than 3,000 cavalry (if we can trust Diodorus' figures). This would be an infantry host as large as the Roman army facing Hannibal at Cannae nearly 200 years later. Accompanying it were 200 warships and 500 supply ships.

The infantry total is probably exaggerated. The cavalry figure in proportion to the infantry is unusually small, and a year later, in 396, Dionysius would field only 30,000 foot with again 3,000 cavalry. Admittedly, many of his allies had by then fallen away and the previous campaign had involved some serious fighting (no doubt with some inevitable desertions), but even so he is not likely to have lost 60 per cent of his original forces in under a year. Thirty thousand horse and foot look like Syracuse's usual military capacity in these years: the same total was recorded during the campaigns of 406–05 and would be again as late as 368. The army that marched out in spring or summer 397 can be estimated, therefore, at a rather more realistic 45,000–50,000 infantry plus Diodorus' believable 3,000 cavalry.[3]

None of these preparations or propaganda claims can have been hidden from Carthage, yet virtually no countermeasures were readied in western Sicily or at home. When Dionysius told his fellow-citizens that the plague's ravages had weakened the enemy, it seems he was right, at least in the short run. Even if Carthage's overseas trade was reviving, the subject Libyans, already heavily oppressed, were seriously restive, as their rebellion a year or two later showed. This was another headache for Himilco the Magonid, still at the head of affairs. As a result, in spite of Dionysius' lengthy and extensive war preparations, there were no field forces in western Sicily to face him, but at most only the city garrisons Himilco had left behind in 405. The result was a calamity for Punic Sicily.

2. Himilco vs Dionysius

The war was launched with a Syracusan ultimatum brought to Carthage by a herald, calling on it to free the Siceliot cities under its power. Whether or not the Carthaginian authorities replied was irrelevant. On Dionysius' orders, the properties, ships and goods of their merchants at Syracuse and other cities were seized. In the subject Siceliot cities, resident Carthaginians were attacked, tortured and probably enslaved or murdered. Dionysius and his army soon arrived on the coast opposite Motya, while his war-fleet and transport ships drew up close by.[4]

Motya's almost circular island, today Isola San Pantaleo, lies in a narrow lagoon between the mainland and a larger L-shaped island (Isola Grande) that shelters it from the open sea. A 1,500-metre causeway to the mainland had been cut by the defenders, so the Greeks' first task was to build a new one or rebuild the old one. Dionysius left his brother Leptines, the fleet commander, in charge of this while he led the rest of his army through the *epikrateia*, intimidating, winning or forcing surrenders (starting with Eryx to the north of Motya) and laying waste the lands of the five places that held out: Halicyae, Segesta and Entella inland east of Motya, and Panormus and Solous further away. This brought in booty but did not change the strategic situation; rather, it gave the Carthaginians time to react.

Manpower had been depleted, but there was enough to crew a fleet. Himilco, appointed again as general, launched 100 triremes and crossed to the Sicilian coast near Selinus, but ignored that city to sail northwards and arrive outside Motya's lagoon at dawn a day or so later. Dionysius, now back in camp opposite Motya, was taken completely by surprise. Then his own resourcefulness and Himilco's lack of tactical élan rescued him. Though a Carthaginian pounce destroyed a few Syracusan ships, drawn up onshore as was normal, Himilco forebore to assail the rest – probably because he was too heavily outnumbered to risk a tight fight in the cramped lagoon – and left the tyrant time to have his abundant manpower drag the Syracusan fleet across the flat headland at the lagoon's northern entrance to the open shore beyond it. Archers and slingers aboard the ships, backed by the powerful newfangled catapults at the water's edge, kept the dismayed Punic crews at bay.

Himilco felt himself stymied. He did not try to send reinforcements into Motya – his hasty departure from Carthage had probably left no time to put soldiers on board – nor retire to Panormus to summon more resources. He had previously sent out a small task force of ten ships to raid Syracuse's own harbour in a bid to draw off at least part of Dionysius' fleet. The raid was highly successful because totally unexpected, but nothing more came of it – its commodore even sailed back to Carthage rather than to his chief outside Motya. All too easily discouraged, Himilco now did the same, leaving Motya as a glittering prize for Dionysius.

As soon as the new causeway was finished, the assault opened. Diodorus' narrative, perhaps drawing directly or indirectly on an eyewitness (the tyrant's friend Philistus may have been there), vividly records the furious resistance of the defenders, some of them Greeks: setting some of Dionysius' lofty siege towers on fire, barricading the narrow streets when attackers broke in, hurling down missiles on them from buildings, fighting hand-to-hand with those who hauled up gangplanks to cross from the siege towers to the equally high buildings, and repeatedly beating back Dionysius' men until at last, in a surprise assault by night, his men entered Motya. Slaughter by the enraged soldiery stopped only when Dionysius – not from humaneness but with an eye to slave prices – encouraged the surviving citizens to flee for sanctuary into their temples and the troops to turn to looting. Greeks who were captured, on the other hand, were killed by the Carthaginian method of crucifixion: a warning to others who might take up arms on Carthage's side.[5]

Resounding as the fall of Motya was – the city never regained its old size or wealth – Dionysius' victory was limited. Winter was nearing, he could take neither Segesta nor Entella, and supplying his large forces no doubt became harder as the year advanced. Conquering western Sicily would require at least another year. He therefore put a Sicel garrison in the ruins of Motya and left his brother to besiege or at any rate watch Entella and Segesta (their defenders seem to have had little trouble holding Leptines off), as well as to command the 120 warships he stationed in Motya's waters. He himself led the rest of the army back to Syracuse.

This proved a mistake. Morale in the *epikrateia* was certainly shaken, but at the same time the disaster of Motya galvanized Himilco and his colleagues at home. Through strenuous and expensive recruitment of Carthaginian citizens, Libyan subjects and Iberian mercenaries, they organized very large new forces. His fellow-citizens 'appointed Himilco king according to the laws' – in other words elected him *sufete* once again (see Chapter 2 §2) – and in spring 396 he sailed for Panormus with an imposing fleet and even more imposing army.

Diodorus' sources agreed on him having 400 triremes and 600 transports, while for the land forces Ephorus redeployed his tried and tested figure of 300,000 infantry. Timaeus, again more circumspect, claimed a more modest 100,000 landing from Africa, then reinforced by 30,000 Sicilians, while both more credibly reported 4,000 horse. As the Carthaginians had determined to deal forcefully with Dionysius' Siceliot crusade, a total of 100,000 or not far below it (including the Sicilian contingents) looks plausible. Himilco also equipped the expedition with 400 war chariots, an old-fashioned military arm still favoured at Carthage (Hamilcar had some in 480, only to lose them at sea), but they are never mentioned in accounts of the campaign.[6]

Dionysius seized the initiative by reinvading the *epikrateia*, where a frightened Halicyae, Segesta's neighbour, yielded to him; but he made no further progress save to re-ravage the region's already damaged countryside. His brother, commanding a supposed 120 warships at Motya, sailed with just thirty to clash with the Punic fleet as it passed by, and sank a number of transports (5,000 men and half the chariotry went down). Then he gave up. To judge from ensuing events, he sailed home to Syracuse. Himilco disembarked his forces at Panormus, soon emerging to recapture Eryx and after that to strike a shrewd blow to the tyrant's prestige by besieging and taking back Motya.

Himilco had most likely sailed from Carthage in the spring. His Sicilian operations before he marched to Syracuse would take up four to five months at most; then he will have encamped outside Syracuse in July or August. Diodorus' account stresses the intense summer heat that beat down during the siege of the city. A theory that the expedition crossed to Sicily much later in 396 and besieged Syracuse over the winter, through to spring 395 and into that summer, has no support in Diodorus' (or any other) narrative: there is no mention or hint that a winter went by. Such later dating requires Dionysius' Spartan ally Pharacidas to be the same man as the Spartan admiral Pharax who operated in the eastern Aegean from 398–96 (in another Spartan war against Athens and also Persia), with Sparta then sending him across the Mediterranean to Sicily in 395. But it was perfectly possible for two contemporary Spartan commanders to have similar names: in that same decade, Sparta's two kings were named Agesipolis and Agesilaus (and the latter's predecessor had been an Agis).

Dionysius, once more sitting outside Segesta, failed to intervene against Himilco's recovery of Eryx and Motya. He avoided battle, even though some of his men wanted to fight. This caution suggests that he commanded nothing like the numbers of the previous year, even before allied defections weakened him further. And if Leptines had taken the war fleet away (necessarily with the supply ships too), it helps to explain why the tyrant began to have trouble with provisions even though he had Sicans and Sicels of the interior as allies. Finally, he found himself so short of supplies that he decided to retire to Syracuse – a 350km march.

Unsurprisingly, this feeble response to Himilco's energy cost him widespread support: the Sicans defected, as did Halicyae. Himilco let him go, for the Carthaginian had his own strategic plan. It may have also been around this time that he settled survivors from Motya, and other colonists, at the harbour called Lilybaeum a few kilometres south of Motya. The new city would become one of Carthage's strongest bastions in Sicily until 241 BC.

Rather than chase the retreating Greeks across country, Himilco marched along the north coast to Cape Pelorias, the tip of Sicily just beyond Messana, while the fleet sailed offshore under his deputy Mago – an able officer now appearing for the first time. A squadron seized the strategically useful island and town of Lipara 20km offshore (and forced the islanders to pay the large sum of 30 talents into Himilco's war chest). When Messana's army, 6,000-strong at most, foolishly marched out against the far larger Punic forces, Mago swooped into the city's famous sickle-shaped harbour and from there broke into Messana through its badly delapidated walls. Most of the Messanians escaped into the surrounding hills, but their city was so literally dismantled by its captors 'that it was impossible to tell that it had previously been inhabited' (a thoroughness that Alexander the Great would apply sixty years later to Thebes in Greece), another taste of how Carthage could deal with opponents and an act probably aimed at undermining the Syracusans' morale. It certainly impressed the tyrant's Sicel allies holding the east-coast strongpoint which not long after became the city of Tauromenium (Taormina): they too went over to the Carthaginians.

Dionysius tried to regain the initiative. He freed slaves at home to crew sixty of his warships (the freedmen must have numbered a good 10,000), strengthened the fortresses in Syracuse's territory, sent recruiters to Greece to hire mercenaries and then, with what remained of his forces – 30,000 foot (about a third of them mercenaries) and rather more than 3,000 horse – moved north. His 180-strong fleet under Leptines accompanied him up the coast to the neighbourhood of Catana. Himilco was well inland, marching around the western side of Mount Etna because the coastal route had been blocked by a new lava torrent. Outside Catana, Leptines was given the chance to fight Mago's approaching fleet, attacked in disorganised fashion and lost 100 ships with – supposedly if improbably – 20,000 men. He and his brother then retreated all the way back to Syracuse to prepare for the inevitable siege.

This was not long in starting. Two-hundred-and-fifty enemy warships, including some just captured, and many hundreds more transport and merchant craft filled the Great Harbour. The Punic grand army ignored intervening strongpoints garrisoned by Dionysius, like Leontini, to advance down to the southern outskirts of Syracuse and there set up camp. For the second time in less than twenty years, the chief city of Greek Sicily was beset by foreign enemies.

Himilco prepared for a long siege, sending transports to Libya and Sardinia to gather supplies and building three strongpoints by the shoreline of the Great Harbour. He rather daringly established his headquarters in the imposing temple of Zeus on a ridge close to the shore, and fortified his nearby camp with stone from the monumental tombs outside the city, including those of Gelon and his wife. He spent thirty days – high summer had arrived – ravaging the surrounding region to spread fear and gather booty, and at some stage he even captured, or at least broke into, Syracuse's mainland quarter called Achradina. There he comprehensively looted the rich temple or temples of Demeter and her daughter Kore-Persephone, goddesses specially venerated in Greek Sicily. This he would soon have cause to rue.

From this point on, as Diodorus took pleasure in recording, Carthaginian fortunes began to turn. The naval blockade was careless at best (or discontinued at worst). First, a thirty-ship Greek flotilla was able to sail in under Dionysius' brother-in-law Polyxenus, bringing 1,000 mercenaries and their commander Pharacidas. Then the tyrant himself and his brother Leptines boldly left Syracuse with another flotilla to meet and escort a provision fleet from elsewhere, probably Locri. Whom they left in charge is not mentioned, but he must have been solidly trustworthy: at a guess, Dionysius' father-in-law Hipparinus. Then ships from the city itself captured a Punic supply ship laden with food and went on to worst an enemy squadron that came out to challenge them. All this suggests that Himilco's naval force was much reduced. Perhaps it was hard to keep the entire 200-strong fleet as well as the army supplied. Perhaps too, with disease now erupting in the army, he feared it could spread to his naval forces. If these were crippled he would be cut off from Carthage, and even Panormus would be much harder to access.

For supply and security, the army was encamped, like Syracuse's Athenian besiegers in 415–13, close to or even on marshland through which the broad River Anapus ran into the Great Harbour, as it still does. The defences of Achradina were also the only feasible points for breaking into Syracuse, apart from assaulting Dionysius' new fortifications on Epipolae and then working down to the inner landward walls of the suburbs, as the Roman proconsul Marcellus was to do in 212. Yet thanks to these calculations, Himilco exposed his army to pestilence. This could have been foreseen:

the Athenians had been hit in 413, and in 405 his own forces were already diseased when he arrived outside Syracuse.[7]

Diodorus' vivid account of the sickness perhaps came from Dionysius' chronicler Philistus: first catarrh, then aches and pains, and severe fever; next dysentery, pustular skin rash and delirium; finally, on the fifth or sixth day, death. This was very likely smallpox, a disease known since the time of New Kingdom Egypt. The impact on the besiegers was catastrophic. Sick men passed the disease on to those who tended them, so more and more of the sick were left on their own. The stench from unburied bodies permeated the camp, where delirious and frantic men roamed, striking out at passers-by. Diodorus' source claimed that half the entire army died. Then and later, the sickness was seen as the gods' punishment for desecrating Syracuse's tombs and temples. Safe within the walls, the defenders were unscathed, watching for an opportunity.

It soon came. Dionysius, now back in the city, decided to sortie by sea and land. Joint operations were unusual in ancient warfare, but his succeeded brilliantly. With eighty warships, Pharacidas and Leptines made a dawn attack on the moored Punic fleet; at the same hour, the tyrant's troops fell on the enemy camp. Machiavellian to a fault, he had 1,000 particularly troublesome mercenaries – he had not paid wages for a long while – attack one sector of the camp along with a Syracusan cavalry escort, only for these then to gallop away and leave the mercenaries to be slaughtered (a trick that a later Syracusan leader, Hiero II, would imitate). The land and sea assaults then converged. Carthaginian warships and merchant ships were set ablaze, others were towed away by exultant Syracusans, and Dionysius penned Himilco between the Greek army and fleet. To drive home his victory, he pitched camp close to the temple of Zeus – Himilco's headquarters.[8]

The Carthaginian knew he was facing destruction. He quietly contacted his adversary for terms: if he and his army were allowed to evacuate Sicily for Africa, he would hand over the 300 talents in his war chest. Dionysius forced a harder bargain. Only the Carthaginian soldiers in the army could leave, once the money was paid. On the fourth night afterwards, the treasure was duly taken into Syracuse, while forty triremes bore Himilco and his citizen troops and crews away. Even if the triremes were packed full, the number of soldiers can hardly have come to more than 4,000–5,000, while the sailors must have been about twice as many. The other survivors of Carthage's once mighty army suffered varied fates. Its surviving Sicel troops largely escaped to their home cities, the Iberians coolly took service with Dionysius – always in need of tough professionals – but the rest, most of them apparently Libyans, were sold as slaves.

Himilco's intelligent strategy had foundered on unintelligent tactics. Rather than send some part of his sizeable forces, which included local contingents who knew the land, to harry the Greeks as they retreated across the length of Sicily to Syracuse, he let Dionysius go safely. Arriving in the Great Harbour by sea and outside Achradina by land, he made no use of the dismay this caused inside the city or of reported discontent there at Dionysius' unimpressive leadership. Instead, he spent a month spreading wastage over Syracuse's neighbourhood and desecrating monuments and shrines, an action which the Sicilians with him could have warned would antagonize rather than cow his adversaries. The Punic fleet in Syracusan waters was lax enough to let Dionysius and his warships come and go, and so too Pharacidas' reinforcements, which Mago could surely have intercepted with some of his 200 triremes.

On land, Himilco could have tried an attack on Epipolae's northern side, for instance at the site called Trogilus (the Santa Panagia gorge or the nearby cliffs below the Scala Greca slope) which Marcellus exploited in 212 – even if only as a diversion while a real assault on Achradina or Ortygia was launched. Instead, both energy and inspiration failed him once he occupied the temple of Zeus. They passed to his opponent, who made brilliant use of them: no great general, Dionysius in war, as in politics, was all the same an unsurpassed opportunist, and blessed with what Cicero was to call one of the essential qualities for generalship – luck. When everything looked lost, abandoned by his allies, challenged by discontented citizens, shut up in his city by vastly greater enemy forces, he kept his nerve and with one decisive blow achieved victory.

Himilco's end was wretched, even though his countrymen did not haul him before the *adirim* for punishment. The disaster in Sicily encouraged a serious rebellion by their Libyan subjects, who subjected Carthage itself to a siege (see Chapter 10). Diodorus and Justin – the latter at tediously rhetorical length – depicted the guilt-stricken ex-general being reviled by fellow-Carthaginians, visiting temple after temple in shabby garb to confess his sacrileges and finally shutting himself up in his house to take his own life. With him ended the predominance of the Magonids, for though he had sons they played no known role in Carthage's history. New factions and new personalities would dominate the republic for the rest of the fourth century.[9]

3. Mago vs Dionysius

The Syracusan war had not closed with Himilco's flight, but the Carthaginians were too busy in Africa to launch another campaign for some years. Dionysius profited from the pause. He had no interest in exploiting Carthaginian agonies by invading North Africa or even occupying Punic Sicily, and none (mistakenly perhaps) in sending funds or weapons to the Libyan rebels. He did take Panormus' neighbour, Solous, when it was betrayed to him, probably as a useful forward outpost should the Carthaginians renew operations. That apart, though, in 395 and 394 he attended to other unfinished business – refounding Messana, settling colonists at the new city of Tyndaris on the north coast (Tindari today), intimidating or inducing many of the Sicel centres into renewed alliance – in particular Agyrium (the historian Diodorus' hometown, modern Agira on a commanding hilltop west of Mount Etna) and its neighbour Centuripa – and conquering others like Enna. Tauromenium, now a Sicel strongpoint on the coast beside Mount Etna, did defy and defeat him. Yet his successes were impressive enough to win an encomium from no less a state than Athens in 394/93, and the damaged inscription recording it fawningly terms him 'ruler [*archon*] of Sicily'.[10]

The Carthaginians thus had time to put down the rebellion in Libya and make new plans for Sicily. The general they appointed to renew operations was Mago, Himilco's admiral in 396, who had clearly not been tainted by his chief's disgrace. Despite his name, he was not, it seems, a member of the Magonid family – no ancient evidence suggests he was – but he must have been a political ally to be made Himilco's deputy, and had stayed on in Punic Sicily after 396. A skilful diplomat, he reversed the Magonid policy of frightfulness. He treated the people of the *epikrateia* mildly (apparently his predecessor had not), won over various Sicel cities, though not Agyrium, and welcomed to western Sicily the many refugees from Dionysius' campaigns.

Three years after Himilco's debacle, Mago relaunched hostilities. The Carthaginians' calculation must have been that they could exploit the vendetta that Dionysius was waging against Rhegium, which had begun to alarm other Italiot states too. Mago, however, had only the forces stationed in the *epikrateia* and some other (probably mercenary) troops. A comment by Diodorus – that Mago's soldiers a year later were 'all carefully supplied with equipment to which they were accustomed' – rather hints that in 393, by contrast, his men were much less well outfitted. It may help account for how the campaign turned out.

Choosing to be bold, Mago advanced across the north coast, bypassing Solous, to ravage the territory of Messana. Possessing Messana would have enabled him to repeat Himilco's strategy in 396, and maybe also win support from Rhegium, which had the extra advantage of a strong fleet; Mago's current naval forces were plainly small or non-existent. He had no time, however, to force or win Messana to his side or woo Rhegium before Dionysius appeared on the scene. Boldness was replaced by caution: the Carthaginian army retreated south-east to Abacaenum, a Sicel city in a valley a few kilometres south of Dionysius' new colony of Tyndaris, which, thanks to him, had gained much of Abacaenum's territory.

Mago's venture eastward had not paid off. He was now probably outnumbered, could not be reinforced easily, if at all, and could retreat to the west only via the coast (which meant passing unfriendly Tyndaris and Cephaloedium) or else through the hills and mountains of central Sicily (with Agyrium and Enna near any route). Either path would be risky. He decided to fight. His army most likely moved down from Abacaenum, near today's Tripi about 15km inland, to the more level terrain between the mountains and the coast. This was another miscalculation. The clash with the Syracusans quickly became a defeat: his losses were small, 800 men, but Mago had to pull back to Abacaenum. He and his men were saved only because Dionysius was keener on assailing Rhegium. The victors marched away, leaving the battered Punic forces to make their way back to the west.[11]

Mago and Carthage were undeterred. Dionysius' ensuing troubles around the Strait of Messina give them time: his surprise attack on Rhegium was beaten off, causing the alarmed Italiot cities to form an anti-Syracusan alliance. The Carthaginians spent the rest of the year recruiting a large army, though it included Libyans – some or all of them probably recent rebels – alongside Sardinians and Italian, no doubt Campanian, mercenaries. The army that arrived in Sicily in 392 supposedly numbered 80,000, but this should be doubted. Large multiples of 10,000 (which was a Greek 'myriad') were a staple of Greek accounts of Punic armies, as we have seen; and this army before long found itself nonplussed by Greek and Sicel forces scarcely more than 30,000 strong. It should not be reckoned at very much above their total, even after it added forces from Sicel allies. Nor had Mago many warships, for reasons not stated; perhaps plague losses had been hard on seamen in Carthage and the Libyphoenician cities.

Mago moved through central Sicily to reach the upper course of the Chrysas, a stream (now the Dittaino) that rose just west of Agyrium to flow down to join the larger Symaethus below Catana. He was in perilous territory: Agyrium ahead of him, Enna to his south, Assorus between these two and Centuripa beyond Agyrium were all hostile. Agyrium's like-named Sicel lord Agyris ruled a large city and a broad tract of surrounding territory, was a keen supporter of Dionysius (especially once the Syracusan promised him more territory), was rich with the property of murdered fellow-Agyrians and could field a strong army to reinforce Dionysius' 20,000 Syracusan and mercenary troops when the tyrant arrived.

As before in the north-east, Mago found himself stymied. He did not want to fight but was harassed by Agyris' forces, who exploited their knowledge of the area to make it hard for supplies to reach him from the west, while his opponents refused to fight a battle. He might well have come to even greater misfortune than at Abacaenum, had Dionysius' own problems not rescued him.

Diodorus' narrative of events is not clear. Either he over-abbreviated his source or sources, or a later editor or copyist over-abbreviated him. Supposedly Dionysius, cautious to a fault, denied his Syracusan troops the chance to fight a battle and argued that the enemy would be beaten by time and hunger, an argument that caused the Syracusans to march away in disgust. To replace them he proclaimed freedom for slaves (Syracusan slaves, obviously), but then the Carthaginians sent envoys to him, so he rescinded the proclamation and made peace, after which Mago sailed home.

This narrative raises questions: why, for instance, did Mago not go on the attack – or else escape back to the *epikrateia* – after Dionysius' own Syracusans went home? His remaining opponents were, at most, the tyrant's mercenaries and Agyris' army. Again, we might wonder how Dionysius expected to have time to levy, train and equip thousands of freed slaves to face Mago; he could not just assume that the Carthaginian would go on biding his time with dwindling supplies beside the Chrysas until Dionysius could come back and attack him.

One view is that matters were more drawn-out than Diodorus depicted: Dionysius following his disgusted troops home (leaving Agyris in the lurch); Mago too dispirited to continue and therefore retreating to the *epikrateia*; and the Carthaginian authorities then sending the envoys from Africa to Syracuse. Yet if the Syracusan army did simply abandon their leader for home, it is hard to understand why Mago should make no effort at all to exploit this. If nothing else, advancing on Syracuse would have encouraged the tyrant's domestic enemies. Equally, even if the tyrant did go home too, protected by his mercenaries, it is hard to see how he could force his citizens to release their slaves for military service. Many slave-owners would be soldiers themselves, and were still armed. Besides, leaving Agyris in the lurch would risk losing him as an ally, maybe even make him an enemy, which could only worsen Dionysius' and Syracuse's situation.

Rather more likely is that the Syracusan troops did not march very far away, but far enough – perhaps to Agyrium – to show the tyrant their displeasure, and Dionysius' slave-freeing was simply a gesture (or a threat) which he dropped after coming to terms with Mago. That general did not venture to force a battle – which was what the angry Syracusan contingent wanted – but offered terms more or less on the basis of the peace of 405, except that Carthage conceded to Dionysius a hegemony over the Sicels and possession of Tauromenium (he had to impose this afterwards by arms).[12]

Carthage's renewed war with Syracuse thus ended unsatisfactorily. Much treasure and effort had been wasted. Mago had opened each campaign with a bold move, but had then run out of initiative. He was unable to make use of his enemy's difficulties – with Rhegium, with suspicious Greek and Sicel cities and with his own Syracusans – and put himself in positions at Abacaenum and the Chrysas that forfeited freedom of manoeuvre. He and Carthage were fortunate that the same difficulties equally limited Dionysius' capacity to retaliate, and that the tyrant clearly also knew his own limitations as a general.

The new peace meant that Dionysius had not been checked; instead he came out of it with enhanced control over eastern and central Sicily. What happened to Agyris and Syracuse's other Sicel allies is not recorded. If the peace terms were matched by reality on the ground, all Sicels' freedom of action was sharply cut back: those outside the *epikrateia* by Syracuse's hegemony and those inside by Carthage.

4. Mago and Himilco against Dionysius

Dionysius went from strength to strength over the next decade. Abroad, he pursued his feud with Rhegium by allying victoriously with the Lucanians, the old foes of the Italian Greeks in the toe of Italy. The Greeks' army was routed in a battle near Caulonia (50km north of Locri) in 389; Caulonia and Hipponium (modern Vibo on the Tyrrhenian Sea) were razed and their citizens mostly transplanted to burgeoning Syracuse; and in the same period he even gained a twelve-year mastery over Croton (Crotone), 160km north of Locri. In 388, the great city of Rhegium itself, besieged by him for almost a year, capitulated and was razed flat. Its remaining citizens were uprooted to Syracuse. Thus, as he had done at Naxos, Catana, Leontini and other places, Dionysius continued Gelon's and other rulers' habit of eviscerating defeated western Greek centres for the aggrandizement of his capital.

At home, he built lavish public works and temples, enlarged the dockyards to house 200 triremes (no mention of quinqueremes), patronized poets and philosophers until they displeased him – supposedly he once sent the visiting Plato to be sold as a slave in Greece – and exercised his own rather limited talents as poet and playwright, only to earn derision when chosen actors presented his poems at the Olympic games. He even quarrelled with his loyal brother Leptines and oldest political ally Philistus, and banished them in about 386. Leptines was soon restored to favour, but Philistus stayed abroad for nearly thirty years.[13]

The tyrant's ambitions ranged much further than the toe of Italy. While keeping clear of other powerful Italian Greek states like Thurii and Tarentum, he used his naval strength to intervene in affairs in the Adriatic region, setting down a colony on the island of Issa (Vis in Croatia) and according to Diodorus, though not to archaeology, at Lissus too (Lezhe in Albania) about 400km further south. He also patronized quality horse-breeding communities in the Veneto region and encouraged the nearby Illyrian peoples to raid the Greek kingdom of Epirus, allegedly with the extra idea (unfulfilled) that they and he should then go on to loot the fabulously wealthy shrine of Delphi in central Greece, the most sacred centre in the Greek world.

The Tyrrhenian Sea off the coast of Etruria also came in for attention, allegedly because of piracy from Caere, the city that had collaborated with Carthage against the Phocaeans of Alalia a century-and-a-half before. With sixty triremes (or 100 in less reliable sources, like Polyaenus), Dionysius sailed from Syracuse in 384 to Pyrgi, the Caeritan port with Thefarie Velianas' shrine to Astarte, and looted 1,000 talents' worth of booty from its richest and most sacred temple. Before sailing home he called in at Corsica to plunder further – exactly like the piracy he claimed to be combating.[14]

Dionysius' true motive, wrote Diodorus, was to finance yet another war with the Carthaginians. If so, his war aim would be to seize as much of the *epikrateia* as possible, perhaps all of it. Carthage was offering no provocation, but the cities under its rule (we are told) were ready to revolt – as before in 397 – and many actually made alliances with him on favourable terms, although we are not told either names or terms. If all this was not just

Syracusan propaganda, Mago's earlier mildness in the *epikrateia* perhaps had soured under a need to squeeze extra tribute out of it to help pay the costs of the last war. Perhaps the unimpressive Carthaginian performance in 393–92 also made some cities think that a new Syracusan attack would succeed and they had better be on the right side.

The likeliest allies for Syracuse would be the Siceliot cities which the peace of 405 had left under Carthage's hegemony, such as Acragas and Selinus. Their relations with their overlord Carthage after 392 are not recorded, but were more likely fractious than friendly. Acragas (like Messana) had reportedly been allied with Syracuse before 394 – perhaps a breakaway attempt that Mago had then deterred – and may have continued to resent its subjection. Selinus, like Acragas, had contributed forces to Dionysius' expedition against Motya in 397. Thermae, with a sizeable Greek population by now, may also have been wooed away.

Even so, Dionysius' plans may not have aimed at a war right away. Enticing away Carthage's Sicilian allies would undermine its military security in the *epikrateia*, its economic and financial proceeds and Punic prestige: losses which, the tyrant might calculate, would squeeze further concessions from Carthage without a war. But Syracuse's wide-ranging projections of power, unprecedented for a western Greek city-state, cannot have left the Carthaginians feeling comfortable. For all they knew, the tyrant would indeed start to focus military attention on the *epikrateia*. To use a fashionable modern concept, they may have fallen into the 'Thucydides trap': the power of Syracuse was growing and Carthage feared its growth.

Diodorus' narrative, the only available one, implies that the war was in fact initiated by Carthage. In 384 or 383, outraged at its subjects' defections, it sent envoys to Syracuse 'demanding back' the defecting states, in other words insisting that he give up the new alliances. When he ignored the call, the Carthaginians reappointed Mago, who at the time was a *sufete*, to command in Sicily and began preparing fresh forces for the war. At the same time, Carthage made an alliance of its own with Syracuse's Italiot enemies. Dionysius responded by dividing his own forces for operations on two widely separate fronts, a posture defensive rather than offensive. It looks as though he was reacting to, not initiating, events.[15]

What we know of this war is skimpy. Diodorus' history covers it in only a few paragraphs: after a vague statement about 'many clashes' and 'continual minor battles', we read of two major battles and then of peace. One theory is that his original account of the war was sharply abbreviated by some later ancient editor with no great interest in Sicilian affairs. Yet Book 15 of the

History is about the same length as preceding and later books, and other wars in it are told in reasonable detail. It is hard to see why an editor should want to prune just the sections on Dionysius' third Punic war. Rather, it looks as though for some reason Diodorus lost interest in giving this war the same coverage as those before it.[16]

His scanty narrative prompts varied views on dates and details. In the narrative, the two major battles, at Cabala and Cronium, are fought only some weeks apart and the new peace follows quite soon. Since Diodorus' date for the outbreak of the war is 383, and after reporting the peace plus some events in the eastern Mediterranean his next date is 382, if taken literally this would cram the war into 383 alone. But it could be argued that scattered bits of evidence in his own work and elsewhere point to ongoing warfare years later. A Punic fleet sailed to southern Italy in 379 or 378 to refound Hipponium with exiles who had escaped Dionysius' net ten years earlier, and Sicily was the pretended destination in 374 of a Spartan fleet putting in at the island of Corcyra (Corfu), its real target. A rapid summary in Justin of Dionysius' wars in southern Italy has been thought to record war events in these years ignored by Diodorus, and so too a one-sentence story in a much later author, Aelian, about Dionysius once losing a huge fleet and army in a gale when he sought to attack Thurii in Italy.

Differing theories result: that the war began in 383 and lasted up to ten years, with much activity in the Italian theatre; or that despite Diodorus, it did not begin before 378 and was preceded by Syracusan campaigning in Italy; or even that there was a separate Punic-Syracusan war in the 370s, between one in 383 and the one (his last) that Dionysius started in 368.

In reality, Justin and Aelian are useless for Mago's new war. Justin's potpourri of Dionysius' Italian wars has him capture Locri, which was actually his steadfast ally throughout (Justin or Trogus really meant Rhegium, taken in 388), then unsuccessfully attack Croton (which in fact he captured along with Rhegium) and also hire Gauls who 'a few months before' had sacked Rome. All these items date these supposed events to 388–87, not five or ten years later. Justin's tyrant then has to hasten back to Sicily to fight the Carthaginian general Hanno – the general not in this but in his last and unfinished Punic war. In sum, the résumé is a mixed-up collection of items accurate and inaccurate, and contributes nothing to what can be gleaned about the war with Mago.

Aelian's story about the tyrant sending 300 triremes full of soldiers to attack Thurii, only to lose them all in a mighty gale, is more fanciful still. Dionysius never had that many warships before 368 – and the figure is suspicious even for 368 – and their loss, plus soldiers, would have cost him over 70,000 men: a colossal blow, which nonethless never appears in any other ancient source. For the new war, therefore, we are left only with Diodorus and one or two anecdotes in Aelian's contemporary Polyaenus, another dangerously erratic anecdote-compiler.[17]

It is best to date the war's start to 383. This is Diodorus' firm date. The various to-and-fro operations ('many clashes' and 'continual minor battles') could have taken up two or even three years: a single year for them is hardly enough. On the other hand, a series of skirmishes and minor battles dragging on into the early 370s is not plausible, or that for a long time Dionysius left operations in Sicily to others while he himself campaigned in southern Italy. That was a risk, political as well as military, which he surely could not take. For Italy, he could appoint someone reliable like his youngest brother Thearidas (Leptines stayed with Dionysius).

The Italian theatre must have been a low-key affair. Carthage had few potential allies there: of the Greek cities in the south, Locri was Dionysius' ally, Rhegium, Hipponium and Caulonia lay in ruins, Croton was under his control and those further north (Thurii, Heraclea, Metapontum and Tarentum) were not involved. The Syracuse-friendly Lucanians took no recorded part in the war. Carthaginian operations in Italy, therefore, may well have been small, and Syracusan efforts limited to defending strongholds and warding off raids. These efforts would nonetheless take a toll on Dionysius' manpower and money, forcing him to stay on the defensive in Sicily too until he could build enough strength to try a pitched battle. This he finally did, arguably, in 381 or 380.

When the war began in 383, Mago took to Sicily 'tens of thousands' of fresh troops, Carthaginian citizens as well as mercenaries and probably (though unmentioned) Libyans. It would be no surprise if his past experiences against Dionysius made him cautious. One focus of operations must have been the cities which Dionysius had enticed, Mago trying to retake them and the Syracusan striving to protect them. Mago might also try to win over Sicel and other native centres allied to Syracuse – Agyrium and Enna, for instance. Neither Panormus nor Syracuse seem to have been threatened at any stage. Most of the manoeuvring and skirmishing, along with the inevitable ravaging and plundering, probably took place in the long-suffering middle regions of the island.

Eventually the main armies came to blows at or near Cabala. Where this was is not known; Diodorus' words 'around the so-called Cabala' imply a region or physical feature rather than a town. The Carthaginians were

Carthage against Dionysius and Syracuse 85

utterly defeated. Among the 10,000 killed was Mago himself, who went down 'fighting splendidly'. Dionysius' prisoners numbered another 5,000. Better still for him, the survivors of the beaten army found themselves encircled by the victors on a fortified but waterless hill, perhaps an abandoned fort. They asked for terms.

The triumphant tyrant demanded that the Carthaginians withdraw from 'the cities in Sicily' – likely Diodorean shorthand for all the non-Phoenician cities – and pay his war costs. Very cunningly (in Diodorus' view), the Carthaginian spokesmen acquiesced in the terms but asked for a truce so that the 'authorities' (*archontes*) could be consulted. Once Dionysius agreed, the army gave Mago a splendid funeral – no doubt visible to the Greek forces – and chose his young son as their new general. He then spent the period of the truce retraining and reinvigorating his troops, and meanwhile talks about peace fizzled out.

Diodorus' narrative leaves a good many things unsaid, quite apart from not naming Mago's son, who was a Himilco if a separate anecdote in Polyaenus involves him (see below). To start with, the spokesmen sent to Dionysius after the battle cannot have come from Carthage: it would have taken days for word to reach Africa and then more days for them to arrive (depending on sailing conditions), while the army stayed waterless, not to mention unfed, on its hilltop. Moreover, official spokesmen from Carthage would have been empowered to negotiate directly, especially given the troops' dire situation, not simply to ask what Dionysius wanted and then seek a truce to take his terms back to the authorities at Carthage. The spokesmen must have been from the defeated army itself.

Another view is that the 'authorities' were those in the subject Sicilian cities (that is, those cities' magistrates and senates), but it fails too. It assumes that the spokesmen persuaded Dionysius that Carthage's Sicilian subjects, on this one occasion, had to be involved in peace terms, and that consulting them could be authorized by the spokesmen, not by the senate and magistrates at Carthage. Neither idea is plausible.[18]

Diodorus' account also does not say that, once the truce was in force, the Punic army was able to move to friendlier ground, but this virtually goes without saying. Mago's son used the interval to retrain and re-enthuse the troops – a feat impossible where it had been trapped. A supposed Punic stratagem told by Polyaenus chimes with this inference. Polyaenus' Dionysius lets the entire army go, supposedly to seek approval for his terms from 'the admiral' (*nauarchos* in Greek, and unnamed). Necessarily, this officer must be somewhere else, perhaps by the sea, though the tale does not say so.

Once the army is safe, the Carthaginians send away Dionysius' envoys. But no Carthaginian *nauarchos* had independent authority to ratify a treaty, least of all one which would cost Carthage most of its Sicilian possessions and force it to pay out great sums of money too, and Dionysius of all people will have known this. Polyaenus more likely distorted whatever source he had read: for instance, his *nauarchos* looks like a mistake for (or misreading of) *archontes*, as in Diodorus.

The most economical conclusion is that the surviving senior Carthaginian officers on the hilltop, Himilco among them, sent some of their number to Dionysius to ask what terms he would offer. He would be well aware that any terms, and especially his harsh ones, had to be referred to Carthage; and equally that the defeated troops could not stay long on their hilltop without water and food. With Mago dead – and it seems with Himilco's *ad hoc* election as general deliberately delayed – the beaten army could appear leaderless and demoralized enough to reassure even a suspicious tyrant. To Dionysius, Carthage would seem to have a Hobson's choice: agree to his terms or see him destroy its army and overrun its *epikrateia*.

Yet Dionysius was outfoxed. Himilco probably did not leave the hill to march back to a coastal site like Panormus or the new fortress-city Lilybaeum – the victors would scarcely allow him a stopping-place where reinforcements could easily arrive – but wherever the new camp was, he proved an inspiring leader. If he did manage to bring in reinforcements without alerting the enemy (for instance from cities in the *epikrateia*), his chances would improve further. In any case, some weeks of hard work restored the army to battle-readiness and inspired the men with a thirst for vengeance. When the agreed period – a month? – ended, Himilco made it clear that talk of peace was over.[19]

The result was a battle at a site called Cronium. If this was a town on the coastal plain just east of Panormus as sometimes thought (on the dubious strength of a coin found on a nearby mountain with the legend *Kronia*), it suggests that Dionysius reacted by thrusting toward Panormus via friendly Tyndaris and Cephaloedium, and Himilco came up to confront him. Wherever Cronium was (this is its sole mention in the historical record), another of Polyaenus' dubious tales has Himilco blind 'the generals of Dionysius' nearby with smoke from blazing timber, so that he and his troops can enter Cronium. The tale implies that Cronium was important enough for the Greeks to besiege it in force and for the Carthaginians to want to save it. What supposedly happened next we are not told.

Obviously such a ruse would have come before the battle, but it should be disbelieved. Himilco's ruse is implausible – he fells an entire wood near the Greek camp without interference, then piles the timber up outside the same camp to set it ablaze, again with no interference. It would be equally implausible that he shut up himself and his army in a town already under siege, whether Dionysius or generals of his were the besiegers. If there was a ruse at all, Polyaenus probably exaggerated or distorted a small one: for instance, Himilco inveigling a relief force into the besieged town (or fort) to save it from capture and perhaps to provoke battle.[20]

In the battle at Cronium, Dionysius suffered a calamitous defeat. His brother Leptines was killed, his army collapsed and the Carthaginians refused quarter to fugitives. Dionysius escaped the slaughter, but 14,000 of his soldiers died. He may have fled back to Syracuse to secure his position there, but any chance of mastering Punic Sicily was gone and even Syracuse's home territory was in danger. Yet Himilco returned to Panormus rather than mount a pursuit. The much-tried Punic army was in no condition to march on Syracuse, still less to risk an extended foray through eastern Sicily, where Dionysius still had allies and forts. The tyrant was saved.

The Carthaginians were already weary of the war. If Himilco had ambition to succeed to Mago's eminence at home, moreover, he would prefer to return victorious and with his hands free to pursue politics. 'Bearing their good fortune in manly [Diodorus probably meant 'gentlemanly'] fashion', the Carthaginians sent envoys, official ones now, to offer Dionysius peace – this time on their terms. He had no choice but to accept.

Their territorial terms were moderate. Both states would hold what they held before, except that Carthage would take over Selinus, its brief flirtation with independence over, and the western sector of Acragas' territory up to the River Halycus (Platani), which meets the sea about 45km to Acragas' west. If the mention of Halycus is right, Acragas' lands even now must have extended even beyond that river – something of a surprise given the city's disastrous fortunes since 406, so Diodorus may have misread what his source wrote. The true sting in Carthage's terms was that Dionysius had to pay 1,000 talents as indemnity, a neat reprisal for his own earlier demand.

Accepting the terms shows that he had run his military resources too far down to risk fighting on. If he tried, his fellow-Syracusans might refuse further obedience; and with the loss of Leptines, and Philistus in exile, his circle of reliable lieutenants must have shrunk dangerously. How he raised the funds to pay the indemnity is not reported, but at least his rule continued over eastern Sicily and the toe of Italy. Even in Italy, though, it soon became precarious the further it extended from Rhegium and Locri.

The new treaty did not precisely restore the earlier *status quo*, for Carthage's *epikrateia* now re–embraced Selinus and extended to the Halycus, with Heraclea Minoa at its mouth. Further north, Segesta, Entella, Solous and probably also Thermae continued to be part of it. The treaty terms, if applied to inland Sicily, would confirm Dionysius' dominance over the Sicels and maybe Sicans, which Carthage had recognized in 392. Yet nothing is heard of them when he went to war with Carthage once more in 368. The Battle of Cronium may have freed them from his control – save perhaps those near Syracuse's territory, like Ducetius' creation Menae (now Minio) – and enabled them to keep out of subsequent clashes for at least a generation.[21]

Thanks to Mago's son, Carthage had effectively checked Syracusan expansionism within Sicily, and soon struck a blow against it in Italy too.

5. Last war with Dionysius

In 379 or 378, a Punic fleet bearing Greek exiles unfriendly to Dionysius sailed to refound Hipponium in southern Italy. This was not the only loss he suffered around the same time, for his mastery of Croton also ended: according to his later namesake Dionysius of Halicarnassus, Croton's subjection lasted twelve years after he took it along with Rhegium. Strabo the geographer in turn reported that the tyrant had planned to build a wall across the toe of Italy, probably at the narrowest point of the peninsula between Scylletium (Squillace) on the Ionian Sea to Hipponium on the Tyrrhenian Sea, 'but the people outside came in and prevented it'. These must have been the Lucanians or their neighbours the Bruttians, displeased at the prospect of any such barrier. Strabo gave no date, but the event could happen only when Dionysius' grip on that area sagged.

Dionysius thus appears to have lost the northern part of his Italian '*epikrateia*'. His setbacks, military and financial, in the just-ended Punic war explain why his reach contracted. Paying out the 1,000 talents, even by instalments, would be a serious drain on his revenues, but no Carthaginian complaints about non-payment are recorded. Nor did he give up hopes of revanche: even though he was growing old, he spent the next ten years rebuilding Syracusan strength for yet another fray. He continued playing a role too, if a limited one, in the affairs of Greece. As an old friend of Sparta, he sent a small squadron in 373, ten triremes, to join its attempted naval takeover of Corcyra, although the Spartan coup failed and all but one of his ships was captured along with their commodore. A few years later, in 369 and again in 368, a still limited but more successful task force, twenty Syracusan ships and 2,000 Gallic and Iberian mercenaries, helped save the Spartans from their newly powerful enemy, the Boeotian League led by the great Theban general Epaminondas.

By then, in one of history's ironic turnarounds, Sparta and Athens were allies, which explains why in 368 and 367 the Athenians gushingly voted to award 'the ruler [*archon*] of Sicily' and his two sons Athenian citizenship, and made a grandiose alliance with him – not explicitly with Syracuse – in which they and he (and his descendants) promised each other perpetual defence and protection. It was pure show. Athens no longer had any ability to wage war as far away as Sicily; Dionysius had other things in train – and in any case was dead before the end of 367. But these gestures illustrated how much Syracuse had recovered its strength, and the tyrant his confidence, in recent years.[22]

The chief cause for his renewed confidence was the condition of Carthage. Soon after the restoration of Hipponium, a fresh and devastating outbreak of plague struck the city. Diodorus claimed that only the Carthaginians in the city were affected. It may be that the epidemic proved less pervasive across Libya if it reached Carthage (and its often overlooked Libyphoenician sister-cities?) via overseas commercial contacts. It did galvanize its Libyan vassals into a new rebellion, which then spread to Sardinia. Harassed by plague at home and mass revolt outside, the Carthaginians 'risked losing their hegemony'. They did succeed in holding on to it, but the task took a long time: Dionysius would choose to return to the fray in Sicily in 368, 'seeing that the Carthaginians were in no fit state for war due to the plague that had befallen them and the Libyans' rebellion'.

Carthage's new general, unnamed by Diodorus, is named Hanno in Justin's *Epitome*, as mentioned earlier. There is no further reference to Himilco. If that was indeed the name of Mago's son, he lost whatever political competition at home followed his return. Hanno is likely to be the same man as the Hanno 'the Great' in the separate *Prologues* for Trogus' history, named as the general who campaigned in this period in Africa (see Chapter 10 §1), even though Justin's account leaves these wars out.

On the other hand, the same account emphasizes that Hanno was not Carthage's dominant leader in 368. 'The most powerful of the Carthaginians at that time' was 'Suniatus', seemingly a Greek form of Eshmuniaton ('Eshmun has given') – and he was a vicious foe of Hanno. Nothing is said of any links that either man might have had with the old Magonid house or with the military father-and-son duo Mago and Himilco. It would be imaginative but unprovable, therefore, to guess that they were the latest competing members of those two families. Crucially, Eshmuniaton's supremacy was domestic; when war came it was his rival who took command. That would provoke Eshmuniaton into making a fatal mistake.[23]

With the Carthaginians still entangled in Libya and by plague, Dionysius decided to strike, on the pretext that 'the Phoenicians in the *epikrateia*' had attacked his territory. This is one of the few pieces of evidence that Sicily's Phoenician cities did maintain forces of their own (as might indeed be expected). It was a pretext which Diodorus firmly characterized as a lie. The Syracusan army, on the historian's fairly believable figures, numbered 30,000 foot and 3,000 horse, plus a supply train. Less believable is that Dionysius launched 300 triremes. If he did, it was his largest fleet since 397, though his army was now smaller; even in 397, he had put only 200 warships to sea. Diodorus' neatly descending military and naval sequence of '3s' (each 10 per cent of the preceding one) looks like a source's – or careless later copyist's – fancy, and it is more plausible to allow the tyrant around 200 ships.

This time Dionysius marched along the south coast to Selinus – Acragas apparently stayed neutral – and easily won over Selinus and also Entella, now held by the ex-mercenary Campanians. He then seized Eryx, just inland from the harbour of Drepana (Trápani). He spread the usual fire and flame across the cultivated countryside, but Segesta and Halicyae, cities in the interior between Entella and Eryx, were left alone, even though they could menace his rear and his land communications when he turned to lay siege to the new fortress-city Lilybaeum on the west coast. From here on, the ambitious expedition started to unravel. Lilybaeum was well garrisoned, probably because Dionysius, moving this way and that across the *epikrateia*, had mistakenly given the Carthaginians time to send reinforcements. The siege stalled as summer turned to autumn.

The tyrant was receiving detailed information about Carthage's military measures and about Hanno from none other than Eshmuniaton, or so the story went later. It did neither Eshmuniaton nor Dionysius any good. Eshmuniaton's incriminating letters in Greek were intercepted, he paid for them with his life and allegedly the *adirim* overreacted by banning all use of Greek at Carthage from then on (if genuine, the ban was soon ignored). Meanwhile, Dionysius gave up the siege of Lilybaeum, then made another mistake. Word came that the naval dockyards at Carthage had gone up in flames, taking the entire Punic navy with them, so he stationed 130 of his triremes in the harbour at Drepana, maybe in preparation for a move against Panormus in the next campaign, and sent the rest back to Syracuse.

The dockyards at Carthage may have burned, but its fleet had been saved. Hanno, or his second in command, sailed over with 200 triremes and took the Syracusans at Drepana completely unaware. Dionysius himself may have been there, as he had not gone home with the other ships. If so, he had to watch the Carthaginians tow away most of his prized fleet. As winter set in, both he and Carthage were ready to make an armistice which stipulated that 'either side should return to their own cities'. This can only mean that the Syracusan forces abandoned the *epikrateia* (Carthage had no cities outside it). Dionysius' invasion had led nowhere.

This in effect finished his last war with Carthage. No preparations seem to have been made for renewing hostilities in 367. Instead, not long before he finalized his ceremonial alliance with Athens, Dionysius – now in his mid-60s – received the glad news that, at long last, a play of his had been awarded first prize at Athens' winter festival, the Lenaea. As Diodorus told it, he celebrated too bibulously and died of alcohol poisoning. By contrast, according to Plutarch, the desperately ill tyrant was sent on his way by a fatal sleeping potion from his doctors, on the orders of his son, namesake and eager successor.

The younger Dionysius had no interest in reviving hostilities with Carthage, although it took a year or two for formal peace to be made. It was brought about largely thanks to the new ruler's respected uncle Dion, son of the elder Dionysius' ally and father-in-law Hipparinus – although the thanks Dion earned was to be exiled to Athens by his suspicious nephew. The peace restored the arrangements that had followed Himilco's victory at Cronium some fifteen years before.[24]

The net balance from forty years of intermittent Sicilian warfare was unedifying. The Magonids' drive to make Carthage the dominant power in the island was blunted in little more than a decade. After that, its aims had to change to the limited goal of keeping at bay Syracuse under the forceful Dionysius, the irrepressible enemy whose own rise to rulership owed much to the wars of Hannibal the Magonid and his nephew Himilco. Dionysius made Syracuse hegemon of eastern Sicily, and the greatest Greek power in the western Mediterranean, at enormous cost and through incessant warfare. How much benefit it brought to ordinary Syracusans is debatable; that it did little good to most Sicilians – Greeks, Phoenicians, Sicels and the others – is not. Flourishing cities were sacked or emptied, communities enslaved or uprooted, farmlands repeatedly looted and ravaged.

The Carthaginians themselves did not gain lastingly from the conflicts after the spectacular plundering of Selinus, Himera and Acragas early on. Not only was the *epikrateia* invaded and looted, and Motya – one of the Mediterranean world's richest trading centres – obliterated, but in North Africa itself, plague was let loose and with it repeated rebellions by Carthage's unhappy subjects. The twenty years of peace that now followed were sorely needed.

Chapter 7

Carthage against Timoleon

1. Carthage and the turmoils of Sicily

Some time after 366, the Carthaginians were finally able to recover control of rebel Libya and shake off the last of the plague that had besieged them for more than a decade. Hanno the Great could take credit for restoring his city's rule over Libya and for the peace with Syracuse, and with Eshmuniaton overthrown he enjoyed at long last the prime position in politics and society. Then, like Malchus, he made the mistake of excessive ambition. To entrench his position, he tried to rid himself of other enemies – as Justin told it, he planned to poison the entire Carthaginian senate at a banquet – but was overpowered and publicly executed. Justin's elaborate tale of schemes of poison and massacre may owe much to Hanno's enemies' propaganda, but something did happen in the 350s (Justin's dating): Aristotle, writing only some twenty years later, mentioned Hanno as one example – all the others being Greek – of 'a great man with capacity to be still greater' who stirred up civil strife 'so as to rule alone'. Justin added that all his sons were executed too, but we shall see that this is another exaggeration.[1]

Carthage's political crisis over Hanno was almost trivial compared to the upheavals that, again in the 350s, started to shake Greek Sicily to the core. Dionysius II did keep his city at peace, both in the island and (after a brief scuffle with the Lucanians) in southern Italy; he even refounded Rhegium, which his ruthless father had razed (his new name for it, 'Phoebia' in honour of Phoebus Apollo, was promptly ignored). Well-meaning at first, before long he came under pressure from conflicting factions among his advisers: one led by his uncle Dion, a friend of Plato and advocate of reforming the tyranny into a (hopefully) merit-based oligarchy, and the opponents of change, the most notable of them Philistus – the elder Dionysius' one-time friend (and current biographer) now back from thirty years of exile.

Though the second Dionysius flirted with Platonic philosophy during a return visit by the eminent philosopher, Dion's eminence and insistence grated. When, in 366, a letter from him to the Carthaginian authorities was intercepted, revealing Dion advising them not to make peace without involving him, his nephew exiled him to Greece. After nine years there, however, the exile made a comeback to energize growing discontent with Dionysius. When he sailed from western Greece in September 357 (the date is guaranteed by a lunar eclipse just beforehand), contrary winds blew his little expedition – under 800 mercenaries in a five-ship flotilla – over to Heraclea Minoa in the *epikrateia*, where a senior Carthaginian general also happened to be: Eshmunhalos (in Greek, Synalus), a guest-friend of his, who welcomed the arrivals.

According to Plutarch, Synalus was 'the Carthaginian ruler' or 'governor' (*archon*) and 'happened to be present' when Dion's flotilla came in, whereas in Diodorus he is the commandant or supervisor of the city. Plutarch's fuller account is more plausible, especially as he was using a narrative by Dion's close friend and companion Timonides. Synalus' rank was probably what Greek writers, in later contexts, termed a *boetharchos*: a subordinate general commanding forces in a Carthaginian-controlled region. As noted earlier, the Carthaginians since Hannibal the Magonid's time maintained regular forces, probably of mercenaries, in Sicily (probably in Sardinia too). It is not likely that Synalus knew Dion was coming – he tried to fight off the Greeks until he learned who led them – but likely enough that he and then his home city were happy to aid an eminent Syracusan leader's crusade to terminate the Dionysian regime.[2]

Dion's crusade succeeded, but only after much time and at heavy cost. Though he quickly ousted his nephew from power, Dionysius held on to Ortygia, the island heart of Syracuse and the family's stronghold, for two years (despite losing old Philistus in a sea battle), while his uncle's rich aristocratic backers bickered and at times fought with radical Syracusan democrats. Dion prevailed but, now virtually tyrant himself, grew more and more authoritarian and unscrupulous. Antagonizing even many of his own supporters, he was murdered in 354 at a dinner party – ironically at the instigation of another Platonic disciple, Callippus of Athens.

A giddy series of short-lived tyrants followed at Syracuse: Callippus, who was thrown out after a year, then two of Dion's nephews in succession, and even Dionysius once more in 346 (he had spent the past nine years at Locri). As Syracuse's hegemony dissolved, confusion, violence and fighting spread over Greek Sicily. Syracuse under Callippus unsuccessfully fought Catana, which had fallen under a shifty Campanian ex-mercenary officer called Mamercus ('Marcus' in Diodorus), one of a fresh breed of city tyrants. An ambitious past friend of Dion named Hicetas took over Leontini and hoped to seize Syracuse from Dionysius, while at some point Centuripa became ruled by a Nicodemus, Agyrium by an Apolloniades (Agyris being dead or displaced) and Engyum and Apollonia, smaller cities north-west of Agyrium, by one Leptines, perhaps a cousin of the deposed tyrant. Little Tauromenium, by contrast, was led by a more amiable character, Andromachus (whose son, born around 356, was the future historian Timaeus). The once great south coast cities, Camarina, Gela and Acragas, had shrunk into near-irrelevance, the prey of stronger powers.

Plato wrote, in a letter soon after the troubles erupted, how he feared that Greek Sicily would be mastered by 'Phoenicians or Opicans' – meaning the Carthaginians or the Campanian mercenaries now active in sizeable numbers around the island. To him and many other Greeks, this meant barbarization and the obliteration of Greek culture.

The turmoils of eastern Sicily were watched closely by Carthage. Dion had friends and enjoyed high regard there, but the outcome of the bitter upheaval that followed his murder could mean fresh problems for the city. There was trouble even in the *epikrateia*: Entella's Campanians had thrown off Punic hegemony, setting a dangerous example to other subject allies. Finally, Carthage determined to intervene once again with military force in Sicily.[3]

2. The arrival of Timoleon

The Carthaginians, arguably, could have chosen to wait longer and watch the Greeks rend one another to pieces, then step in to impose an island-wide dominance with minimal effort. Instead, they moved to push this process along. Recalcitrant Entella was a relatively minor concern. More importantly, in 345, they probably became aware that Leontini's aristocratic Syracusan exiles, seconded – reluctantly – by Hicetas, decided to appeal to Syracuse's mother-city Corinth for help against the returned Dionysius. Before long they certainly learned that help from Greece was on its way, though not perhaps until later that this consisted less impressively of an elderly Corinthian aristocrat, Timoleon, and a small force of 700 mercenaries (whom he had to recruit personally) on ten ships. Even so, any level of mainland Greek intervention was enough to galvanize Punic attention.

Politics at Carthage possibly played a part. Hanno the Great's elimination allowed other leading men to compete for primacy; and in spite of Hanno's fall and even though sons and kinsmen of his perished too, his faction was not uprooted. One son, Gisco, survived in exile (we do not know where) awaiting fortune's next turn. A new and successful forward thrust in Sicily would be a political boon to the leaders who urged it.

Mago, the general appointed for the expedition, and Hanno the admiral, his presumed deputy, were either the chiefs of their faction or men whom that faction trusted. They could argue that the current chaos among the Greeks posed an opportunity that would never be repeated. Further encouragement came from none other than Hicetas, who had no enthusiasm for a Corinthian competitor – he wrote to Corinth to warn off Timoleon – and declared himself openly Carthage's ally once it in turn decided to act.

Punic envoys were sent off to woo as many other Sicilian tyrants as possible into either joining in or at least staying neutral, and indeed many did remain aloof from what followed. Diodorus added that the Carthaginians 'made friendly approaches to the allied cities in Sicily', a remark not very clear but probably referring to those Elymians and Sicels still its allies: Segesta, for example. Entella had broken away and the Carthaginians would not want to see others do so too. The 'friendly approaches' (assuming that Diodorus did not simply misinterpret his source) could be promises that Mago would not put demands on them, or at any rate demands out of the ordinary, for manpower or money.

The expedition in 344 amounted, wrote Diodorus, to 50,000 troops, 300 war chariots with 2,000 spare horses, and 150 warships. Plutarch's numbers are higher for troops (60,000) and match Diodorus' for the warships, but have nothing about chariots or chariot horses. As often in Greek accounts of Punic armies, the infantry figure may be too high. Surprisingly, cavalry are not mentioned at all. Equally surprising is to find war chariots still in a mid-fourth century Punic army, but as they were still in use in Persian armies, Mago possibly took the idea from there. Some of the many Greek mercenaries he hired could have done earlier service in the eastern Mediterranean against – or in the pay of – Persia. In 341, chariots would be wheeled out for service again. As for the 2,000 horses, possibly Diodorus' source or Diodorus himself mistook Mago's cavalry numbers as spares for chariots.[4]

The Punic commanders felt they had little to fear from the approaching Timoleon. Already 65, his one noteworthy action had been to have his brother assassinated when the brother tried to make himself tyrant at Corinth. Since then he had lived out of the public eye for twenty years. Choosing him to lead the mission to Sicily, and with such small resources, suggests that his fellow citizens viewed the venture unenthusiastically. His mercenaries were not only few but tainted, for the only ones he could obtain were men who had taken part in pillaging Greece's most sacred site, Delphi, a decade before. Few Sicilian or Italian Greeks showed support for the enterprise either: besides the Syracusan exiles, only Rhegium was openly, and Andromachus of Tauromenium secretly, well-disposed. The rest waited on events.

The Carthaginians and Hicetas together tried to nip Timoleon's enterprise in the bud. First, a Punic trireme with official spokesmen caught up with his flotilla at Metapontum on the southern Italian coast (he ignored the warning they brought). Next, a squadron of twenty warships anchored outside Rhegium to await him there. Messengers from Hicetas disembarked with a proposal: Timoleon should dismiss his forces and become, on his own, Hicetas' colleague. Timoleon learned, too, that three days earlier his would-be friend had pushed Dionysius II back into Ortygia and was master of mainland Syracuse. Instead of yielding to the demands and threats, he gave the messengers and the Punic ship-captains the slip with the help of the Rhegines, who distracted them at an almost farcically long-winded public assembly until Timoleon's flotilla had sailed. Avoiding Messana, now neutral or even pro-Carthaginian, Timoleon then hurried down to Tauromenium, where Andromachus declared his support. A Carthaginian envoy who arrived by ship to threaten the Tauromenitan leader with destruction if he did not send the newcomers away was himself sent on his way, unsatisfied. The time was probably March 344.[5]

A complex skein of military events followed. Mago in the west had moved on Entella, annihilating a small rescue force from Galaria (a Sicel place thought to lie in the hill country near Enna – and if so a long 170km from Entella) and compelling the Entellans to return to Punic obedience. He also sent off a naval squadron to Syracuse's two harbours to encourage his new ally Hicetas and dismay Dionysius, though otherwise it did nothing of note. But while the Carthaginian was busying himself with insubordinate old allies in the *epikrateia*, Hicetas – underestimating the newcomer again – handed Timoleon a golden opportunity.

The little city of Adranum, close to Campanian-held Aetna on the southern slopes of Mount Etna, was divided between citizens favouring Hicetas and others keen on Timoleon. Why Hicetas judged it worth his personal attention is not obvious, but he marched there with 5,000 men and encamped outside. That evening he was promptly surprised by Timoleon, who arrived from Tauromenium with a force now grown to 1,200 (or barely 1,000 in Diodorus' telling) to rout the Syracusan army as it ate dinner. Hicetas lost 900 men – 600 of them taken prisoner – and had to stagger back to Syracuse.

Neither Hicetas nor the Carthaginians had actually declared war on Timoleon: they and he were at war with Dionysius II, still in Ortygia, and they had tried to frighten off Timoleon or win him over. It was Timoleon who abruptly launched hostilities (a point ignored by our sources), though no doubt Hicetas, like Mago, did already see him as a potential foe. His victory at Adranum certainly brought benefits: not only did that city and another small place, Tyndaris on the north coast, declare for him and give him soldiers, but so did one more consequential, Catana under its tyrant Mamercus. When the news reached Corinth some days later, his home city made haste to ready ten more ships, donate money, enlist 2,000 mercenaries and 200 cavalrymen – Greece had plentiful mercenaries looking for work – and send them out to reinforce him.[6]

3. Sorting out sources

What followed is much debated, because Diodorus' account and Plutarch's diverge.

In Diodorus' telling, Timoleon now makes a lightning swoop on Syracuse ahead of Hicetas, and a paragraph later we read of Timoleon holding part of that city while Hicetas stands at bay in its mainland suburbs, Achradina and Neapolis, and Dionysius II remains in Ortygia. At Hicetas' request, Mago then arrives with his army and fleet in full strength to blockade the city by land and water. At this point, first Mamercus of Catana (in Diodorus he is called Marcus) 'and then many of the forts' (undefined) declare for the liberator. Next, the Corinthians man ten warships and send them over with funds, much to Timoleon's relief and even more to the Carthaginians' alarm, causing Mago to pack up and sail away to the *epikrateia*. 'With Hicetas isolated, Timoleon overcame his enemies and mastered Syracuse,' we are told: this therefore enables him to move north to capture Messana, which had gone over to the Carthaginians. Before long, Dionysius hands over his island citadel to the liberator on condition of being released into exile in Greece.

Plutarch's lengthier narrative offers a very different sequence of events. In this version, Mamercus and others join Timoleon's side right after his victory at Adranum (but no mention of 'forts'). Later on, Timoleon is still busy at Adranum and Catana, for during a sacrifice at Adranum he narrowly escapes assassins sent by Hicetas. But before this, Dionysius in Ortygia has negotiated with him to hand over his island stronghold and go into exile; as the first stage in the handover, Timoleon infiltrates 400 soldiers into Ortygia in small groups to escape notice. This is what causes Hicetas to send assassins against him and then call in the Carthaginians. Mago's fleet fills the Great Harbour and – horror of horrors to the Greeks – 60,000 barbarian troops encamp in Syracuse itself. Ortygia holds out against attacks, Timoleon holds his nerve, and Mago and Hicetas make further mistakes until, as the setbacks mount, Mago abruptly packs up all his forces and sails away to Libya.

Diodorus' version is problematic. To start with, if Timoleon went to Syracuse straight after Adranum, it is hard to see which part of it he might occupy: at that stage Hicetas held both the mainland suburbs and (we learn later) the plateau of Epipolae, which must mean he also held the Euryalus fortress. Second, in having the full Carthaginian fleet and army already at Syracuse before Mamercus and others declare for Timoleon and Dionysius hands over Ortygia, Diodorus is less convincing than Plutarch, who has Mago's forces arrive only afterwards.

Diodorus' odd statement that, with Mago gone and 'with Hicetas isolated, Timoleon overcame his enemies and mastered Syracuse', is a clue to what has gone wrong in his telling. It comes while his narrative still has Dionysius lodged in Ortygia and after Mago has departed; Ortygia's handover to Timoleon is not reported until later. For Diodorus, therefore, at this stage Timoleon is still confronting both Dionysius and the 'isolated' Hicetas, making nonsense of the claim that he has overcome his enemies and become master of the city. His next supposed act, to break off action and march north to take Messana, again makes unsatisfactory sense in such circumstances.

Plutarch's narrative on this is not just fuller but more logical too. The Corinthian reinforcements arrive in Sicily some time after Dionysius has handed over Ortygia to Timoleon's men. Timoleon meets them at Catana and takes over Messana, while a countermove by Mago and Hicetas to attack Catana by sea is reversed when Timoleon's Corinthians now holding Ortygia boldly sally out and seize Achradina. Then Timoleon marches south for Syracuse with all his forces, prompting Mago to decamp and leave Hicetas on his own. Hicetas is now indeed 'isolated'. Diodorus' odd statement fits this context and not any earlier one.[7]

His narrative of events has, in effect, mislocated several of the events between the battle at Adranum and Mago's disappearance. That has produced anomalies like his improbable claim that Timoleon holed up in some unidentified, and unattacked, corner of Syracuse after the victory at Adranum, and the equally bizarre declaration (even before Dionysius has surrendered Otygia to Timoleon) that the Corinthian leader had 'isolated' Hicetas and 'mastered Syracuse'. The mislocatings may be due to scrambling, or just misreading, what his sources reported. For Timoleon to advance all the way to Syracuse directly after Adranum and capture some part of the city is a fuzzy and false doublet, anticipating his later takeover of Ortygia.

On the other hand, Diodorus' mention of freedom-yearning 'forts' declaring for Timoleon is too incidental and undeveloped to be an invented touch. Like the linked mention of 'Marcus' (Mamercus), it should be believed. But both events should be placed in the early stage of Timoleon's actions, after his victory at Adranum. This may be a clue to what did happen after the victory.

'Forts' that were freedom-yearning must in reality have been lesser cities under Syracusan hegemony. Several of these lay west and south of that city: for example Menae (Minio) west of Leontini, Acrae (Palazzolo Acreide) in the Hyblaean hills only 35km west of Syracuse, Casmenae near Acrae and, to Syracuse's south, Notum and Helorus, all of them known as under Syracusan dominance in various periods. Arguably, Timoleon marched to, and won over, at least Menae, Casmenae and Acrae while Hicetas was retreating by another path to Syracuse with his shattered army. These places would be valuable to Timoleon both for some extra troops and for keeping watch on Syracuse. Once he had won their backing, he could return to Adranum and Catana to assemble other allies' forces. There he would receive the news that fresh forces from Corinth were on their way.

4. The enigma of Mago

Clearing up the discrepancies and problems in Diodorus' and Plutarch's versions allows a tighter, and clearer, sequence of events to emerge.

After the Battle of Adranum, Syracuse was still divided between Dionysius in the island fastness of Ortygia and Hicetas holding the mainland sectors and Epipolae with his remaining troops. A squadron of Carthaginian warships sent by Mago and Hanno patrolled the two harbours, though they could not stop all access to and from Ortygia, as we shall see. Outside Syracuse, Leontini was also on Hicetas' side, for he was to retreat there when his position in the city finally became untenable. Timoleon's prospects may have looked dim even now, but several major developments swung fortune over to him.

First, Dionysius, in gloomy confinement in Ortygia (also called the Nesus, or Island), made contact with him to put a startling offer: if granted a safe exit into Greek exile, he would hand over the Island with its arsenal, all his stored treasure and his 2,000 remaining mercenaries. His life had little meaning left: he was shorn of power, and his wife and most of their children had been savagely slaughtered at Locri after his return to Syracuse two years earlier. His offer was accepted, for Timoleon's brief was to end the tyranny at Syracuse, not kill the tyrant.

To elude the Punic ship patrols, the liberator infiltrated his 400 men into Ortygia in small groups led by two fellow-Corinthians, Eucleides and Telemachus. They found a wealth of military equipment there: artillery and other engines, horses, missiles and armour for fitting out no fewer than 70,000 men. Most of it probably dated back to Dionysius II's war-obsessed father. They also took command of his mercenaries, while the ex-tyrant and his last few friends left in similar secrecy to go to Timoleon at either Adranum or Catana. The fallen ruler then, or the following year, sailed with a small portion of his wealth to Greece, to spend the rest of his life at Corinth in increasingly shabby circumstances (Plutarch's biography of Timoleon tells quite a few anecdotes).[8]

Ortygia came into Timoleon's hands less than fifty days after he landed in Sicily. So Plutarch reported, and the time-span is believable once Diodorus' confused event-sequence is cleared up. Timoleon landed at Tauromenium probably in March 344, struck and routed Hicetas at Adranum before his opponent had any idea he was approaching – two weeks after landing would be enough – and before long again was in contact with Dionysius in Ortygia. By the end of April or early in May, he can have slipped his 400 Corinthians into the Island and brought out the ex-tyrant. Then it would be early in the summer of 344 that the great expeditionary fleet and army of Mago and Hanno arrived to occupy Syracuse's harbours and mainland to link up with Hicetas and blockade and harass the Corinthians and Dionysius' 2,000 mercenaries in Ortygia. These were able to hold out in the strongly fortified Island, despite hunger and enemy attacks, because Timoleon at Catana sent them loads of grain on small boats that eluded watchful Punic vessels, especially in rough weather. This siege will have continued for some time over the summer, until Hicetas and Mago made another mistake.

Deciding to stop this irritant and deal once and for all with Timoleon and his allies, they embarked their best troops to assail Catana from the sea. But as soon as they sailed from Syracuse, Neon, the current Corinthian commander in Ortygia, sallied forth against Achradina's unwisely relaxed garrison, expelled it and took over the well-stocked suburb. Hicetas and Mago had just disembarked their men near Catana when a rider came up with the news of the coup. That brought the two commanders back in haste, the Catana mission aborted. Yet still they made no sustained effort against Ortygia or Achradina. Counterproductively, their mercenaries had struck up fairly friendly contacts with those of Neon during the desultory blockade of Ortygia.

Timoleon now left Catana, perhaps for Tauromenium, to meet the reinforcements arriving from Corinth under two officers, Deinarchus and Demaretus. These had initially been held up at Thurii because Hanno was watching the southern Italian coast with a squadron (they stayed there long enough for their hosts to go off to fight neighbouring Bruttians), but had then marched overland to Rhegium while storms at sea kept the Carthaginians away – probably the same weather that had enabled the grain rations to slip through to Ortygia. Hanno thought them marooned there, abandoned his patrolling when calm seas returned and sailed to Syracuse, whereupon the Corinthians crossed safely to Sicily. With them, and apparently peaceably, Timoleon took over Messana, which (perhaps from enmity with Rhegium) had allied with Carthage but had no Punic protection. Finally, he marched south for Syracuse, still with limited forces: 4,000 men according to Plutarch. He obviously planned to link up with the troops holding Achradina and Ortygia.[9]

The day before he reached the city another event happened, one totally unexpected, perhaps the most extraordinary event in all of Carthage's Sicilian wars. During lulls in hostilities at Syracuse, the Greek mercenaries on both sides had became friendly – both liked to go eel-fishing along the shore – and Neon's men scolded their opponents for serving 'the basest and bloodiest people', whose aim was not to reinstate Hicetas but to seize Syracuse for themselves and 'barbarize' it. The criticisms struck such a chord with their hearers that (we are told) they excited suspicions in Mago about possible treachery. Ignoring Hicetas' pleas, he struck camp, embarked his army and sailed off to western Sicily.

Timoleon swiftly seized the opportunity to attack Hicetas in the Neapolis suburb. He must have done so within a couple of days of arriving, rather than lose momentum. The attack was launched with some skill: he moved from the River Anapus area to strike Neapolis from the south, a Corinthian officer named Isias stormed out of Achradina to hit Hicetas on the other flank, and Deinarchus and Demaretus led their Corinthians to seize Epipolae. If the garrison of Euryalus held out at all, the men there would soon see that they were isolated and it made sense to join the general retreat which ended at Leontini. Timoleon let them go. The date was probably sometime in the late summer or early autumn of 344.[10]

It was unique for an undefeated Carthaginian general to abandon a war despite having ample resources, an experienced ally and a heavily outnumbered enemy. Mago had supposedly long been wanting to abandon the campaign, though Plutarch's reasons for this are nebulous: that Mago judged Timoleon's forces far superior in quality to Hicetas' and that he abandoned Sicily 'under no human calculation'. More recent views vary.

One sees him simply as lacking initiative and too readily discouraged. Another is that he was recalled to put down the insurrection of Hanno the Great; but that is best dated a decade or so earlier, nor is Mago mentioned in connection with it; and in any case, after he returned home he killed himself. In another view, he had been sent only to restore control over a rebellious *epikrateia*, but had been drawn eastward into the Greek brawls out of friendship for Hicetas. All the same, an armament of many thousands of soldiers (even if not up to 60,000) plus most of the Punic navy, not to mention 300 war chariots, was uncommonly large to deal with just a regional rebellion.

A rather more plausible explanation sees Mago suspecting that Hicetas, like Dionysius before him, was in contact with the approaching Timoleon – contact later masked with a tale about eel-fishing mercenaries – to make a deal behind the Carthaginians' backs. Rather than risk betrayal, Mago arguably called time on his expedition. A supposed clue is that when Timoleon, upon reaching Syracuse, launched the assault on Hicetas' positions, his forces – still outnumbered even with the just-arrived Corinthians – quickly defeated the defenders and bundled them out 'without any of the Corinthians being killed or even wounded' (thus Plutarch). A sign that the assault was just a prearranged show?[11]

This suggestion, though plausible-looking, fails to persuade. While Hicetas was still defiant, his men may have been less so after the sudden disappearance of their Carthaginian allies. The story that not one Corinthian was hurt (pretty clearly referring to the newly arrived reinforcements) certainly looks like upbeat embroidery by Timoleon, keen to bolster further support at Corinth. It is not a clue that the attack was fake. Had Hicetas come to a secret pact with Timoleon, he could simply have pulled out and retired to Leontini without costing his troops casualties; and Timoleon would hardly have lost face in treating with him for the bloodless conquest of Syracuse.[12]

The explanation may be that, seeing Timoleon's earlier successes and the broad uninterest of Sicilian tyrants in resisting him despite Carthage's urgings, Mago decided that his city's interests would be served no less well, but less riskily, by once again leaving the Sicilian Greeks to fight among themselves. They would still end up, he might reckon, too weak to trouble the *epikrateia* or even resist future Punic domination. Such calculations would prove mistaken, but only in later hindsight. With Dionysius gone and Timoleon offering a new start, support at Syracuse for Hicetas had waned too: a further discouragement.

For Carthage, the war was over, in practice though not in name. Mago may have left some forces in the *epikrateia*, perhaps under Hanno, but he sailed home with the rest. At Carthage he met a frenzy of hostility over his strange conduct of operations, enough to drive him to suicide. His infuriated fellow-citizens nailed his corpse to a cross, a gesture showing they had wanted him tried by the recently created court of One Hundred and Four and crucified.[13]

The fiasco of an expedition which had begun so well and ended so bafflingly may also have sharpened factional rivalries in Carthage. Hanno disappears from the record. The next Sicilian expedition was led by two others, Hasdrubal and Hamilcar, nor did they sail until 341 at earliest (in other interpretations, not until 340 or even 339). Preparations for the new expedition were certainly thorough and took time, but three years look too long even so, unless there were other hold-ups. Dissension among political factions over whether to reintervene at all against Syracuse under its new ruler, or when, or by whom, may have slowed them down.

5. The battle at the Crimisus

Although Diodorus unhelpfully parcelled out Timoleon's progress up to his takeover of Syracuse over the three years 344–42 – at least partly a result of his flawed order of events – and then brought the second Punic expedition to Sicily in 339, he was right to indicate that substantial time passed before Hasdrubal and Hamilcar came to Sicily. Plutarch's account, once again fuller, confirms a substantial interval. They show how ceaselessly active Timoleon was both in Syracuse (where he was in effect the new tyrant) and across eastern Sicily, in the two-and-a-half years after Hicetas's expulsion.[14]

The most critical challenge was Greek Sicily's impoverishment and depopulation after a dozen years of upheaval. Syracuse's *agora*, or forum, on the Achradina mainland close to Ortygia, was deep enough in grass for horses to graze. Within most other cities, Plutarch wrote, deer and swine ran wild (though this looks like hyperbole). Appeals were sent to Corinth and other Greek states on both sides of the Aegean for exiles to come home and new settlers to join them; Corinth promised to pay their travelling costs, Timoleon granted them land, and in time some 10,000 men (plus families) crossed the sea to Syracuse. Larger numbers would come over the next few years.

Timoleon almost at once launched a reform programme to set up a constitution for Syracuse, bringing a pair of eminent Corinthian theorists, Cephalus and another Dionysius, to help him work it out. It was apparently a limited democracy, maintaining the citizen assembly (which even the tyrants had kept) but checking it with an aristocratic council and, no doubt, strong magistracies. The new political system would give Syracuse passably stable government for more than twenty years.

His more immediate task, though, was dealing with Hicetas and other regional despots. With them he had successes and failures. Hicetas beat off his attack on Leontini and even tried – unsuccessfully – to recapture Syracuse when Timoleon moved inland against Leptines of Engyum and Apollonia; after that, Timoleon left Leontini alone. Plutarch's biography tells the move against Hicetas differently, and almost certainly wrongly: Timoleon 'compelled Hicetas to abandon the Carthaginians and agree to demolish his citadels and live as a private citizen in Leontini'. In reality, Hicetas was still master of that city later when Timoleon once more moved against him – this time successfully. Plutarch's statement looks like a flawed, and mislocated, report of contacts between the two men in early 341: at that time, Hicetas agreed to contribute troops for Timoleon's confrontation with the second Carthaginian expedition (a promise not mentioned by Plutarch), possibly also promising to retire into private life: promises he had no intention of keeping.[15]

Timoleon's campaign against Leptines, on the other hand, did bring that tyrant to heel. He was shipped off to Corinth to hobnob with his fallen cousin, and his cities regained their freedom. Yet Timoleon had to leave still others alone – Nicodemus in Centuripa, near Agyrium, and Apolloniades of Agyrium – along with the loutish Campanians of Aetna and, of course, his ally Mamercus of Catana. He must also have lost control of Messana, for that city is later found under the uncooperative rule of one Hippon.

Dionysius II's treasure was a windfall for the new regime, but not infinite. Timoleon spent money rebuilding and refurbishing Syracuse, which included levelling the tyrants' palace, citadel and even the elder Dionysius' tomb. He also had to help the incoming settlers establish themselves and, of course, had to keep his mercenary troops properly paid (probably his Corinthians too). The claim of freeing Siceliots from their tyrants meant that liberated cities were not sacked or their lands ravaged. Eventually funds ran low. The Syracusans sold off the statues of past notables to raise money (who bought them we are not told), but Timoleon went so far as to put up every private house for sale, then invited their owners to buy them back – a procedure that can hardly have been popular, even though he justified it as for the good of the state.

Another, more inviting source of funds was Carthage's *epikrateia*. The Corinthians Deinarchus and Demaretus were sent out with 1,000 of their men on an extensive plundering raid, with gratifying results. Although only a small force, the Corinthians certainly had free rein to roam and ravage – 'they passed their time amidst plenty', wrote Plutarch – and the loot they gathered, when Timoleon sold it off, enabled his mercenaries to be paid their accumulated arrears. So we are told, anyway, though later on some deserted at a critical moment, claiming they had not had their pay. According to Plutarch, the Corinthians also induced 'many cities' to revolt from the Carthaginians; but no names are offered and some places may simply have made a show of declaring for the Greek side to avoid a sack. The comment about the raiders enjoying plenty in the west does suggest not a short rampage through the *epikrateia* but a much longer visit, as a later item in his narrative may confirm.

Diodorus' version of the raid adds some other details or else transmits a source-report different from Plutarch's, for it also has Timoleon himself coming west. If he did, it would be with extra troops, for he assailed and captured Entella, executing its fifteen pro-Carthaginian leaders. Moreover (we are told), 'many' Sicel and Sican cities under Carthaginian rule asked to become his allies – again, no names are given – although it is very unlikely that important native Sicilian places did (Segesta, Halicyae or Eryx, for instance). More propaganda can be suspected in this claim, and in the accompanying claim that all the Siceliot cities now enthusiastically embraced his cause. In reality, even those that did so soon showed an enthusiasm decidedly lukewarm.[16]

Amid all this there were Carthaginian generals in the region, but they 'were managing the war ignobly', as Diodorus put it. Hanno may have been left in charge, or else lieutenants of *boetharchos* rank, but evidently defence forces in the *epikrateia* were too few to intervene, too fearful, or both. At Carthage, resolve firmed to deal once and for all with Timoleon and the Sicilian Greeks. His wide-ranging policies of restoration and repopulation – all of them tending (at any rate in foreign eyes) to return Syracuse to Dionysian-level dominance over Greek Sicily – could only sharpen

Carthaginian conviction that Mago had made a gigantic mistake. Without a resolute response, Carthaginians surely feared, they could ultimately forfeit their western Sicilian territories and allies to a revitalized alliance led by Syracuse.

Greek propaganda afterwards insisted that this time Carthage planned to drive all the Siceliots out of Sicily. Of course that would have been physically impossible, not to mention unnecessary, as all that was needed was to make sure that Syracuse was kept weak (or maybe resettled with Punic colonists) and other cities kept obedient. It would be economically damaging too, for it would take decades at best before the emptied regions could be fully repopulated and redeveloped. On the other hand, to crush Syracuse and its allies, rid Sicily of Corinthians and other meddlers, and rely on garrisons and Sicel allies to rivet Punic hegemony over the Siceliots were (or would look like) sensible and feasible aims.

Once again, as in their preparations for 480 and 406, the Carthaginians devoted time and care to readying forces. New warships and quantities of military equipment were manufactured. After at least a year of strenuous and costly build-up, an army reportedly 70,000-strong was ready to take the field in spring 341, together with 200 triremes, while 1,000 transport ships bore 10,000 horses, war chariots, artillery and grain. Diodorus' and Plutarch's descriptions of the battle that followed make no mention of cavalry: if correct, then the new generals must have chosen to substitute war chariots, in unknown numbers, for horsemen (a major mistake). The infantry total, as often before, may be exaggerated (Polyaenus gave it from some source as 50,000). Nonetheless, Carthage was so undoubtedly determined at all costs to deal with its Siceliot problem that the number must have been large.

This army was special. As well as Libyan conscripts and mercenaries from Iberia, Gaul and Liguria (and very likely other places, such as Sardinia) – but no Greeks – Carthaginian citizen troops had been enlisted. Diodorus' narrative presents the 'Sacred Corps' (in Greek, *hieros lochos*) of 2,500 gorgeously equipped infantrymen, while Plutarch's features 10,000 splendidly armed and impeccably drilled Carthaginians, all bearing white shields and forming the van. We should infer that along with the Sacred Corps, and perhaps emulating it on this crucial expedition, another 7,500 citizens served, almost as impressively equipped. Silver, and especially gold, fittings made the armour of the 10,000 glitter when they advanced in disciplined array. For so many Carthaginians to take the field (and with over 30,000 others crewing the warships), feeling in the city must still have run high over the repeated frustrations in Sicily, even two years and more since Mago's humiliation.[17]

News of the massive expedition spread fear across the island. Timoleon found it hard to recruit even Syracusans for the new campaign: in the end, only 3,000 men of the city he had liberated heeded his call to join the 4,000 mercenaries in his service. Hicetas did contribute some troops too – a remarkable turnaround, whether from a belated feeling of solidarity with fellow-Greeks or simply from distrust of Carthaginians after his treatment by Mago – and places like Adranum, Engyum and Apollonia might want to show their support too. Contrastingly, Mamercus of Catana was a non-contributor, to judge by his actions later.

Even those who did send troops were frugal: Diodorus' figure for the army is 12,000 all told, with a comment in Plutarch indicating that 1,000 of them were cavalry. A contingent of light-armed may be missing from these totals, as such a force is found afterwards in the battle at the Crimisus. Timoleon would not wait for any more troops: he was intent on taking the war to the *epikrateia* rather than letting the Carthaginians fall on his allies. The odds he and his men faced were virtually as unfavourable as three years before, when he marched with 4,000 from Messana against Hicetas and Mago, but this time there was no prospect of the enemy suddenly decamping.

Some of his troops began to panic. In the neighbourhood of Acragas, 1,000 mercenaries mutinied, complaining about being unpaid (they may of course have exaggerated or lied) and being led to slaughter by a madman. They then set off back to Syracuse. Their spokesman Thrasius declared that Timoleon had brought them eight days' march from Syracuse to certain annihilation. This does not mean that the battle with the Carthaginians was fought on the ninth day: no one on the march somewhere near Acragas could forecast when it would happen. But a mostly infantry army would need at least eight days for the 210km or more from Syracuse to Acragas, even when moving with urgency and even if wagons or pack-animals bore the men's armour and other kit (as was regular in Roman armies). The battlefield, it turned out, was by the River Crimisus (the Belice), probably close to Entella: that was about 110km north-west of Acragas, another four to six days' march through hilly country.[18]

Hasdrubal and Hamilcar had disembarked at Lilybaeum and, 'on learning that their *epikrateia* was being ravaged, rapidly and angrily advanced against the Corinthians'. If Plutarch's wording is accurate and not just clumsy writing – the reference to 'the Corinthians' suggests accuracy – Deinarchus' and Demaretus' raiding force was still doing the rounds of western Sicily in spring 341, as Plutarch also suggested earlier. Now the Corinthians would leave as fast as possible, maybe to join Timoleon as he advanced and so bring in a valuable though unrecorded final reinforcement.

It looks as though Hasdrubal and Hamilcar felt no need for urgency, apart from scaring off the raiders. The news of their landing would have taken a few days to reach Syracuse, so even if Timoleon then set out as fast as possible – perhaps picking up allied contingents en route – they could still have penetrated into central Sicily by the time he suffered the mercenary mutiny near Acragas. Instead, he found them still within, or on the edge of, the *epikrateia*.

Possibly they wanted to draw him closer, so that after a defeat he would be cut off far from friendly territory and the way would lie open to them to invade the east of the island, against minimal opposition. Yet it seems the Carthaginian generals, encamped for a night or more beside the Crimisus, had no idea that the Greeks were so close. They may, though, have learned that Timoleon was in the area, just as he had learned the same about them. To find him, they set the army in motion next morning. It was the 24th of Thargelion, the Athenian month that ran from late May to late June, and the day was early in June.

When Timoleon's marching men reached the top of one of the hills above the river, a thick summer haze meant they could hear but not see the Carthaginians, nor did the Carthaginians see them. The Greeks rested until midday, when the haze rose to unveil an extraordinary opportunity. The enemy chariots and part of the Carthaginian citizen array were across the river. The rest of the citizen troops, and with or behind them the other contingents, were in the stream or waiting their turn to ford. Timoleon dressed his ranks and ordered a charge down the hillside.[19]

The Greek allies and some mercenaries formed the army's two wings, while he himself in the centre led his Syracusans, most of the mercenaries and no doubt his Corinthians under Deinarchus. All three divisions advanced in serried ranks, shield to shield. Ahead of them galloped the cavalry under Demaretus, aiming to strike the Carthaginian infantry before these could form up. But according to Plutarch's not entirely clear account – the only one with details – the horsemen were blocked from the Carthaginian infantry by the Punic chariots 'racing in front of the array'. It was the Greek infantry that came to blows with the Carthaginian infantry as these were forming up.

Timoleon, meanwhile, signalled Deinarchus to skirt the chariots and attack the Carthaginians in the flank. The signal must have been conveyed by trumpet calls (if so, Timoleon's trumpeters were in step with him), but how the cavalry got past the chariots can only be guessed. Maybe these large four-horse vehicles were hard to turn around quickly – but turn away they surely did, at least after the Greek cavalrymen had passed and perhaps in an effort to pursue them: the oncoming Greek infantry certainly did not run into them. Timoleon's light-armed fighters could have taken part too, harassing chariot-horses and their drivers with javelins and spears – and it need take only one badly injured or slain horse to wreak havoc on its team.

On the infantry clash, Diodorus and Plutarch diverge. According to Diodorus, 10,000 Carthaginians were already across the Crimisus when the Greek infantry met them, shattered them and made them flee, but the main Punic army now reached the battleground and stabilized the struggle. Plutarch says it was the 10,000 who held their ground, repelled the Greeks' spear thrusts and forced a combat of sword against sword. This is more likely, but it leaves unanswered what the rest of the Punic infantry was doing, and what had become of the chariots and Deinarchus. As a possible scenario, the light-armed infantry and Deinarchus' riders succeeded between them in neutralizing the chariots and harassing the flanks of the 10,000 infantry while the rest of the Carthaginian army – all foot-soldiers, it seems – was still lining up (or milling around) to ford the Crimisus. Meanwhile, the sky began to darken with a threatening storm.

Hasdrubal and Hanno could have used some of these still uncommitted elements to cross at points further up and down the river, so as to swing in and envelop Timoleon's infantry, or the chariots might have tried the same manoeuvre once Deinarchus had bypassed them. But perhaps the army was too unwieldy for any nimble pivoting, or the Crimisus offered no other viable crossing points nearby – or else the generals simply reckoned that, once they got the rest of their men across at the same spot while the 10,000 were engaging the Greeks, it would be no great difficulty to fan out and crush Timoleon with overwhelming numbers. They would surely have succeeded, had not the heavens intervened.

As thunder and lightning erupted overhead, a ferocious storm of wind, rain and hail rolled across the countryside, again from the east, striking Timoleon's army from the back but hitting the Carthaginians frontally. Very quickly the Crimisus began to flood, spilling over its banks, and then the surrounding hillsides poured down more flash-floods.

The 400 Carthaginians in the lead of the citizen division, no doubt the front company of the Sacred Corps, were overthrown by their opponents, and as the rest fell back under the Greeks' pressure they started to slip and

Freepost Plus RTKE-RGRJ-KTTX
Pen & Sword Books Ltd
47 Church Street
BARNSLEY
S70 2AS

✂ DISCOVER MORE ABOUT PEN & SWORD BOOKS

Pen & Sword Books have over 4000 books currently available, our imprints include: Aviation, Naval, Military, Archaeology, Transport, Frontline, Seaforth and the Battleground series, and we cover all periods of history on land, sea and air.

Can we stay in touch? From time to time we'd like to send you our latest catalogues, promotions and special offers by post. If you would prefer not to receive these, please tick this box. ☐

We also think you'd enjoy some of the latest products and offers by post from our trusted partners: companies operating in the clothing, collectables, food & wine, gardening, gadgets & entertainment, health & beauty, household goods, and home interiors categories. If you would like to receive these by post, please tick this box. ☐

We respect your privacy. We use personal information you provide us with to send you information about our products, maintain records and for marketing purposes. For more information explaining how we use your information please see our privacy policy at www.pen-and-sword.co.uk/privacy. You can opt out of our mailing list at any time via our website or by calling 01226 734222.

Mr/Mrs/Ms ....

Address...

Postcode .... Email address ....

Website: www.pen-and-sword.co.uk   Email: enquiries@pen-and-sword.co.uk
Telephone: 01226 734555   Fax: 01226 734438
Stay in touch: facebook.com/penandswordbooks or follow us on Twitter @penswordbooks

Right: 1. Parade armour from Ksour es Saf (near Sousse), Tunisia: bronze breastplate, 4th–3rd centuries BC. Now in the Bardo Museum, Tunis. *Source:* Wikimedia Commons 25/3/2019: author Jona Lendering, Livius.org 13/10/2018

Below: 2. Scale-armour suit (reconstructed), found in Lake Trasimene: probably Roman, possibly from a casualty of the battle in 217 BC. Carthaginian infantry of the period, and perhaps earlier, will have worn similar battle-dress. *Source:* reproduced from *The Armour of Imperial Rome,* by H. Russell Robinson (London: Arms and Armour Press, 1975): the publisher has ceased to exist and all efforts at tracing the original copyright holder have been without success.

Above: 3. Countryside outside Thugga (Dougga), with the Tower of Artaban (a Numidian prince, *circa* 120 BC) on hillside. Carthaginian grandees may have been buried in similar towers. *Source:* Wikimedia Commons 25/3/2019: supplied by UNESCO as part of a GLAM-Wiki partnership: https://commons.wikimedia.org/wiki/File:Dougga_Thugga-130247.jpg

Left: 4. View from the 'Hannibal quarter', on the southern slope of Byrsa hill; developed in 190s BC. Carthage's enclosed ports in the middle distance, and Jebel Bou Kornine in the background. *Source:* Wikimedia Commons 25/3/2019: photo Karl Schreiber, 2014: https://commons.wikimedia.org/wiki/

Right: 5. Relief portrait of Polybius from Kleitor in the Peloponnese, set up by T. Flavius Polybius, a descendant. *Source:* Wikimedia Commons 25/3/2019: relief from Kleitor, Greece (second century AD): 1881 photograph: http://ia311337.us.archive.org/3/items/mitteilungen06deut/mitteilungen06deut.pdf

Below: 6. View (1958) over Carthage and the headland of Megara (modern La Marsa-Gammarth), with the late third-century BC enclosed naval port and Admiralty Island in foreground. *Source:* Wikimedia Commons 25/3/2019

7. Carthaginian copper alloy coin (fourth century BC?), with head of Tanit and horse standing before palm tree. *Source:* Wikimedia Commons 25/3/2019: photographer Suffolk County Council Archaeology Service, Andrew Brown, 2010-02-01 19:43:36: Filename: KDG SF-958525.jpg

8. Syracusan silver coin, with head of Persephone and dolphins: legend SYRAKOSION ('[coin] of the Syracusans'): period of Dionysius I. *Source:* Pinterest 25/3/2019

9. Stele of Aristion, a Greek hoplite (infantry soldier), made by the sculptor Aristocles *circa* 510 BC, now in the National Archaeological Museum, Athens. He wears a leather cap, breastplate, short tunic and greaves; traces of original paint survive. *Source:* Pinterest 25/3/2019

10. Votive stele at Carthage, dedicated to Baal Hammon and Tanit. *Source:* Wikimedia Commons 25/3/2019

11. Syracusan silver *decadrachma* (10-drachma coin), *circa* 400 BC. *Source:* Wikimedia Commons 25/3/2019 (commons.wikimedia.org/wiki/File:Evainete_Decadrachme_de_Syracuse.jpg): author Stéphane Degroisse: http://www.mba-lyon.fr

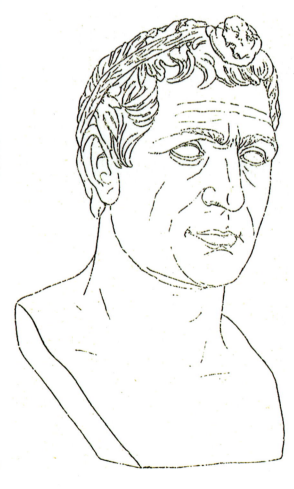

12. Supposed head of Agathocles (line-drawing by J.J. Bernouilli, 1886): original in Musei Vaticani. *Source:* Wikimedia Commons 25/3/2019: https://commons.wikimedia.org/wiki/File:Agathokles_Musei_Vaticani.jpg

13. Syracusan silver *decadrachma*, *circa* 317–311 BC, with head of Apollo and Apollo (as sun-god) in chariot: legend SYRAKOSION. *Source:* Wikimedia Commons, 25/3/2019: author Stella: https://commons.wikimedia.org/wiki/File:Dekadrachm_-_50_Litrai_-_Agathocles_of_Syracuse.png

14. Syracuse, viewed from the Euryalus fortress on Epipolae. *Source:* Wikimedia Commons 25/3/19: photo: A. van Loon, 2014: https://www.flickr.com/photos/94609149@N05/15316553538

15. Epipolae plateau, Syracuse: Euryalus fortress at eastern (left-hand) apex, Scala Greca cleft at top right; note cliffs edging the plateau on both sides. *Source:* Google Earth satellite image, 7/4/2019: Google Maps.

Above left: 16. Carthaginian infantrymen on the march: fourth-century BC scarab: author's photograph.

Above right: 17. Barcid-era silver coin, *circa* 221 BC, Spain: head of Melqart, depicted as Heracles: author's photograph.

slide on the soaked and muddy ground. Men who lost their footing and fell found their armour letting in – and keeping – mud and water, and their weapons hard to handle. How Timoleon's troops kept their footing is not told. Disorder spread through the Carthaginian division, and then through the troops trying to cross behind it. 'All of them turned towards the river,' Diodorus wrote, 'horsemen and infantrymen all together, and the chariots too adding to the confusion' as the Greek cavalry herded the collapsing formation further into the stream. Fallen men were trampled underfoot or drowned, then bodies piling up in the water worsened the terror and chaos. The disaster was complete when the relentless rain transformed the Crimisus into a furious torrent that swept away desperate and exhausted men struggling in its depths.

The rest of the army, even elements that cannot yet have fought, became a frantic mob. Survivors either fled, with Greek cavalry and light-armed in pursuit, or surrendered. Their camp was taken. The toll of casualties was catastrophic: the Sacred Corps had been destroyed, no fewer than 3,000 citizens were dead – the greatest loss of life in battle yet suffered by the city – plus 7,000 other soldiers, and another 15,000 were prisoners (10,000 of them appropriated by Timoleon's men). The survivors struggled back the way they had come to seek safety at Lilybaeum.

The spoils of battle were just as enormous: 200 chariots taken, the rest swept away in the flood, and the camp's wealth of goods and transport animals seized. Most of the costly and (for many) lethal body-armour was swept away too, but Timoleon's tent by the battlefield over the next few days was surrounded by 1,000 enemy breastplates and over 10,000 shields, his share or the public share of the plunder. The victors were stunned at the richness, quality and sheer quantity of the booty; it took two full days and part of a third to bring everything in. There was enough, even after the soldiers took their share, for Timoleon to send some of it to Syracuse and other Sicilian cities to adorn their temples, and the finest part of it to Corinth. A few fragments of the Corinthian inscription set up with it have been found, listing Greek cities with contingents in his army.[20]

6. Gisco and peace

A single day's fighting had undone Carthage's long, thorough and costly preparations. The disastrous news provoked horror, fear that the victors would follow up by invading Libya and grief at the loss of so many citizens. Hasdrubal's and Hamilcar's fates are unknown, but must have been unpleasant. A political somersault followed. Since the aristocrats currently running affairs had proved themselves incompetent in warring with Syracuse, the exiled Gisco, son of the executed Hanno the Great, was recalled and elected general – according to Polyaenus, 'general with supreme powers' (*strategos autokrator*), the phrase applied to Greek leaders who often turned into tyrants like Dionysius the elder. Polyaenus all the same wrongly described Gisco as brother of an unjustly executed 'Hamilcar', and so his Greek phrase should be treated with caution. Gisco was elected general, and no doubt it was clearly understood and perhaps formally enacted that his authority was superior to any other general's; he may also have been chosen *sufete* with the same understanding.

Polyaenus also told of a peculiar performance by the returned exile. Gisco had his old enemies brought to him in chains, made them lie prostrate before him and set his foot – lightly – on their necks three times. He then freed them without further harm. The act, if genuine, was unique in Carthaginian history; if it did happen, it could be a clue that Gisco had spent his exile in Egypt with its grandiose monuments of triumphant pharaohs treading on beaten foes. Pharaohs did not let their foes go (they preferred them skinned alive), but Gisco was intent on calming factional strife so as to focus on the crisis in Sicily.[21]

Timoleon had followed up the Greek victory with a fresh rampage by his mercenaries through the *epikrateia*, then by expelling Thrasius' faithless thousand from Sicily (they were afterwards massacred by Bruttians, to Diodorus' and Plutarch's joint satisfaction). He soon had to deal, too, with his increasingly unhappy allies Hicetas and Mamercus. Realising that they now stood less chance of keeping their power with his blessing, they colluded in appealing to Carthage for military help to resist him.

Gisco's return from exile and his fresh military preparations would have taken up the rest of the year. It was probably in spring 340, then, that the new leader sailed from Carthage with seventy warships and troops who, rather surprisingly, again included a plentiful number of Greek mercenaries. In Punic Sicily he may well have found remnants of Hasdrubal's and Hamilcar's defeated army, but even so his forces were not large enough for him to try any bold moves. However, he had decided that Carthage's priorities now were guarding the *epikrateia* and ending the war. As a result, envoys left Carthage with him, or not long after him, charged with seeking the best terms they could from Timoleon.

It might look contradictory for Carthage to try for peace and, at the same time, to ally with Hicetas and Mamercus, for by now those two irrepressible leaders were openly at war with their former friend Timoleon. Yet Gisco had to show that his city was not a totally spent force and that he could add to Timoleon's harassments if there was no peace. One sign of this was to send a force of mercenaries to Mamercus. They were probably sent by sea to join him near Messana, and helped him score a success over a body of other mercenaries despatched overland by Timoleon to reinforce that city: 400 were killed. It was no great triumph, but it showed that Carthage could still project military force across the island. Meanwhile, in the west, Gisco himself sprang an ambush to wipe out some of the plundering Greeks near Ietae (Monte Iato), in a steep valley 30km south of Panormus.

Peace came closer. Neither side reopened direct hostilities with the other, and Gisco's envoys at Syracuse waited while Timoleon dealt first with Hicetas and then with Mamercus and Mamercus' ally Hippon of Messana. Hicetas' defiance – he even raided and looted Syracusan territory when Timoleon was away – ended when his own soldiers handed him over. Timoleon was vengeful: he executed not only the fallen tyrant but also his young son, and allowed the still more vengeful Syracusans to put his wife and daughters to death. Then he attended to Mamercus, whose last stand was beside a stream near his city; his army included the troops he had received from Gisco, most of whom were killed in the ensuing defeat. Mamercus found brief refuge at Messana, but Timoleon – tireless despite ageing and losing his sight – besieged and took the city. Hippon was left to his embittered fellow-Messanians to be publicly and painfully executed, while Mamercus was taken to Syracuse, tried by its citizens and 'paid the brigands' penalty', as Plutarch put it (without saying what that was).

At some point too, Timoleon concluded terms with the Carthaginians. In Diodorus this comes before he suppresses Hicetas (no mention of Mamercus), but Plutarch's more circumstantial narrative puts it directly after Mamercus' defeat and before the fall of Messana. Plutarch must be right: troops sent by Gisco, even foreign mercenaries, could not still be fighting alongside Syracuse's enemies after peace was made. The Punic envoys at Syracuse could have travelled up to meet Timoleon in his camp at Mylae, on the north coast near Messana; Gisco himself might have sailed over from Panormus to meet the man who, against all conceivable odds, had defeated his predecessors and was steadily re-establishing order and peace over Greek Sicily. The time was probably late summer or early autumn in 340.

The treaty, limited and not punitive, recognized Carthage's control of western Sicily up to the River Halycus (the Platani), guaranteed that emigrants from the *epikrateia* to Syracuse could bring their families and goods, required Carthage to stop aiding tyrants hostile to Syracuse and declared 'all the Greek cities to be free'. The real point of this freedom-proviso would be to guarantee autonomy to Heraclea Minoa (on the eastern bank of the Halycus but in practice within the *epikrateia*, as before), Selinus further west and Thermae Himeraeae east of Panormus. Indeed, a later treaty with Syracuse, in 313 when Carthage had a stronger hand, placed these three under its rule 'just as they previously had been'. This must imply that they had not recently been, although they had been subject even in the time of the younger Dionysius (as Dion's encounter with 'Synalus' at Selinus showed). We may surmise that Timoleon's treaty set them free. Freedom for such places, naturally, would last only so long as peace prevailed and Sicily's two dominant powers avoided strife.[22]

Nevertheless, the treaty made a sound settlement of affairs. Agreeing to freedom for all Greek cities declared, in effect, that Syracuse would respect the autonomy of the other Siceliot states: and certainly the – admittedly scrappy – record of events in the late 320s shows this was true of Acragas, Gela, Messana and Thermae. The Halycus border, and very likely the northern Himeras River east of Thermae, put Entella and other places taken by Timoleon back under Carthage's hegemony. Allowing people from the *epikrateia* to migrate to Syracuse (this would include not only Greeks anxious to move but others too, like pro-Syracusan Entellans) was an easy concession by Gisco. It also chimed with Timoleon's repopulation programme. As for ceasing support for tyrants, Gisco could see that the various petty despots left around eastern and central Sicily had no real prospects.

Carthage's Sicilian war of 344–40 was a futile effort that could well have been avoided. At the cost of tens of thousands of dead, wounded and enslaved, and unknown quantities of money, it ended as it began: Carthage controlling the west of the island, and the Sicilian Greeks – even if battered and thinned out – free to manage and mismanage their own affairs. On the Carthaginian side the war had been spectacularly badly handled. All but the last of its generals showed themselves incompetent and muddle-headed, failing to exploit what (fairly few) opportunities they were offered and out of their depth in dealing with a masterful political and military tactician like Timoleon, while Gisco's performance was merely average. His best achievement was the even-handed treaty which established another twenty-five years of peaceful coexistence with the Siceliots. The calm proved vital, for his city's next struggle with them would be the worst of all.

Chapter 8

Carthage against Agathocles

1. The advent of Agathocles

Gisco's advent marked the return to primacy in Carthage of the family of Hanno the Great. Greek and Roman writers knew little about these leaders or the republic's affairs over the next quarter-century. Polyaenus (drawing on an unknown source as usual) lauded Gisco's moderation, valour and kindly nature. Political competition among aristocrats was not suppressed, to judge from stray items in other sources. Around 318–17, the ranking general in the Sicilian *epikrateia* was one Hamilcar, but not Gisco's son of the same name. The first Hamilcar involved himself in Syracusan politics, as we shall see, and fell foul of his government as a result: Justin's *Epitome* suggests that political intrigues at Carthage contributed. He was then replaced by Gisco's son, who in due course would have his own difficulties with the home authorities as competitive politics there grew sharper.

Although peace had been achieved in Sicily, the stunningly sudden fall of the long-established Persian Empire to Macedon's Alexander the Great between 334 and 323 was alarming to the Carthaginians, especially as the king not only sacked Carthage's mother-city Tyre in 332 but threatened a Carthaginian embassy, there to pay customary honours to Melqart, that he had future plans to conquer their city too. (Carthage had stirred his ire by accepting some Tyrian women and children as refugees.) Besides, by annexing Egypt, Alexander brought Macedonian power into Africa.

A Carthaginian named Hamilcar was supposedly sent to infiltrate the king's entourage and learn his western plans, but upon coming home after Alexander died he was put to death, accused of betraying his city's interests. Alexander's early death certainly came as a relief. The new Macedonian Empire was almost immediately dismembered into different realms by his lethally competitive generals, and Egypt's new Macedonian ruler Ptolemy I had no interest in (or opportunity for) westward thrusts – apart from taking control over Cyrene, which, in any case, he left to a more or less autonomous Macedonian governor named Ophellas.

At home, the losses suffered at the Crimisus needed time to mend, and this helps explain Carthage's peaceful handling of affairs in North Africa and the overseas territories. The *epikrateia* recovered from the harm inflicted by Timoleon's raids, to judge from recent studies of how Selinus came into a new era of public building and vigorous housing projects. The styles were not Greek but Punic, showing that the city's new residents came from elsewhere in the *epikrateia* or North Africa.[1]

In Greek Sicily, making peace in 340 with Carthage and then uprooting the last remaining tyrants and troublemakers were Timoleon's final steps as war leader. Centuripa and its neighbour Agyrium were liberated. The unruly Campanians of Aetna in the same area were killed or enslaved, to be replaced no doubt by some of Timoleon's immigrants. By 339, all of Sicily was at peace, the programme of repopulation well under way and a remarkable reflowering of the much-harassed Siceliot cities began. It embraced even Acragas, Gela and Camarina on the south coast. In the end, a reported 60,000 Greek men transferred themselves to the island, many or most with wives and families. Archaeological evidence may even suggest that the sources' figures are (very unusually) an understatement; or perhaps the flow of newcomers went on into the 320s, after the sources stopped counting.

Timoleon could not have single-handedly established the Siceliots' social and economic revitalization (much as Diodorus and Plutarch liked to suggest it), but without his leadership it would have been less extensive. So when he died a few years after resigning his authority in 339, Greek Sicilians joined with Syracusans in giving him a magnificent funeral and memorial. He was remembered with almost universal esteem by Greeks and Romans as a selfless crusader, a model of integrity and a great commander and peace-bringer.[2]

Yet the Greeks of Sicily soon made it clear that they could not stay at peace among themselves for long, any more than their kinsmen in Greece could. As the 320s wore on, Syracuse, unquestionably the greatest city in the island, soured its relationships both outside and at home. While the Carthaginians watched, Syracuse went to war with Acragas and turned friendship with many other Greek and Sicel cities into antagonism – Morgantina 120km to its west, Herbita north of Enna, Messana and Rhegium are mentioned. At home, the Syracusans suffered steadily worsening political divisions between a dominant faction of aristocrats, called the Six Hundred, and their enemies who were, or claimed to be, democrats.

The two trends fuelled each other. The Six Hundred seem to have become dominant after sending forces to Croton, in southern Italy, to help repel fresh attacks by the region's Bruttians around 330. The oligarchs' dominance was opposed by one of that expedition's popular and forceful officers, Agathocles, whose older brother Antander was one of the three generals. Antander, incidentally, would be Agathocles' most enthusiastic supporter throughout his life (and his biographer afterwards).

After the Bruttian campaign, Agathocles did not return to Syracuse. Born in 361 or 360, he was the son of an exile from Rhegium who had settled at Thermae Himeraeae in the *epikrateia*; his father later moved his family to Syracuse after Gisco's treaty with Timoleon. The middle brother of three, Agathocles soon made his mark there as a fearless soldier and attractive politician, as well as a rich one through marrying the widow of a wealthy Syracusan who had backed his career (rather as Philistus had backed Dionysius eighty years before). But he stayed on in south Italy for some years after 330 as a mercenary commander and champion of democratic politics. Eventually fortune favoured him again. By rescuing Rhegium from a new Syracusan attack around 322, he contributed to bringing down and expelling Syracuse's oligarchs, then played a growing role on the democrats' side in a civil war ensuing between them and the exiles, whose leader was named Sostratus.

At this point Carthage became interested in Sicilian Greek affairs once again. With Alexander the Great safely dead, Gisco's faction may have felt that they could afford to act. As aristocrats themselves, it was preferable to side with Sostratus' Six Hundred rather than with populists, and so the general in the *epikrateia*, Hamilcar (not Gisco's like-named son), was authorized to send Sostratus help. Whatever it was – most likely a small mercenary force – it failed to decide the struggle, which seems to have dragged on for some years. The fighting left many, perhaps most, Syracusans so unimpressed that they followed Timoleon's precedent by appealing to Corinth for another referee. Corinth's nominee Acestorides came, was elected general and, briefly, settled matters. First, Agathocles as chief troublemaker was expelled once more, then the oligarchic exiles were recalled, and peaceful relations with Carthage were restored.

Yet nothing could keep Agathocles down. Rather than disappear into exiled obscurity, he established himself at Morgantina to gather an army from that inland city and others – most of which must have been Sicel centres – and make himself a nuisance, according to Justin's unusually detailed but fairly believable narrative. How long he kept up the pressure is not clear, but eventually he seized Leontini and 'began to besiege' Syracuse itself – although, given the city's massive fortifications and the likely size of his forces, it could hardly be a real siege but more a pattern of harassment. Even so, the restored Six Hundred again sent to Hamilcar for protection.

He brought it, only for Agathocles to trump them, persuading the Carthaginian to broker a reconciliation between the two sides and then go away. Justin's tale of the devious Syracusan promising Hamilcar on oath to help him in his turn gain power at Carthage is as unconvincing as the added claim that Hamilcar then supplied Agathocles with 5,000 African troops to use in a coup. Hamilcar was a member of the dominant faction and stayed on in the *epikrateia* for years to come. But he agreed to Agathocles' proposal to mediate, and the new leaders of the Six Hundred, whatever they really thought about reconciling with him, had little choice but to agree. Agathocles not only returned to Syracuse but, after swearing an oath to respect the democratic constitution, was elected 'general [*strategos*] and guardian of peace' in Diodorus' phrasing; or in that of the rather later chronological inscription the Parian Marble, '*strategos autokrator* of the defences in Sicily'. The Parian Marble dates this to the Athenian archon-year 319/18.

The reconciliation lasted a couple of years, with Agathocles apparently behaving himself. Yet the final step inevitably came. When other opponents of the reconciliation started gathering forces in the island's central uplands, he brought his personal army into Syracuse on the pretext of preparing to campaign against them. A ruthlessly amoral coup followed. The leaders of the Six Hundred were arrested and executed; and then Agathocles launched a pogrom against the rest of their supporters across the city. Over two days, his troops slaughtered 4,000 Syracusans in their streets, houses and temples. Another 6,000 escaped or were expelled to Acragas and other cities. One of them, spared by Agathocles, was an old friend named Deinocrates. But all victims' properties were seized and shared out among the killers. It was no surprise (and there was no opposition) when their commander was 'elected' by cowed surviving Syracusans as *strategos autokrator* without time-limit. The Parian Marble put it succinctly: in 316/15 'Agathocles began his tyranny over the Syracusans'.[3]

2. Agathocles frustrating Carthage

Hamilcar soon found that Agathocles was far from peace-minded and even less trustworthy. The tyrant soon confirmed his control over most of the region inland from Syracuse, where the Sicel states were largely friendly.

Other leading Greek cities – Messana, Gela and Acragas – were rightly wary of him. Exiled survivors of his putsch, at Messana and Acragas especially, reinforced the wariness. He soon showed that it was justified.

The Messanians, anxious to keep him at bay, paid him the large sum of 30 talents for a Syracusan-held fort (the site is unstated), but after taking their money he refused to hand it over, repaying them instead with a land and sea lunge at Messana early in 314. It was thrown back, but Agathocles then used his ships to seize nearby Mylae on the north coast, a small but strategic site. He launched a new siege of Messana later in the year at harvest time, but was frustrated again: first by the vigorous defence of its citizens and resident Syracusan exiles, then by the unexpected arrival of envoys from Carthage. These warned him that he was violating Timoleon's treaty, no doubt meaning its proviso that the Greek cities should be free. Agathocles could not yet risk clashing with Carthage. He gave up not only the siege but the fort, and instead went over the mountains to Abacaenum to rivet control of it in his usual way – killing forty or more leading opponents.

The intervention that saved Messana made clear that Syracuse's activities were closely watched by Carthage, through information coming most likely from merchants and travellers via Panormus and Lilybaeum. Where Hamilcar was in 314 is not mentioned, but even if he was in the *epikrateia*, the *adirim* and *sufetes* at home – and Hamilcar himself – may well have judged, rightly, that ambassadors from Carthage laying down the law to Agathocles would have stronger effect. It is less likely that Hamilcar's mild attitude towards the Syracusan was so disapproved by Carthage that now he was bypassed. Of course the Carthaginians must have begun debating how to deal with a new Syracusan leader determined to make Syracuse great again. But a diplomatic démarche needed to be backed by the implicit threat of intervention by forces from the *epikrateia*, and Hamilcar continued in charge of these.

Messana's last-minute rescue galvanized the other Greek cities outside Syracusan control. Pressed by their Syracusan exiles, the Acragantines took the lead in forming an alliance with Gela and Messana to prepare for war. The allies opted to seek yet another generalissimo from homeland Greece – Timoleon's memory was still vivid, and Siceliot leaders suspect as would-be tyrants – but their hope proved misplaced. Seeking a selfless champion, they made the mistake of recruiting Acrotatus, a Spartan prince who turned out to be imperious, unsympathetic and self-indulgent. He took his time reaching Acragas in 313, via Tarentum, which lent him some warships; then as *strategos* of the alliance he did nothing worthwhile militarily and before long, as criticisms mounted on all sides, he thought it a good idea to murder Agathocles' old foe, the exiles' most prominent leader Sostratus, whom he distrusted. This brought down Acrotatus' own ramshackle position: to avoid being killed in his turn, he fled back to Sparta. The Tarentine ships went home and the anti-Syracusan drive collapsed.

Agathocles was biding his time so as to consolidate his position and his forces. Quite likely it was his initiative again that drew in Hamilcar, still in 313, to broker a peace settlement between Syracuse and Acragas, Gela and (according to Diodorus) Messana. Its terms, again according to Diodorus as the sole source, are a surprise: 'of the Greek cities in Sicily, Heraclea, Selinus, and in addition Himera [meaning Thermae Himeraeae] to be set under the Carthaginians as they were before, and all the others to be self-governing with the Syracusans having hegemony.' It is a surprise because the west Sicilian Greek cities – independent in recent decades, as shown earlier – did not figure in Diodorus' account of events. Their sudden appearance here might suggest that they too had rashly joined the anti-Syracusan alliance; more probably they had played no part but were Hamilcar's price for settling the Siceliots' brawling.

Another surprise is that Diodorus' list of signatories includes Messana, for not long afterwards his own narrative reveals it as the last remaining holdout against Agathocles, with embittered Syracusan exiles flocking there for that reason. Messana perhaps agreed at first to Hamilcar's mediation but then refused to accept being placed under Syracuse's hegemony; or perhaps it did not take part at all, and was wrongly put on the list by Diodorus' source or Diodorus himself.

In practice, the peace was a triumph for the Syracusan tyrant. Without needing to take the field, he was recognized as hegemon of Greek cities he had not yet mastered. With much or most of Sicel territory already under his control, Syracuse's domination now stretched – at least in the treaty – across nearly all eastern and central Sicily, virtually recreating the lordship that Dionysius the elder had achieved after 382 and his son had lost. Nonetheless, Agathocles remained dissatisfied. Nominal overlordship was one thing, imposing it on places like Messana and Acragas another.[4]

Also dissatisfied were Hamilcar's countrymen. Instead of an agreement that re-established the settlement agreed on with Timoleon, now they faced a Siceliot superpower led by a blatantly opportunistic despot, who depended on expansionist success to maintain his despotism. Justin's over-compressed account, which treats the two Carthaginian interventions (in 314 and 313) as one, then has Carthage's allies complain to that city about

Hamilcar's spinelessness – supposedly after Agathocles has raided the *epikrateia* unopposed – and the Carthaginian senate votes to recall him, but not right away. In Diodorus we read merely that the Carthaginians 'had censured Hamilcar over the treaty'; Agathocles' raid on the *epikrateia* comes later. This sequence must be right. The anger at Hamilcar was unfair (and, as Justin notes, he was not given a hearing). What other policy he could have followed is not obvious; allying with the Acragantine coalition to make war on Syracuse might not have been approved at home either. The Carthaginians lacked appetite for a new collision with Syracuse, as they showed when facing Agathocles' next Siceliot aggressions in 312/11.

The drive to recall Hamilcar looks like embittered home politics. In Justin's bald narrative, the *adirim* hide their decision to recall him 'until the other Hamilcar, son of Gisco, should come back from Sicily'. What Gisco's son was doing there is not stated. If the curt item is accurate – and there seems no reason to think it wrong – he may have been serving as his namesake's *nauarchos* or, more likely, had been sent over to act with Hamilcar in negotiating with the Greek states, rather as envoys (including him?) had done the year before.

Whatever the second Hamilcar's role, it need not follow that he agreed with how his namesake solved the confrontation between Agathocles and his opponents. Justin's account implies he did not, and when he took over the Sicilian command he certainly acted very differently. The first Hamilcar may have also been part of the dominant faction, but a faction can readily break up under stress, especially if others are attacking it. Although the evidence is very limited, it looks as though Gisco's political grouping, dominant since the aftermath of the Crimisus disaster, started to splinter from 314 or 313. It would shatter just a few years later.[5]

3. Carthage at war with Agathocles

Agathocles was building up sizeable military forces, centred on a permanent mercenary corps of 10,000 foot and 3,500 horse, and copious funds, though not much of a fleet. His interest in keeping to the just-concluded agreement with Hamilcar and the hostile Greek cities was short. It lasted only into the following year, 312, or – if the run of events in Diodorus is followed rather than his Athenian archon-years – into 311. It does look more likely that Agathocles restarted his aggressive ways in 311.[6]

First, he moved against Messana one more time. He intimidated the city into forcing its many Syracusan exiles to leave and opening its gates to him, and then allowing him to execute Messanians he counted as enemies. Along with citizens of Tauromenium whose lives he also cut short, 600 men were killed. Then Messana was put into the power of its own returned, and safely pro-Syracusan, exiles. The Syracusans forced out of the city retreated inland to form a small army of 3,000 infantry and 2,000 cavalry, the large proportion of cavalry reflecting the aristocratic status of so many of the tyrant's enemies. Led by his ex-friend Deinocrates, they stayed in touch with Carthage too, where the navy was on standby and preparations began for a fresh intervention into the troubles of Greek Sicily.

Agathocles next turned on Acragas, 'intending to take control of that city too', according to Diodorus. But before he could reach it – he had probably taken his time and avoided the exile army on the way – a Carthaginian force of sixty warships reached Acragas' coast. This swift countermove implies that the Acragantines had rushed an appeal to Lilybaeum or Panormus and that the Carthaginians were ready to respond. Whether the ships brought any troops is not stated, but the warning to Agathocles was clear. This was a step they had not taken just now for Messana, probably because Acragas had agreed to the previous year's settlement terms – Messana had not. As the Carthaginians could have foreseen then, and as Agathocles now confirmed, new conflict was unavoidable, for the strength of his autocracy rested on expansion and exploitation.

For the same reason he could not tamely afford to accept a humiliation. So he turned away from Acragas to invade Punic Sicily: some places were stormed and others won over, but Diodorus' account gives no names. It also gives no explanation for why the invaders were not opposed, even though there were local forces in the *epikrateia*. Perhaps, with the previous Hamilcar dead and the son of Gisco yet to arrive, a hiatus at the top of the *epikrateia*'s military administration paralyzed action.

Reputation at least partly restored and booty gained, Agathocles then stopped the exile army from taking over Centuripa, and his generals Pasiphilus and Demophilus soon afterwards kept them out of Galaria too. Both cities were then cleansed in standard Agathoclean style, with wholesale executions of suspect opponents.

Meanwhile, Carthage's new war began unimpressively. Fifty ships, not triremes but perhaps penteconters, sailed into the Great Harbour of Syracuse – as mentioned before, Agathocles had little naval strength – more to shock the citizens than to achieve anything practical They then left, after needlessly mutilating the crews of two merchant ships from Athens. Next, according to Diodorus, Agathocles learned that a Punic force had established itself on Mount Ecnomus, a high coastal ridge beside the River Himeras 30km west of Gela (now alongside the city of Licata). But when he marched over to face them, the newcomers refused to come down and fight, so he went home.

This odd story is in fact suspect. Afterwards, Diodorus' narrative opens the next stage of events by describing the Sicilian situation virtually as new. Agathocles was constantly building up his might, the Carthaginians heard that 'he was taking control of the cities' and so 'they resolved to undertake the war more effectively'. All this, of course, had been going on for more than a year already. Next we are told how the new general, Hamilcar son of Gisco, made a storm-tossed crossing to Sicily and reinforced his army there with local allied troops, while Agathocles carried out a typically vicious takeover of Gela. Quite abruptly we then find Hamilcar and his entire army on Mount Ecnomus – with no mention of how he reached it (by sea, or over land?) – and Agathocles positioning his own forces across the Himeras at a fortress called Phalarium. There followed a furious battle in which Agathocles was badly defeated.[7]

That earlier supposed occupation of Mount Ecnomus looks like the historian's mistake, perhaps from trying to conflate at least two sources whose dating or arrangement of events differed. The likely course of events in late 311 was that having disciplined Centuripa and Galaria, Agathocles returned to Syracuse to prepare for Hamilcar's expedition; advance reports of it could scarcely fail to reach Syracuse. Then it was with the start of spring 310 that Hamilcar sailed for Sicily.

The army he brought was not large: 2,000 citizen troops (some of them aristocrats), 10,000 Libyans, 1,000 Etruscan mercenaries and as many Balearic slingers. It was also unlucky. Storms sank no fewer than sixty of Hamilcar's 130 triremes and cost him a large number of men, including some of his fellow-aristocrats, but once in the *epikrateia* he added mercenaries and local allies to the army. He also sent home a call for fresh troops. These measures would take some while, for foreign mercenaries in particular could not simply turn up at very short notice, but by the summer Hamilcar had 40,000 foot and nearly 5,000 horse. He even scored a minor success at sea: a Punic squadron captured twenty ships of Syracuse's fairly small navy in the Strait of Messina.[8]

Agathocles, a little surprisingly, left him alone. Had he marched into western Sicily as soon as word of Hamilcar's landing came, he would have found the Punic army still relatively small and badly shaken. Instead, distrusting his own allies, he marched only on learning that Hamilcar had reached Gela's territory, no doubt en route to Ecnomus. Agathocles' immediate reaction was to move not against the Carthaginians but against Gela. Taking it by stealth, he massacred (we are told) 4,000 suspect Geloans, piled up their corpses in ditches outside – plainly to arouse terror and obedience – and seized their and other Geloans' goods. After that he took up position at Phalarium to watch Hamilcar. The season was that of Sirius the 'Dog Star': the height of summer, with the Sicilian harvest just starting.

The battle that followed began with clashes between foraging troops from either army, continued with an almost-successful Greek assault against the Carthaginian camp, but ended when Hamilcar's reinforcements from Africa arrived on the scene and turned the tide. Agathocles lost 7,000 men killed and an unknown number captured – the best and largest part of his army, according to Diodorus. Hamilcar lost 500 dead. He may have deliberately brought on the fight, for the timely arrival of fresh troops seems more than just luck. A story in Polyaenus' *Stratagems*, without mentioning site or date, has him trick his opponent by leaking false information about his army's supposed low numbers, knowing that reinforcements were approaching; Agathocles' resulting heavy casualties point to Polyaenus' battle being this one.

Hamilcar's follow-up, though, was not brilliant. Agathocles in effect outmaneouvred him strategically, shutting himself up in Gela with what was left of his army and daring the Carthaginians to a siege or an assault. Rather than ignore or mask Gela and march on Syracuse, where parts of the walls were in bad repair and the defenders still in shock, Hamilcar spent some time outside Gela deciding what next to do. Then he moved inland to receive reportedly rapturous overtures from city after city, Greek and Sicel, all eager to throw off Syracusan rule and become Carthage's allies: Camarina, Leontini, Catana and Tauromenium 'immediately', then 'after a few days' Messana, Abacaenum and 'many others'.

Hamilcar thus missed the chance – perhaps his best chance – of winning the war fast. Having kept him away until the harvest could be gathered in and repairs begin to Syracuse's fortifications, Agathocles was free to return home and prepare both for the expected siege and for his unprecedented counterstroke: invading Libya.

Preparations were efficient and harsh, as was Agathocles' way. Kinsmen of suspect citizens were conscripted into his invasion army as virtual hostages, forced loans exacted from merchants and temples stripped of valuables. More killings followed: after encouraging dissatisfied well-off citizens to exit Syracuse with their possessions while there was time, he sent out mercenaries to kill them (a sign, incidentally, that there were no Carthaginians outside) and seize their goods. So Diodorus claimed, at any rate; Justin numbered the evacuees at 1,600 but mentioned no massacre. Next, Agathocles freed and conscripted as many able-bodied slaves as he could find.

He calculated that the last thing the Carthaginians would expect was enemies on their own doorstep. This should lead the oppressed Libyans to revolt, relieve the pressure on his home front and – always important – yield plentiful plunder. Certainly the only other time Carthage had been directly attacked had been by Malchus two centuries earlier: and it had capitulated. A successful invasion would also impose terms that the invader would dictate. By contrast, staying in Syracuse would lead to nowhere but ruin. Timing was vital. Though Hamilcar had not yet arrived to besiege the city – Diodorus' detailed account makes that clear – some Punic warships were already patrolling outside.[9]

A question of dating arises. The battle at the Himeras was fought in June close to harvest-time, while Agathocles and his invasion force sailed one day before an eclipse of the sun dated to 15 August 310. Six to eight weeks might seem too short for all his preparations, military, financial and political. One interpretation therefore is that the battle was fought in summer 311, so leaving rather more than a year before the expedition sailed. There is the added point that Syracuse reportedly faced a food shortage by August 310, even though, after his defeat at the Himeras, Agathocles had ordered the harvest grain to be brought in.

Yet Diodorus' detailed narrative has no year-long interval before the expedition left, and no Punic siege either. Justin's claim that Syracuse was already surrounded when Agathocles left is no more convincing than his other suggestion that the tyrant had lost not one but two battles. Over six, seven or eight weeks while Hamilcar was somewhere else – taking defectors' plaudits at Catana, perhaps, or Messana – Agathocles could not only have enforced his funding and security measures but have brought in fresh soldiers, especially mercenaries, along with conscripting fellow-Syracusans and their slaves. Despite losing maybe 10,000 men dead or captured at the Himeras, he both left an 'adequate' garrison in Syracuse under his brother Antander and an experienced mercenary, Erymnon of Aetolia, and sailed with over 13,000 soldiers. It is not likely that both forces were just the survivors of his defeat.

The August food shortage may have been caused, at least partly, if Agathocles' and Antander's soldiery and – not to be forgotten – the ships' crews had priority with supplies. Moreover, even without an actual approach by the Carthaginian army, some, maybe many, fearful people in the surrounding countryside would migrate to the city to be safe, adding to demands for food.[10]

The invasion plan was of course kept secret. Only those who needed to know were told, starting with Antander. According to Justin, the tyrant simply told his assembled citizens that 'he had found the road to victory' and they should steel themselves for a siege – just a short siege. This item may be true, for the preparations could not be completely hidden, least of all in equipping and manning the necessary ships. By August he had sixty ships and 13,500 troops ready.

These figures in Diodorus raise another question, this time of logistics. For sixty ships to carry 13,500 men, each would need to take on board 225 men, with arms and provisions, plus its crew. This was impossible for triremes. Yet the ships (or some of them) were triremes, for after Agathocles burned them in Africa, the Carthaginians sent some of their bronze rams to Hamilcar in Sicily. The only explanation must be that Agathocles had not only sixty triremes but an unknown number of transports, and that the entire fleet did succeed in eluding their Punic pursuers.[11]

Enemy ships on watch outside the harbours made it problematic even to sail from Syracuse, but Agathocles agilely seized the opportunity when they were distracted by a fleet of approaching grain ships. It is surprising enough to find such shipping still able (or anyway hoping) to reach the city, but still more so that the Carthaginian flotilla let itself be so easily deflected. Agathocles, who no doubt had ordered the shipment (maybe from southern Italy), probably had word of the ships' coming and stood ready to make use of it. Accompanied by his sons Archagathus and Heracleides, the tyrant won enough of a head start on 14 August to leave the regrouping Carthaginians behind. Nor did they press the pursuit once night fell.[12]

The eclipse next day is calculated as passing over northern Sicily, which suggests (but does not prove) that the expedition passed through the Strait of Messina and then along the north coast, rather than via Cape Pachynus and Sicily's southern side. Yet the northern route would take the fleet past both Panormus and Lilybaeum, the naval as well as military strongholds of the *epikrateia*. If so, the Carthaginians there were as lax about urgency as the flotilla commander outside Syracuse and Hamilcar himself outside Gela. At best they may have sent word to Carthage about the expedition: for as the Cape Bon shoreline came into Agathocles' view at daybreak, after six days and six nights at sea, so did a Carthaginian fleet – unless this was the flotilla from Syracuse still in pursuit.

The invaders barely made it to shore, but then drove off the enemy ships with missiles. For the first, and only, time in the history of its Greek wars, a Greek army set foot in Carthage's heartland.

4. Africa invaded

As detailed by Diodorus before the army's first battle some weeks later, Agathocles led 6,000 Syracusans (these must have included the freed slaves), 3,000 Greek mercenaries and 3,000 Samnites, Etruscans and Gauls (mercenaries again), plus the tyrant's personal division of 1,000 – again surely mercenaries – and 500 archers and slingers. There had been no room for cavalry. It was an extraordinarily small force for assailing a state which, when pressed, could field tens of thousands of troops, but Agathocles was equally extraordinarily self-confident. Once the men were ashore, he had them (to their horror) set the beached ships on fire as an offering to Sicily's divine patrons Demeter and Kore-Persephone. It relieved him of having to guard them against capture and stressed to his followers that there could be no going back except in triumph.

They had landed at Latomiae ('the Quarries') close to the Cape Bon promontory – the quarries, at modern Al Huwariya, are still in use – and marched south through the wealthy peninsular countryside. The troops' amazement, and greed, at its orchards, vineyards, farming estates and fine villas shines vividly through Diodorus' telling. Agathocles took his time, first stopping at a city which Diodorus' text calls Megalepolis ('Great City' in Greek) to capture and destroy it with ease; then moved on to treat another, named Leukos Tynes ('White Tunes'), in the same fashion.

Megalepolis is not mentioned again by that name at least for seven hundred years, but then appears in a fifth-century AD list of African Christian bishops. Its position in the list suggests that it could be Uthina, near modern Oudna 45km south of Carthage. Leukos Tynes was not Tunes (Tunis) near Carthage, for this soon appears separately as Agathocles' headquarters. But neither can it have lain 2,000 *stadia* (400km or so) from Carthage, as Diodorus' text has it; that would put it as far away as today's Constantine in Algeria or Gabès on the Lesser Sirte gulf.

An Egyptian papyrus fragment of a history of Agathocles' wars offers a clue: Leukos Tynes lay next to a height which dominated the road eastward to Neapolis (Nabeul, on the gulf of Hammamet) and the plain around the height. This fits the lofty Jebel Bou Kornine, 576 metres high, beside a seaside town called Naro in Roman times and no doubt before: today's Hammam Lif, 40km from Carthage via Tunis. Naro should qualify as Leukos Tynes, and Diodorus' 2,000 *stadia* probably as a later copyist's mistake. All these towns were far from Latomiae and close to Carthage, but the tyrant had taken the Carthaginians utterly by surprise. His advance was unopposed until they could organize a home army. That would take some time: a month or more, even if there were ready stockpiles of arms and equipment in the city and able-bodied residents to recruit.[13]

The Carthaginians had suffered panic when the Greeks disembarked – they thought that Hamilcar's expedition had been wiped out – and learning the truth still left them in desperate straits. Bizarre as it seems, there were no regular defence forces in being in Punic Africa. Carthage, and doubtless other communities, had what in effect were citizen militias – citizens who had done some military service, or at any rate training – and probably stocks of armaments, although the elaborate fortifications and equipment stockpiles described by Appian may not have existed yet. But levying men to fight, drilling them to bear arms and keep ranks, and readying equipment, cavalry horses and supplies needed energy and breathing-space. All this would account for how Agathocles and his men, though laden with more and more plunder, were able to march over several weeks and 150km from Latomiae to the environs of Carthage before a Carthaginian army came out to face them.

Political infighting made matters worse. Hamilcar son of Gisco's predecessor had fallen foul of the *adirim*; the son of Gisco himself had let slip the chance of attacking Syracuse directly; and worst of all he had now let Agathocles leave Sicily with his invasion army. Enemies of the once-dominant faction were now, it seems, its equals in competing for political support and office. This had an impact on who should hold command to face Agathocles. For the first time in their history, instead of selecting a single general the Carthaginians appointed two: a Hanno and a Bomilcar, who paradoxically belonged to mutually hostile families.

This choice aimed to prevent either leader from using his position to make himself tyrant, which (Diodorus claimed) Bomilcar was avid to do. He, according to Justin, was nephew to the previous Hamilcar and would later denounce his fellow-Carthaginians – just before they executed him – for their cruelty not only to himself but to his uncle Hamilcar, to Gisco the exile and even to Hanno the Great. If that story is true, Bomilcar was part of Hanno the Great's family and faction. His colleague, then, would be from the strongest rival group, and had a brief to keep watch on Bomilcar no less than on the Greeks.[14] Diodorus claimed that the army which eventually left Carthage was made up of Carthaginians alone (including the revived Sacred Corps) because there was no time to bring in troops from Libya or allied cities. Contradictorily, his account of the battle that followed includes a role for Libyan troops: so either his claim was a careless mistake or, more charitably to Diodorus, the recruits included Libyans living in the city or fleeing there to escape the Greeks. Justin's version fills the army solely with 'rustics' while ignoring both Bomilcar and the Sacred Corps. Hanno and Bomilcar had 40,000 (in Diodorus) or 30,000 foot (in Justin), plus 1,000 horse and 2,000 war chariots. The horses must have been stabled in the city or hurriedly brought in from the countryside.

Somewhere outside Carthage, Hanno and Bomilcar deployed their men, with Bomilcar on the left wing narrowing his front because of higher ground on his flank. His Carthaginian soldiers formed the front ranks, the Libyans those behind. One suggestion is that this position lay just outside Tunes/Tunis (then a small lakeside town) on its northern side, in the narrow plain between today's Parc du Belvédère and the La Rabta suburb. If so, Agathocles had advanced northwards past the inland side of the salt lake just south of Tunis, the Sebkhet Sijoumi, since low hills lie between that lake's other side and the coast. But a rather likelier site is the fairly level terrain between those low hills and the coast at Radès. The hills edge this flat ground on its western side and, about 5km distant, only the small height of the Radès Forest lies between the ground and the coast.

This is more or less the site of the Battle of Ad Decimum fought almost exactly 850 years later in September AD 535, where Justinian's general Belisarius defeated the Vandals in the Byzantine reconquest of Libya. If so, when the Carthaginians came out Agathocles was still at or near Leukos Tynes, which (the same Egyptian papyrus fragment shows) had been made a strongpoint by the Greeks. Now he advanced to fight.

In the battle, the two Carthaginian divisions acted more or less separately. The cavalry and chariots were quickly eliminated by Greek missiles. Then Hanno's division with the Sacred Corps was broken after a hard fight and Hanno was slain. Bomilcar's wing, by contrast, had barely engaged when he sounded a retreat, causing his Libyan troops to panic and the entire army to dissolve in flight back to Carthage. The number of troops killed varies in the sources between 1,000 and 6,000; the Greek dead from 500–2,000 – apart from Orosius claiming only two. Instead of pressing a pursuit, Agathocles chose to loot the enemy camp, where (wrote Diodorus) the Greeks found not only valuables but wagons loaded with no fewer than 20,000 manacles intended for the invaders. His next move was to occupy Tunes proper, 16km from Carthage, to block land access to the city. He also had two small ships built, at Tunes or Leukos Tynes, and despatched one to bear the news to Syracuse.[15]

Bomilcar's abrupt withdrawal from the field was afterwards put down to treachery: ending the invasion would also end the crisis for Carthage and disrupt his political schemes. Still, after the battle he was not punished for retreating – though there must have been plenty of recriminations from his political enemies – and he remained general until 308, in fact the sole general in Punic Africa. He had perhaps been slow to engage with the foes in his front because of difficult ground, and then on seeing Hanno's defeat decided that retreating and saving his part of the army was better than useless valour. Instead, the entire army suffered a rout. From Carthage he rushed an urgent call to Hamilcar in Sicily asking for some of the troops there to be sent home, and meanwhile he kept what was left of the beaten army behind Carthage's walls. This left the countryside and towns largely at the invaders' mercy, a freedom Agathocles would soon exploit.

Within the city, the Carthaginians decided to appease their angry gods with religious rites that included one which, in Diodorus' telling, has remained notorious. First, acknowledging that they had been lax in their cult worship, they sent off large offerings of money and precious goods to their mother-city Tyre. Then they resorted to appeasing 'Cronus' (Baal Hamon) by sacrificing 500 children from elite families, casting each child from his bronze statue into a blazing fire-pit beneath. This dramatic episode may be true, caused by feverish terror at their army's defeat and with the Greeks now less than a day's march from the walls. That it was a regular rite at Carthage does not of course follow: mass child-sacrifices are never reported in other crises, like the Romans' initially victorious invasion fifty-odd years later or the Truceless War of 241–37. Killing foreigners to placate heaven was another matter: Himilco the Magonid had sacrificed a foreign child in 406, and prisoners from Agathocles' army would die in vengeful flames in 307.[16]

Agathocles in reality had no prospects, nor plan, for attacking the city. His original army was down to 13,000 at most, or maybe just 11,000. Even if he now beefed it up by arming his ships' crews with captured Punic weapons – they would be fit enough, and supposedly he had given them fake weapons before the battle to make his forces seem bigger – he would still have only some 20,000–30,000 men, fewer than the surviving troops in the defeated army. Carthage's fortifications were strong: it was virtually impossible to storm and, without a blockading fleet, impossible to starve out. It was important therefore for the Greeks to win allies and resources.

Expecting Bomilcar to stay behind his walls, the tyrant chose to garrison Tunes with part of his forces and march with the rest to Byzacium, the region to the east along the gulf of Hammamet. It was still the archon-year 310/09 (says Diodorus), but his victory had been many weeks after the expedition landed, making Tunes secure would take time and even in North Africa the winter months would bring cold temperatures and rain to keep both sides inactive. When Agathocles did set out into Byzacium, probably in spring 309, city after city, Libyphoenician and Libyan, was stormed or surrendered. He began with Neapolis 20km south of Curubis, then Hadrumetum 100km further down the coast and, after that, Thapsus another 50km to the south. Towns in between offered submission too, so that by about mid-year, Agathocles was master of over 200 places, or so Diodorus claimed. The tyrant perhaps made this boast in reporting to his home city base, but the figure was no doubt overblown and also must have included scores of small villages across Byzacium.

According to a dubious story in Diodorus' account, while besieging Hadrumetum, Agathocles learned that the troops in Carthage had sortied, taken his camp and were attacking Tunis: but then he scared them back into Carthage (and frightened the Hadrumetans into surrendering) by lighting night fires on a mountain that could be seen from both cities to create the illusion that a big army was on its way against each. All the same, even though the northern crest of the Zaghouan range (50km from Tunes in a direct line and 75km from Hadrumetum) is reportedly visible from both cities, the Carthaginians' supposed craven panic rings false. They had no reason to think that the invaders' forces had suddenly and hugely multiplied, nor that these would choose to climb over the top of a steep mountain range to reach Tunes.

Moreover, we soon read in Diodorus of a second sortie by the Carthaginians, after their Sicilian reinforcements arrive and once Agathocles has set off again, this time to subdue inland Libya. Now they besiege Tunes again and capture other Greek-held positions, only for the tyrant to hasten back once more and defeat some of their troops. Two foiled attacks on Tunes in his absence and two unexpected and victorious ripostes by him are too many to be plausible. The earlier one, coloured with blazing mountains and sudden panics, is very likely fiction, although perhaps a real fire on the Zaghouan heights (lit by marauding Greeks?) grew in later tellings.[17]

It may also have been during 309 that Agathocles sent off a detachment to fortify the headland site of Aspis (Kelibia), an east-coast strongpoint only 35km across the peninsula from Latomiae. Aspis, later called Clupea by the Romans (both words mean 'shield'), would give him the shortest sailing route to Sicily, and Strabo credited him with settling colonists there. In 310 he would hardly have risked lessening his forces by doing so. As word of his successes spread, he also began to attract local support, for instance from a Libyan 'king' named Aelymas who joined him at Hadrumetum. Aelymas was probably lord of a Libyan city or group of cities in Hadrumetum's hinterland, with territory in the plains around the mountains that lie 50–100km inland.

There was need of larger forces. Over the year or so since his original victory, the scope of Agathocles' operations was widening. Thapsus was over 220km from Tunes, and to keep hold of the captured towns he would have to leave at least small garrisons in them. Apart from Libyan defectors, mercenaries from overseas may have been attracted once they could acccess ports under Greek control. Greek professional soldiers were willing to travel: around the same time, Ophellas of Cyrene was enticing many from Athens and elsewhere for a scheme to join in the war.[18]

Agathocles' further plan was to thrust into Libya's heartland. This offered the Carthaginians the real opportunity just mentioned. Once he moved off into the interior, Carthaginian forces came out to besiege Tunes and retake several other Greek-held positions. These actions look like the ones sketched in the fragmentary papyrus from Egypt, for the moves it reports come before another section that refers to Hamilcar in Sicily in 309 (see §5 below). Troops 'occupied the hill overlooking Leukos Tynes and, by fortifying this, caused a great deal of trouble to Agathocles' men', which confirms that the town was still held by the Greeks. 'Shutting these off from the roads to Neapolis and to the east, and foraging over all the nearby plain', they clearly managed to bottle up the Greeks there. And 'marching with the other division to the [communities] upland ... they caused these to desert from the Greeks and brought them again back into their [that is, the Carthaginians'] alliance' – probably a reference to Aelymas and his followers, repentant of their passing flirtation with the other side. If Aelymas' territory lay inland from the Hammamet coast, that area would be the 'upland' reached by this second Punic division.[19]

As also mentioned above, the Carthaginians underestimated Agathocles. He returned at speed to take their forces by surprise – apparently those who had advanced into the uplands – and killed or captured some thousands of them; then turned on Aelymas, who in his turn was defeated and killed. Yet the Carthaginian forces did not scurry back into their city. Diodorus' next report on the war in Africa, after narrating events in Sicily, reveals the two sides encamped not far apart and Agathocles having serious trouble with his own troops, even after resoundingly encouraging news came from Syracuse, that Hamilcar was dead and Agathocles was being sent his head.

5. The destruction of Hamilcar

The expedition to Africa had not greatly helped Hamilcar against Syracuse. To press the city to give in, the Carthaginian general sent envoys twice: first to claim that Agathocles' invasion had been destroyed (the envoys displayed some bronze rams from the ships Agathocles had burnt), then to offer security for Antander and the other leaders if they handed over Syracuse. Despite much debate, neither overture was accepted.

Both Diodorus and the previously mentioned Egyptian papyrus fragment report the Syracusans' excitement and fear after the first embassy, contrasting with the resoluteness of the authorities. The fragment adds the detail of how one Diognetus, 'corrupted by Hamilcar and the exiles', urged the Syracusans to come to terms, but was bundled out of the shocked assembly on Antander's orders and denounced as a troublemaker. According to Diodorus, no fewer than 8,000 Syracusans opposed to the regime were expelled and took refuge with Hamilcar. After the second embassy, Diodorus continues, the 'cowardly' Antander wanted to give in but was overruled on the urging of his colleague Erymnon. Antander's silencing of Diognetus does not make his later weakness a fiction of Diodorus (or Timaeus): after all, the second Punic offer would save his own skin.[20]

When word of Agathocles' victory near Tunes came in to buoy the defenders' spirits, Hamilcar at last brought his troops up to attack the city. Instead of an easy capture, however, they were thrown back. Soon afterwards, he received the order to send 5,000 men home. As this followed Agathocles' victory in about October 310, winter would now be approaching in Sicily, so Hamilcar would reasonably choose to end operations for a time. His next moves are reported in the new archon-year 310/09, and the renewal of campaigning can thus be placed in spring 309.

Sometime earlier he had been joined by Deinocrates with some, or all, of the exiles' army. That would explain the papyrus' comment about Diognetus' alleged corruption, though Diodorus does not mention Deinocrates until the start of the new offensive. Appointing the exile-general as his cavalry commander, Hamilcar began by imposing control over 'the rest of the districts' – the territory belonging to Syracuse – and tightening the naval blockade to prevent any fresh food shipments. Then, destroying the crops in the fields on the way, he marched for Syracuse intent on occupying the area of the Olympieum (the great temple of Zeus on the harbourside hills 2½km south of the city walls).

Diodorus' text now gives him 120,000 infantry and 5,000 cavalry: for the infantry a shameless exaggeration, or perhaps a copying mistake, as in 310 he had had 40,000 foot and most of the 5,000 then sent home would be infantry. Once the exiles' army joined him, he may have had (or said he had) 50,000 infantrymen, while his cavalry were back to 5,000. A regular siege with such forces and the naval blockade should have been enough to strangle Syracuse, for the city was cut off from outside relief and already suffering a food shortage.[21]

Hamilcar had a better idea. Allegedly inspired by his accompanying priest, whose sacrificial offerings intimated that if he attacked at once, he would dine in Syracuse next day – dining being a symbol of victorious relaxation – he now planned a night assault on the walls near the Olympieum. This may be a later fiction, but he did have practical reasons for rapid action. With the summer heating up, and Hamilcar no doubt aware of Himilco's and his men's plague-devastation in 396, he might well wish to bring the siege to a swift end rather than await a slow one.

The manoeuvre did not go to plan. Not only was it mismanaged from the start, but the Syracusans were forewarned: no great surprise when his army included so many Greek exiles plus plentiful camp followers. Hamilcar's attack force moved forward in two bodies, one of his own troops and the other of Greeks. The two bodies were not perhaps the entire army but two chosen divisions, for the route was narrow and rocky; there was no way of concentrating the whole army for an assault. If so, the rest of it was following some distance behind to exploit the capture. In Diodorus' account, a ragbag collection of camp followers and even a baggage train accompanied the attackers, all looking forward to booty and all pushing, jostling and even brawling over the right of way. But even for a general much less experienced than Hamilcar, this would be no way to mount a surprise attack by night. Any extra equipment the attackers carried must have been for immediate use, like ladders and grapnels. The account seems to conflate their advance with that of the entire army, including its baggage train and irrepressibly noisy civilian followers.

As the attacking force neared the walls – Dionysius' fortifications around Epipolae, edged by steep rocky ground – it was struck by a totally unexpected onslaught from 3,000 Syracusan infantrymen and 400 cavalry. They had been positioned in the Euryalus fort to wait for the right opportunity. Confusion and panic spread through the attackers' ranks, then panic turned to flight. Some men leapt or were flung down cliffs, which suggests that the fighting started directly along the walls and steep edges of Epipolae. The disaster fell chiefly on Hamilcar's division, for Deinocrates and his troops got away. The death toll is not mentioned, but must have been large. Most catastrophic of all for the Carthaginians, Hamilcar was surrounded and captured as his soldiers fled.[22]

The Syracusans were vengeful. During the following day, their captive was forced to walk in chains through the streets, viciously tortured as he went, and finally beheaded. As the later story told it, the priest's prophecy was thus fulfilled but, like so many others, not as its hearer had foreseen. Antander sent the head by speedy ship to his brother. The Carthaginian army retreated, apparently to the *epikrateia*, under unnamed commanders. Although for a while Syracuse remained blockaded by Punic warships and almost lost another grain convoy to them, this was virtually the end of Carthage's Sicilian war. With more than enough trouble to cope with in Africa, it guarded the *epikrateia* but played little part in the hostilities that continued to divide and ravage Greek Sicily.

6. The destruction of Ophellas and Bomilcar

Diodorus' vague attention to the details of Carthage's defence of Libya leaves the military scene there in limbo for the rest of 309. The port to which a ship brought its grisly trophy, Hamilcar's head, is not named, but could have been Aspis or Neapolis. Agathocles then triumphantly rode out with the trophy to show it off outside 'the enemy encampment' and reduce the Carthaginians there to dismayed grief. The scene was played around Tunes (as the next episode in Diodorus reveals) and it can be deduced that a truce was in force, for otherwise a general as prudent as Agathocles would not have ridden to within voice-range of his foes. He and his army were in Tunes, and the Carthaginians were encamped probably on the isthmus between that town and their city.

A truce is also implied in the next event reported: a drunken dinner in the tyrant's quarters in Tunes which ended in his elder son Archagathus spearing to death one of Agathocles' trusted officers after an insult (rather in the style of Alexander the Great drunkenly killing his loyal friend Cleitus a few years before). The whole army mutinied, embittered not only by the murder but by continued lack of pay – profitable campaigning had evidently stopped. The troops even elected new generals (unnamed) and listened favourably to offers of pay and bonuses that arrived from the enemy, most likely via itinerant merchants or deserters (or stentorian soldiers outside the camp). It took all of Agathocles' persuasive powers, plus a pretended suicide-attempt, to save the situation, but he then rallied the army for a surprise and successful attack against the Carthaginians who had come out of their camp to welcome – they thought – defecting troops. Nevertheless, a couple of hundred Greeks did leave him for the other side.[23]

Any ceasefire was obviously finished, yet the positions at Tunes stayed the same. Both sides' attention shifted elsewhere. The Carthaginians (still with Bomilcar in charge) sent off a force 'to win over the Nomads who had defected', more precisely a people called the Zouphones. This prompted Agathocles to lead a sizeable force of his own in pursuit—8,000 foot, 800 horse and (rather oddly) 'fifty Libyan chariots', which cannot have been much use in the operations that followed.

When he caught up with the enemy, encamped in hilly country sliced through by deep rivers, the Zouphones discreetly kept apart from the fighting, then plundered Agathocles' baggage train and absconded while he and men were busy routing the Carthaginians and killing or capturing over 1,000 Greeks in the enemy's service. The captured Greeks – half of them Syracusans – were promised their lives but, in Agathoclean fashion, massacred afterwards. He then returned to Tunes.

The 'Nomads' episode is puzzling on a number of counts. It is not clear why the Carthaginians exerted themselves to win back 'Nomad' communities – were these genuine nomadic peoples wandering around Libya or a Diodorean source's term for Libyans? – rather than tackle enemy-held centres like Uthina, Neapolis and Hadrumetum, not to mention Tunes, on their own doorstep. The Zouphones are not known from any other evidence, but the hilly region with plentiful streams is thought to be the Bagradas valley a good distance inland (100km and more west of Tunes). The further inland he pressed, the more dangerous for Agathocles, nor is it obvious what benefits such an expedition would offer except some booty. Very obvious by contrast were the perils of taking part of his forces far from the coast, leaving his less than charismatic son Archagathus to deputize for him at Tunes facing possible new enemy attacks.[24]

In fact, after their defeat inland the Carthaginians went back to doing nothing. Yet Agathocles' war was scarcely making progress either. This led him, still in 309, to send an invitation over to Cyrene, whose Macedonian governor Ophellas was more or less independent of his nominal superior Ptolemy, ruler of Egypt. Ophellas, ambitious for a grander destiny than a small African province, was happy to accept Agathocles' proposal that he should bring an army to Libya to help subdue Carthage. The carrot dangled before Ophellas was that he would then become ruler of Libya and his new friend would return to Sicily to be master there.

For an experienced soldier and old companion of Alexander the Great to believe in the sanctity of an Agathoclean promise is a surprise, but in fact it looks as though Ophellas had long had his own thoughts about western expansion. Now if not earlier, he began advertising in Greece for recruits, selling the scheme as not just a military expedition but more a major colonising programme, and drawing thousands of Greeks – many with families – to sail to Cyrene to take part. When in 308 he set out, he led 10,000 infantry, 600 cavalry and 600 fighters to man 100 war chariots, together with another 10,000 camp followers and the families of many of them. This extraordinary host had to move overland along the desert coast of today's Libya, a 1,600km trek mostly over sand and rock and (we are told) harassed by poisonous snakes, until after nearly three months it reached Byzacium and trod a further 400km north to Tunes, probably in July or August 308. How many of the non-combatants completed the march is unknown (at one stage the travellers had only the fruits of the lotus palm to eat).[25]

Once the two leaders met, it did not go well for Ophellas. The arrivals were certainly welcomed and their needs attended to, but when most of the newcomers went out foraging, maybe a few days later, his new ally made a sudden attack on their camp and slew Ophellas. Agathocles claimed that his new colleague was plotting against him, which may have been true, just as much as Agathocles surely plotted against Ophellas. The dead man's soldiery, now leaderless, were won over with lavish promises of rewards. For the non-combatant men, and no doubt the families that many had brought, he had no use, so he placed them all on merchant ships, together with plunder that he had gathered, and sent the fleet off to Syracuse. Few vessels reached there, for storms sank some and drove others to the Italian coast and an unknown fate.[26]

The Carthaginians had not tried to intercept Ophellas' expedition, though they must have known of it and, according to Diodorus, were aghast at its size and impressive display once it arrived. They were involved in troubles of their own in the city, which came to a head at the same time as Agathocles liquidated his ally.

Bomilcar was still the commanding general at Carthage after two years, and still plotting to seize tyrannic power. Supposedly he had got 'the most eminent citizens' out of the way by sending them on the recent inland expedition, but even so he did not get around to his actual coup-attempt until later. Diodorus' history, drawing on a well-informed Greek source, gives a vivid though tight account of what happened, emphasizing strongly that the two coups, Bomilcar's and Agathocles', took place at the same time and yet each in ignorance of the other. It looks as though his source was at pains to rebut claims (originally by the tyrant's brother-biographer Antander?) that the two had conspired to synchronize their separate coups.

After holding a military review 'in the New City as it is called, a short distance from old Carthage', the general took a select body of the soldiers – 500 Carthaginians and 1,000 mercenaries – to move through the streets in five companies, declaring him 'tyrant' and killing any who opposed them as they headed for the *agora*, Carthage's forum or market square. The New City, a sector outside the original walls probably built up during the fifth century, may have stood on the lower slopes of the Megara plateau, beyond the old burial grounds on the slopes and with its villas, gardens, and orchards further back. The broad wooded hilltop above today's suburb Gammarth Supérieur could be where the military review was held.

The putsch quickly foundered. Though other Carthaginians first thought that the Greeks had broken in, able-bodied citizens soon rallied, surrounded the *agora* and began to pick off Bomilcar's men with missiles from the tall buildings around it. Many of the loyalists must have been soldiers who had been in the military review and then been dismissed home, a remarkably stupid blunder of Bomilcar's if so. The thinning band of rebels had to force their way out and retreat under fire all the way back to the New City, finally escaping to a hilltop (maybe the same hilltop) while the thoroughly aroused and armed citizens prepared for battle. The rest of the Carthaginian leadership, anxious to avoid a disaster that could benefit only Agathocles, preferred to offer amnesty to all on oath, and the crisis ended.

Once Bomilcar himself was in the authorities' hands, however, they ignored the oath, tortured him and crucified him. According to Justin this was done in the *agora*, and Bomilcar lived long enough to excoriate the crowd of his fellow-citizens for their treacherous treatment of his predecessors Hanno the Great, Gisco and the earlier Hamilcar, the latter 'because he preferred to make Agathocles their ally rather than their enemy'. This denunciation looks genuine enough (there was little reason for Trogus to invent such details), signalling that Bomilcar was another member of what had been – but after this was no longer – the pre-eminent family and faction in Carthage. Meanwhile, his fellow-citizens still had their durable Greek adversary to deal with.[27]

7. Agathocles fails in Africa, wins in Sicily

Ophellas' and Bomilcar's removals left Agathocles master of the strategic situation. Carthage stood at bay with almost no allies nearby and very little territory outside the city itself. Cleaning up the political mess left by Bomilcar must have taken time, along with rebuilding its military capacity, which probably included hiring new mercenaries from abroad. As a result it was months before fresh Punic armies could take the field. In the meantime, the invaders dominated most of Libya with forces strengthened by the army from Cyrene and, we can surmise, some fresh mercenary infusions As noted earlier, mercenaries could disembark at Aspis and other Greek-held coastal cities. Certainly, despite the inevitable wear and tear of years of campaigning, the Greek forces during 308 remained large – large enough, in fact, to breed overconfidence.

Agathocles followed up his coup against Ophellas by besieging and taking Utica, Carthage's sister-city 40km further up the coast. Utica had supposedly thrown off an alliance with him, but none was mentioned earlier; more probably Diodorus misunderstood his source. Though a small city, Utica was tough. Agathocles had to use siege engines, with captured Uticans as human shields, to break through the walls. He then had everybody in the city slaughtered, plundered it thoroughly and left a garrison in it while he marched north to do the same to Hippou Acra (later called Hippo Diarrhytus, today Bizerte). According to a cryptic report in Diodorus, he first defeated the locals in a sea battle – the first indication that now he had something of a war fleet – before storming the city.

These victories not only won much-needed booty for his always touchy troops, but brought over many of the Libyan peoples, as eager as ever to rid themselves of Carthaginian domination. The new setbacks for Carthage probably took place in the later months of 308 and maybe the start of 307 (especially if the winter weather allowed some operations). Relief came unexpectedly. Early in the new year, Carthage's tormentor sailed back to Sicily to cope with a worsening situation there, leaving the bulk of his forces in Libya under his son Archagathus.

Hamilcar's defeat and death, and Carthage's own troubles at home, had cut back Punic Sicilian efforts to no more than the ongoing (but not always effective) naval blockade of Syracuse and the protection of the *epikrateia*. Warfare against Syracuse continued to be waged from then on partly by Deinocrates and the exiles' army (over 20,000 strong by 307 and still growing), and partly – and separately, a poor recipe for success – by a revived Acragas and its general Xenodicus. During 308, with a slogan of freedom and autonomy for the Sicilians, Xenodicus' Acragantines liberated city after city across the centre and south: Gela, Enna, Leontini and Camarina the most notable, along with Carthaginian-held Herbessus. But they then ran into a Syracusan army smaller than their 11,000-strong force, and were so totally beaten that they went home and stayed there.

Agathocles reached Sicily soon after with 2,000 men from his army in Libya. Advancing energetically from Selinus, he first subdued Heraclea Minoa, then – avoiding Acragas – marched away to the north coast to take his birthplace Thermae (he allowed Thermae's Punic garrison to leave in peace). It was probably along this march that he won Segesta as an ally; the Segestans, now or earlier, must have decided that Carthage had been weakened enough by events in Libya for them to break away. Next he took over Cephaloedium and Apollonia on the coast further east. Because the Apolloniates resisted, he massacred them. But when confronted by Deinocrates – now styling himself 'guardian of public freedom' and enjoying wide Siceliot support – he marched away to Syracuse and turned his attention to the Punic naval blockade there.

It is not obvious why Carthage's sole forward effort at this stage of its war with Syracuse was this blockade. It seems to have had no effect on the city's maritime supplies; and where the ships docked, obtained provisions and sheltered from bad weather is a mystery. The thirty-strong flotilla proved as insouciant as before. With seventeen triremes and a newly arrived Etruscan squadron of eighteen others – Antander, or an able lieutenant named Leptines, must have negotiated previously for this – Agathocles so completely routed the Carthaginians that, Diodorus wrote, he won Syracuse full security and fresh access to traders, so ending famine and shortages.

Meanwhile, his war with the other Sicilian Greeks went on in oddly erratic fashion. His general Leptines invaded Acragas' territory, drew Xenodicus out and defeated him again, but then left Acragas alone. Another general, Pasiphilus, was by now in charge of Gela and nearby cities in the south-east. Deinocrates sat somewhere else in the island – the centre or north-east seems likely – with a constantly enlarging army and many (unnamed) cities in his power, yet gave Agathocles no trouble. In practice, the two despots – the 'guardian of public freedom' was as much a *tyrannos* as his rival – kept up a wary peace, which in fact lasted while Agathocles returned to Africa to deal with looming disaster there. In view of what happened later, we might suspect that their *de facto* armistice was due to more than weariness.[28]

It must have been late in summer 307, or early in the autumn, that Agathocles had alarming news from Libya. Left there by his father to oversee the war and clearly confident of Greek strategic supremacy, Archagathus had detached a force under an officer named Eumachus to sweep inland for booty and, perhaps too, to deter allied peoples there from responding to any blandishments from Carthage. Eumachus took a city which Diodorus' Greek text calls Tocae and must be Thugga (Dougga) in the uplands above the Siliana River, 130km south-west of Carthage; then other places with names not attested in any other source – Phelline and Meschela – and after them a second Hippo Acra, which in Roman times was Hippo Regius, the see of St Augustine seven centuries later and today Anaba on the coast of eastern Algeria. The raiders pleased themselves by supposing that the 'very large city' of Meschela was a Greek colony, but this did not stop them from gathering as much booty as they could to take back to Tunes.

So delighted with the plunder was Archagathus that he soon sent Eumachus out again, beyond the region of his previous *chevauchée*. This time the raiders had only limited success, with greater resistance from the peoples of the Numidian highlands. Diodorus' source supplied vivid if not entirely convincing descriptions of these peoples and their habits (for instance, we are assured that in three inland cities the region's apes lived side-by-side with the residents). Fearing disaster, Eumachus decided to go back to base, but now trouble awaited him and his superior.[29]

With Bomilcar out of the way, the Carthaginians were at last able to turn to dealing with the invaders. Three generals, Hanno, Hamilcar and Adherbal ('Atarbas' in Diodorus), marched out at the head of 30,000 men, leaving a strong garrison to hold Carthage. The claim in Diodorus that one reason for their departure was to ease the supply situation in the city is not very convincing, since Carthage could always be supplied by sea: the Greeks had no fleet to blockade it. His second reason, that they expected to hearten their allies, must really mean that they hoped to win back their allies and subjects: they did not have many of these left, according to Diodorus himself.

The third and main reason supposedly was to make the Greeks divide their own forces and move farther away. The three generals therefore separated their forces into three corps and went off in different directions.

Arguably it would have been better to confront Archagathus directly. His forces cannot have been larger than theirs, and probably were smaller. He could have been bottled up in Tunes, his communications with Greek-held and allied cities – and Agathocles – cut off, and were he to come out and fight he would have slight chance of a victory. Besides, a lengthy siege or blockade of Tunes might well have made the mercenaries in the Greek army finally rethink their loyalties.

Instead, probably in mid-307, Hanno marched into 'the central region', Adherbal to 'the cities on the coast' and Himilco to 'the upland areas'. These last must be the Bagradas valley and its surrounds, including places like Thugga; Himilco probably aimed to intercept the returning Eumachus as well as win back local Libyan support. The coast cities may have been Utica and Hippou Acra, recently captured by Agathocles, or else were the cities on the gulf of Hammamet like Neapolis and Hadrumetum, whose Greek garrisons had been left very much on their own for more than a year except for a passing handshake from Ophellas' army. The 'central region' would then be the broad lands around the River Catadas (Meliane), studded with Libyan cities like Uthina, Nepheris and further south Thuburbo (Henchir Kasbat).[30]

Diodorus' fuzzy record of operations does not say why Archagathus let them go past Tunes. It would have been in the Greeks' interest to try to stop the enemy from fanning out across Libya (especially when one obvious target was Eumachus). Instead, he reacted by scattering his own forces. A captain called Aeschrion pursued Hanno, another body went to 'the coastland' – this must mean following after Adherbal – and Archagathus himself set out in a direction not stated, possibly aiming to intimidate the communities around the lower Bagradas from severing their association with his side, maybe hoping also to link up with Eumachus.

His efforts foundered. Himilco intercepted Eumachus, who, laden with booty, was lured into an ambush outside 'a certain city' (Diodorean fuzziness again). Of the 8,800 raiders barely seventy escaped. Hanno dealt similarly with Aeschrion, ambushing and killing him along with 4,000 of his infantry and 800 horsemen. Only some of the survivors managed to join Archagathus, whose corps, we are told with unusual exactness, was 500 *stadia*, or 60km, away. What the force sent by Archagathus to the coastland did is not reported; at least no defeat is mentioned, but then he recalled it to Tunes along with the remnants of the other divisions. Only a few places remained garrisoned, no doubt to keep open communications with Sicily. Archagathus did still have several thousand Libyan troops too – mercenaries or volunteers – but their loyalty to a struggling cause was uncertain. In any case, he and his surviving officers were out of their military depth. He sent frantic messengers over to Syracuse summoning back his father.

Agathocles – incongruously depicted by Diodorus as now leading a cheerfully unbuttoned lifestyle at Syracuse – acted quickly. Ruthless as always, he seized and massacred 500 fellow-Syracusans who he feared might work in his absence to bring back Deinocrates. As there was no longer a Punic blockade of the city, he had no trouble sailing, though the size of his flotilla and any accompanying soldiery is not given. Where he disembarked in Libya is also not given. Even if a Greek garrison still held Aspis, that was a long ride (over 100km) from Tunes through increasingly hostile country and with Adherbal across the route. In view of what happened later, Leukos Tynes or some other nearby coastal point is likeliest, unless he sailed right up to Tunes, passing the southern walls of Carthage without being sighted.

What was left of his army was now caged in and around Tunes. The Carthaginians were all on high ground that was hard to access. Himilco held the hills and passes to Tunes' north, south and west, with his camp 100 *stadia* (20km) away. Adherbal's camp was 40 *stadia*, just 8km, from the invaders: maybe on the hill of today's Cimetière du Djellaz, south of Tunis, to block any attempt to escape to Cape Bon or Byzacium. Hanno most likely had joined Himilco.

The cornered invaders now consisted of only 6,000 Greek infantry, the same number of Gallic, Samnite and Etruscan mercenaries, and 1,500 cavalry. The 10,000-strong Libyan contingent, in its own encampment, was rightly distrusted, while another force of 'Libyan chariots' (the 'six thousand' figure in Diodorus must be corrupt) played their usual ineffective role in the battle. Forced by growing hunger and discontent in his army to launch an attack on the Carthaginians – Himilco's troops most likely – Agathocles, after a hard fight, was beaten back into his camp, losing 3,000 dead and many taken prisoner. The Libyan troops looked placidly on.[31]

A very strange sequence of events followed. During the night after the battle, the victorious Carthaginians in their camp began a ritual of sacrificing in fire prisoners chosen as thanksgiving to the gods: a ritual much like the one which Diodorus recorded them performing in 310 with children of their own after Agathocles' initial victory. A sudden wind sprang up and blew flames across the camp's flimsy tents and huts, causing confusion, fear and then deaths among its troops. This was just the moment when half of Agathocles' Libyans started to move across in the dark to join the Carthaginians. These panicked, thinking that the Greeks had taken advantage of the blaze to launch an attack: the Punic army collapsed into a mob struggling – and then fighting – among themselves in desperate efforts to flee across the isthmus to Carthage. Reportedly no fewer than 5,000 men perished in the disaster.

Agathocles' battered and weary army could not take advantage of this, for it promptly fell into a catastrophe of its own, again thanks to the Libyans. These had turned back when the Punic camp went up in flames, but to the Greeks the uproar and fire led them to assume that the advancing troops were the Carthaginians on the attack. Panicking in their turn, they began to run, a panic that turned into disaster when the Libyans came up. As among the Carthaginians, fighting broke out, ending only after 4,000 were killed. Although the survivors returned to camp (and the Carthaginians in turn were too shattered to try a real attack), the ragtag force that was left cannot have numbered more than 5,000–6,000.

Agathocles saw that it was all over. He made plans to leave Africa, deserting his men and, if Diodorus is to be believed, even his son Archagathus, whose loyalty he distrusted. Archagathus found out and had his father arrested, but the ordinary soldiers then insisted that he be freed; no doubt most could not believe that their leader would abandon them. Of course he did so at the next opportunity, this time taking only a few friends – and neither son – in a transport vessel that bore them to Sicily. It was the time of the setting of the Pleiades, around the start of November 307.

In the uproar that followed in the Greek camp, the men seized and killed both Archagathus and his brother Heracleides. According to Diodorus, the killing was done by Ophellas' men, in Justin by a Syracusan ex-friend of the tyrant named Arcesilaus. The army elected new generals and accepted generous terms from the Carthaginians: 300 talents in money, enrolment in Punic service at regular pay rates or, for others, settlement in the *epikrateia* at Solous. Some of the remaining Greek garrisons in Libya nonetheless held out, hoping for rescue – again we are not told which, though Aspis, the stronghold nearest to Sicily, may have been one – but were soon forced to surrender, in their cases to death or slavery.[32]

8. The end of the war

With Libya lost, Agathocles was determined to make sure of his position in Sicily. Outside Syracuse it was far from secure. Deinocrates controlled much of the east, probably from Catana and Messana to the north coast (Diodorus' narrative is blank on details). Agathocles' own general Pasiphilus had turned against him at Gela and declared for Deinocrates. Acragas and the Punic *epikrateia* stayed aloof from these squabbles, but of course Agathocles was still at war with the Carthaginians and he needed money.

He handled the situation with a ruthlessness exceptional even for him. When he learned what happened to his sons, he had Antander at Syracuse kill – in public, on the shore – all the relatives of the Syracusans who had accompanied him on the expedition. Agathocles himself collected troops in western Sicily, marched to Segesta (now allied to Syracuse) and there, on a pretext of treachery, carried out a bloodbath: inflicting savage tortures on wealthy Segestans to get at their possessions, massacring most poorer citizens and selling off the surviving women and children as slaves in Italy. Having emptied Segesta of its 10,000 citizens, he handed it over to deserters and, with Stalinesque irony, renamed it Dicaeopolis, 'Justice City'.

These achievements took him into spring 306. At this point he did, briefly, lose confidence in his prospects – or so it seems. He contacted Deinocrates to offer to give up power at Syracuse and keep only Thermae and Cephaloedium. This may have been simply a move to gain time. However, Deinocrates was (in Diodorus' view) not eager to return to Syracuse as a merely ordinary citizen. He haggled too long about terms. Meanwhile, Agathocles was also negotiating, probably via Panormus, with Carthage, making peace and freeing himself to deal with the exiles and their general.

The peace of 306 was a remarkable win for him. His sole concession was the inevitable one: 'the Carthaginians to recover all the cities previously under them'. This meant yielding Segesta (which soon regained its name, and maybe some surviving citizens), Thermae, Selinus and Heraclea Minoa: but that simply returned to the situation of both the agreement with the earlier Hamilcar in 313 and Carthage's peace with Timoleon in 340. On the other hand, his benefits were handsome. Only two were stated: Carthage would pay him 300 silver talents (or, in Timaeus' account, half that) and 200,000 measures of grain – this proviso a sign that Syracuse was still suffering food shortages even though the Punic blockade was over. Not stated, but plain, was that Carthage recognized the tyrant as ruler of Syracuse; implicitly, it would not intervene again in his actions against Siceliot – or Sicel – states outside the *epikrateia*.

With no risk of Carthage interfering, Agathocles moved fast and boldly against the exiles. He was probably in touch with elements among them who had lost enthusiasm for their increasingly authoritarian leader, and others who simply wanted to end the crusade and go home (a group noted by Diodorus). Agathocles gambled. He marched from Syracuse with 5,000 foot and 800 horse to challenge Deinocrates' claimed 25,000 infantry and 3,000 cavalry – numbers surely overblown in Diodorus – and defeated them at an unknown site, thanks to a timely switch of sides by 2,000 of the exile army and panic then spreading through the rest. Deinocrates and the cavalry escaped, and before long the beaten champion of public freedom was pardoned by his old friend and made a general in the Syracusan army. A large body of his infantry, at least 4,000 strong, fared far less well. Once they surrendered on a promise of amnesty, Agathocles massacred them.

Deinocrates' next employment (it took two years) was to go after and kill Pasiphilus, and bring that apostate's cities back under the tyrant's control. Agathocles cherished his old friend and foe until his own death nearly two decades later. Sometime around 305, meanwhile, the tyrant – still 'general with supreme power and guardian of the city' – decided to follow the current example of Alexander the Great's successor generals: one after another, starting in 306, each successor gave himself the title of king (*basileus*), as did Agathocles.

Like theirs, his kingship was a mark of supremacy, not of territory. Far from being just a king of Syracuse, Agathocles was master of virtually all Greek Sicily from 305 up to the Halycus and northern Himeras rivers, and overlord of the Sicel interior too. Only Acragas may have kept its independence, but it was a minnow by comparison. Agathocles had restored the Sicilian empire of Dionysius I and riveted it still more firmly on its subjects.

Carthage had escaped the greatest threat so far to its existence more by good fortune than military or naval skill. Like too many previous commanders, the generals in both Sicily and then Libya made mistakes – Hamilcar son of Gisco's maladroit night-attempt on Syracuse being only the most glaring – and lost opportunities, above all the clumsy failure to stop or chase Agathocles' armada leaving Syracuse in 310. Political tensions at home also interfered with the republic's war efforts, most discreditably of all when Bomilcar's abortive putsch stymied any chance of exploiting the crisis that Agathocles caused outside Carthage by murdering his new ally Ophellas (if nothing else, the Carthaginians could have thought of offering the new arrivals inducements to defect).

For much of the time, the Carthaginians actually showed minimal enthusiasm for the war. Although they had saved Acragas from the tyrant in 311, they limited further action to a squadron briefly showing the flag in Syracuse's waters. It took his raid into the *epikrateia* to prompt their armed response. Then Hamilcar son of Gisco, cautious to a fault even after winning the battle at the Himeras, took his time about moving on Syracuse, not only while the beaten tyrant was holed up in Gela but even after he had left Syracuse for Libya.

This hesitancy persisted even after Agathocles invaded Africa. Once Hamilcar was defeated and killed, they let the Syracusan exiles and Acragas carry on the war in Sicily, apart from the fairly inept flotilla prowling outside Syracuse, which was not renewed after the tyrant came back and defeated it. In Libya, once the invaders had established a firm footing in Tunes and other captured cities, Carthaginian efforts to dislodge them were sporadic at best. Instead, the Carthaginians preferred to work around them: Bomilcar's idea of strategy was to send out a force to overawe the 'Zouphones' and other 'Nomads', and later the trio of his successor-generals spread out across the countryside rather than move directly against Tunes. When Agathocles attacked Utica and Hippou Acra – Carthage's oldest and nearest sister cities – no help came out from Carthage on land or by sea to either city or to strike at Tunes in his absence.

Punic hesitancy and poverty of strategy contrasted with Agathocles' resourcefulness, risk-taking skills and energy, through which he out-manoeuvred them as regularly as he did his other opponents. As a general he was as prone to losing battles as to winning them, but as a leader he was undeniably charismatic to both soldiers and civilians from the start of his long career. Carthage had had no leader like this since, at best, Mago in the 390s and 380s. At the same time, it had none as wedded as Agathocles to cold-blooded killing of opponents and suspects. These varied and conflicting qualities of the tyrant forced on Carthage a war that it did not want, dragged it into the severest danger it had ever faced and in the end – at serious cost in lives, goods and treasure to all its participants – saved the city-state and its possessions from destruction.

Chapter 9

The Sicilian stalemate: Pyrrhus and Hiero

1. The woes of post-Agathoclean Sicily

Agathocles spent the last decade-and-a-half of his life interfering in southern Italy with repeated but unprofitable military ventures, creating a warfleet and with it winning temporary possession of the island of Corcyra before ceding this (with one of his daughters) to the flamboyant Demetrius the Besieger. In his final years, and though he was into his seventies, he supposedly started to prepare yet another war with Carthage, only to be struck down by a painful illness (some said poison from an ambitious grandson). Bizarrely, his last act before dying in 289 was to abdicate and allow his fellow-Syracusans to re-establish a democratic regime.

The democratic restoration, like the rest of Agathocles' legacy to Sicily, proved bitter. Syracuse soon collapsed into civil war, while the cities that Agathocles had controlled regained their independence one by one – most of them falling under home-grown tyrants – and before long began to make war on one another quite in the traditional style. This was much the same self-destructive cycle as when Syracuse's hegemony had disintegrated in the 350s and 340s. It was a situation which, inevitably, prompted Carthage to renew military interest in the Siceliots.

The peace of 306 had left Carthage free to reassert its dominance over Libya and western Sicily, and of course its position in Sardinia had never been challenged. Who was in charge of the republic's affairs, now and for the next sixty years, is not known. It may be that the faction or factions around the successful generals of 307, Hanno, Adherbal and Himilco, were able to dominate the state for a time, as had happened often in the past. Certainly Carthage kept an eye on what went on in Greek Sicily, and Agathocles' naval build-up in the 290s probably put it on alert (whether he did have a fresh Punic war in mind or not). His death must have been welcome news in 289, but did not relax Punic attention. The need, or temptation, to become involved once more arrived very soon, and again Syracuse was the focus.

Agathocles' Campanian mercenaries, based at Leontini and hankering for Syracusan citizenship, found a leader in the dead tyrant's favourite,

Menon, after he murdered one of Agathocles' grandsons to take over their command. Threats coming from Leontini then led the Syracusans in turn to elect as general one Hicetas (perhaps a descendant of Timoleon's adversary). Nothing much happened at first. Menon's men avoided battle and Hicetas avoided assaulting Leontini. But the Carthaginians acted fast. Whether Menon sent an appeal to Panormus or received an offer he could not refuse, Punic troops arrived on the scene, to the Syracusans' utter consternation.

Hicetas may have supposed that Carthage would be glad to see Agathocles' unruly soldiery disciplined or destroyed; hardly that it would take their side. When Punic troops in large numbers appeared near Leontini, he was forced to negotiate. As a result, the mercenaries returned to Syracuse and the city had to hand over 400 hostages to the Carthaginians. This was the first time we read of hostages being exacted from a Siceliot state, but what became of them later is not recorded, nor what became of Menon. Hicetas' backdown satisfied the Carthaginians, but once they had gone away strife and stress erupted at Syracuse itself, as the Campanians were still denied citizenship. In the end, probably sometime in 288 or maybe 287, these agreed to leave for their Italian homeland, made their way northward to Messana and there seized the unsuspecting city, killing or driving out the menfolk and taking over their wives and children.

This treachery was not unique for Campanian mercenaries. As mentioned before, early in the elder Dionysius' tyranny another Campanian body had done the same thing at Entella. The takeover of Messana would one day lead to momentous developments in Mediterranean history; but for the time being its effects stayed within Sicily. The mercenaries named themselves 'the Mamertines' (after the Campanian war-god Mamers, equivalent to Rome's Mars) and made Messana a rogue state, raiding their neighbours' territories, Syracuse's included, for booty. Their plundering ranged as far as Gela and Camarina – they even drove the Geloans from their city – yet for some years the major states in the island found it more congenial to leave them alone or even seek their help. They made such an impression on other Campanians that a decade later, in 278, another contingent misused its position as guardian of Rhegium to do the same there, much to the embarrassment of the Romans, who had placed them there to ward off the invading Pyrrhus of Epirus.

A fresh crop of tyrants emerged across Greek Sicily during the 280s. One Tyndarion became master of Tauromenium, Leontini succumbed to a Heracleides, while at Acragas power was taken by an ambitious citizen named Phintias, who set about extending Acragas' reach in obvious competition with Hicetas' Syracuse. Even Agyrium, 120km away, came under Phintias' control, although Enna (between the two) avoided that fate by calling in a Punic garrison. Hicetas rose to the challenge, leading to a vengeful – and, it need hardly be said, totally unnecessary – war across the increasingly devastated eastern Sicilian countryside. But when Hicetas defeated the Acragantines, Phintias must have made peace, for his adversary next went to war with the Carthaginians.

Hicetas' reason for this fresh venture – unless it was sheer overconfidence, as Diodorus alleged – may have been that the Carthaginians were troublingly close to Syracuse and its neighbours now that they held Enna. The River Terias (the San Leonardo today), where Hicetas fought them and lost, rises south-west of Leontini to flow down to the sea below Catana. A brief excerpt from Diodorus mentions only the Carthaginian victory, but it looks as though they had moved to attack Leontini, or, perhaps, to support it if it was trying to cut free of Syracuse's domination, for Hicetas' defeat did enable Leontini to gain independence. When Pyrrhus arrived in Sicily some years later, the city was ruled by one Heracleides.

Diodorus' order of events implies that Phintias also recovered freedom of action. He gathered up the homeless Geloans to settle them at a new city beside Mount Ecnomus, which with disarming immodesty he named after himself (Licata today). Neither he nor his enemy, though, lasted much longer. Phintias' harsh rule led to breakaways by some subject cities – Agyrium, Diodorus' homeland, is the only one named – and he himself then met his end on the tusks of a boar he was hunting. He was replaced by another tyrant, Sosistratus, who soon seized an unprecedented opportunity: he helped Thoenon, Hicetas' garrison-commander in Ortygia, oust that ruler, and then himself took over Syracuse. Thus in 279 (Hicetas had ruled for nine years), Acragas and Syracuse found themselves under a single master.

Sosistratus promptly fell out with Thoenon, who no doubt had expected to rule Syracuse himself as an ally of the Acragantine. Thoenon was still occupying Ortygia with his mercenary forces; Sosistratus could not dislodge him, for Syracuse's 140-strong navy was docked in Ortygia. They patched up their differences only when they faced a new and potentially ruinous danger.[1]

Carthage had decided to act. Its main reason for opening a new Siceliot war was probably the political alignment of Syracuse with Acragas, flimsy as it was since only Sosistratus held it together. But were it to become a firmer bond, that would pose an obvious threat to the *epikrateia*. The Carthaginians may also have reckoned that if they let too much time pass inactively, their position in Sicily could worsen further. Pyrrhus, king of Epirus, was in Italy heading Tarentum's war against the Romans, but his widely suspected ambition for a broad western Mediterranean realm (one of his many wives was Agathocles' daughter) would be enough to perturb Punic policymakers.²

2. The war with Pyrrhus

The Carthaginians acted on several fronts. Late in 279, an admiral named Mago sailed to Italy with a fleet of 130 ships, first to the mouth of the Tiber, from where he offered to aid the Romans against the king. Just what aid he meant is not specified, but it would probably have been money, grain for the legions and perhaps mercenaries. Although he was turned down, the Romans did agree to a pact with Carthage under which either state would include the other in any agreement with Pyrrhus, and could aid the other against attack by him (he was seeking peace with the Romans). Mago then sailed to meet the king, probably at Tarentum, ostensibly to offer to mediate between him and Rome. But as peace between those two could leave the way open for Pyrrhus to focus on his Sicilian project, offering mediation was an empty show and Pyrrhus knew it, just as the Roman senate had known that the aid-offer to them was meant to keep the war going.

Carthage's next measures were naval and military. A short excerpt from Diodorus tells of the Carthaginians transporting 500 troops (Romans, apparently) to Rhegium, which was then used as a base for some small actions against Pyrrhus' local allies and for patrolling the straits to prevent him from sailing across to Sicily. These moves should date to early 278. The patrol flotilla comprised thirty ships, no doubt detached from Mago's fleet and stationed at Messana; the Mamertines were cooperative. If the troops were indeed Roman (Rhegium already had a Roman garrison), this small – and unimpressive – operation was the sole offshoot from the Punic-Roman pact. Neither state was anxious to have the other's forces campaigning in its own regions of interest.³

Larger offensive moves were occurring. In late spring or early summer 278, a fleet of 100 Carthaginian warships, which must again have been Mago's, appeared in Syracuse's Great Harbour. On land, an army supposedly 50,000 strong arrived, under an unnamed general, to form the latest siege of the oft-beleaguered city. The army's march across the island alarmed Heracleides of Leontini. He, Thoenon, Sosistratus and maybe also

Tyndarion of Tauromenium sent off pressing appeals to Pyrrhus to come over and 'help them drive out the Carthaginians'.

Their fright meanwhile paralyzed any resistance of their own. Syracuse, for example, still had a navy of 120 decked and twenty undecked ships – Pyrrhus took over all of these when he did arrive – yet made no effort to challenge the 100 Punic ships blockading the harbour. Sosistratus and his fellow-tyrants between them had over 20,000 soldiers, for these too were made available to the king when he came. They had known that the Carthaginians had been preparing for war, yet they did not join forces against them or try now to harass the besiegers. Instead they chose to wait for outside deliverance.

Pyrrhus was ready to listen, since by now his Roman war was going nowhere. The Romans had rejected his offer of talks even after two severe defeats, and his victories had cost him so many of his own troops that he quipped ruefully and famously, 'if we win one more battle against the Romans we shall be totally annihilated.' Once preliminary contacts through his chief adviser Cineas had been made with the appellant Siceliots, ignoring his Tarentine allies' protests he sailed for Sicily in the second half of 278, after two years and four months in Italy. The only mention of his expedition's size is a badly copied sentence in the text of the later historian Appian, giving him 8,000 cavalry and some elephants: perhaps Appian had in fact written 8,000 infantry and 800 (or the like) cavalry. This would be a fairly small force to lead against the Carthaginians, but Pyrrhus had to leave troops to hold Tarentum and other strongpoints, and he counted on large Siceliot support.[4]

With sixty warships he crossed to Tauromenium without trouble – so much for the Mamertines and the Punic naval patrols – and once he disembarked his troops he was greeted with remarkable outpourings of rapture from Sicily's Greeks. Siceliot reinforcements started to come in. When he set out down the coast for Syracuse, the Carthaginian fleet, which was now for some reason down to only seventy ships, and army chose discretion over valour and decamped.

This spineless reaction was as strange as the earlier Mago's similar performance in Timoleon's time. The Punic forces failed to exploit the weeks (or months) between their arrival at Syracuse and Pyrrhus', even though their Greek opponents were divided and demoralized. They even left the large Syracusan fleet safely alone. Then, confronted by a military hero of Mediterranean-wide fame, the Carthaginians apparently lost their ardour for the war they had begun. Their forces retreated to the *epikrateia*, to wait there for the inevitable counterattack.

Pyrrhus prevailed on Syracuse's warring despots to shelve their differences, added his new allies' forces to his own – 4,500 supplied by Leontini, probably a thousand or two from Tauromenium and the several thousand men in Syracuse – and readied the stores of equipment he found in Ortygia as well as the Syracusan fleet. His preparations may have taken up the winter of 278/77, but in spring 277, at latest, he set out for Acragas, to be welcomed there by Sosistratus and a contingent of 8,000 foot and 800 horse. The men of Enna also joined the expedition after driving away their Punic garrison.

With an army of 30,000 infantry, 2,500 cavalry and some elephants, and with his 200 warships keeping pace along the coast, he then marched westward to invade the *epikrateia*. One place after another fell: Heracleia Minoa despite a Punic garrison, probably too Mazara west of Selinus ('Azonae' in Diodorus), then voluntarily Selinus, Halicyae, Segesta and 'many other cities'. He had to take Eryx by force, but after that Ietae nearby (called Iaetia by Diodorus) joined him. This left the way clear to assault and capture Panormus, the finest city of the *epikrateia*. The entire region was thus occupied by the king and his Siceliot allies, with the sole exception of Lilybaeum.[5]

At this point, if Diodorus' and Plutarch's accounts give the right sequence of events, the Carthaginians gained a respite. Pyrrhus turned on their allies the Mamertines, at the opposite end of Sicily, defeated them in battle and captured some of their strongholds. He must have left troops to occupy western Sicily, but after beating the Mamertines he returned not to the west but to Syracuse. The Carthaginians used the time to reinforce Lilybaeum with troops, heavy weapons and food. At the same time they sent envoys to the king, asking for his terms and making it clear that they were ready to pay a large amount for peace, and even to provide him with ships, obviously for a return to Italy. Negotiating with him without bringing in the Romans breached the recent pact, but Carthage was plainly too anxious for peace to worry about that.

The peace overtures were not a mere ploy to gain time for Lilybaeum, as it was Pyrrhus' attention-switch to the Mamertines that allowed the fortress-city to be made impregnable. Nor did the Carthaginians use his absence to attack the forces he left behind or try to retake any of the cities he had captured. Carthage's unenthusiasm for war with him could not be clearer.[6]

The peace offer came to nothing. Pyrrhus first insisted that the Carthaginians abandon all the *epikrateia* save Lilybaeum, then changed his mind. According to Diodorus, both his Epirote entourage and the Sicilian allies' representatives demanded that Carthage abandon the island completely. According to Plutarch, Pyrrhus was set upon invading Libya (no doubt with his late father-in-law's near-success in mind). Instead of negotiating, he hurled attack after attack on Lilybaeum, only to be driven back each time. After two months of this he gave up and focused instead on readying a fleet for Libya.

Circumstances and his own miscalculations ended this project too. During 277, his relations with the Sicilian Greeks changed for the worse. To gather ships' crews for his invasion fleet he resorted to high-handed methods, because volunteers proved too few: the allied cities were ordered to furnish more men and suffered penalties if they did not. Other oppressive measures followed as the Siceliots, maybe disappointed at the stalemate outside Lilybaeum or worried about what a major invasion of Libya might entail, began to lose their earlier enthusiasm for the cause and as Pyrrhus began taking steps to buttress his authority over them.

The list of his injustices (offered by the historian Dionysius) is long and maybe exaggerated: properties confiscated to be given to the king's friends, army officers arbitrarily made magistrates of cities, lawsuits and other cases interfered with, and then as things worsened, garrisons placed in suspect cities and suspect citizens there put to death. How many cases of injustice actually happened we are not told, and generalizations were easy for his critics, but even if only a few occurred they would have given wide offence.

Pyrrhus' most self-defeating miscalculation was to turn against the leaders who had invited him over, Sosistratus and Thoenon. Apparently he suspected them of covert contacts with the Carthaginians. Sosistratus got wind of his danger in time and fled from Syracuse – to Acragas presumably, unless Pyrrhus had put his own men in charge there too – but Thoenon was put to death. This unleashed pent-up resentments felt by Siceliot aristocrats at least, who now viewed him as another Agathocles. 'A fearful hatred arose against him in the cities,' wrote Plutarch, and some states (again no details) turned to the Carthaginians and some to the Mamertines. At the same time, Carthage sent fresh troops and ships over to Sicily, no doubt via Lilybaeum. They did not try to bring the enemy in the *epikrateia* to battle, but used harassment tactics to demoralize them and destabilize Pyrrhus' faltering occupation.[7]

With his dreams of a Sicilian realm dissolving, the king accepted appeals from his allies in Italy to return to save them from Rome. At some stage, most likely during winter 277/76, he pulled out whatever forces he had in the *epikrateia* and in allied cities as he prepared to vacate the island.

Naturally, the plan could not be hidden. The Carthaginians readied their Sicilian fleet and alerted the Mamertines. When in spring 276 his warships and transports reached the Strait of Messina, the Punic fleet intercepted them and sank or took several (though Appian's claim that only twelve of 110 warships escaped looks fanciful). Then after he reached southern Italy, 10,000 Mamertines attacked his army as it marched for Tarentum and badly mauled it before he could drive them off.[8]

This was the inglorious finish to a military and political campaign that had briefly achieved more against the Carthaginians in Sicily than any before it. Pyrrhus had also briefly threatened Carthage with a repeat of its still-recent Agathoclean trauma. That his grand designs failed was thanks more to his own bad handling of resources and allies than anything the Carthaginians did. Their efforts against his arrival were piecemeal and easily given up, they put up not very much resistance when he finally invaded the *epikrateia* and afterwards they bungled their opportunity to make an end of him in the straits.

They were happy enough to see him go and were doubtless pleased to learn how he went on to suffer defeat by the Romans, return to Greece for further ambitious adventures and finally perish in a street in Argos in 272 when trying to storm that city. By then, Carthage had settled its own affairs in Sicily and its struggle with Syracuse.

3. Hiero of Syracuse

Disappointingly sparse details survive for Sicily's next few years. The Carthaginians clearly regained control of the *epikrateia*, but they could not conciliate all of its communities. A dozen years later, in 263, a Roman army's thrust into western Sicily was welcomed by the Segestans, who claimed kinship with the Romans on the optimistic ground that they too were descended from Trojans. Halicyae, the other important Sicel city, went over to Rome at the same time without needing such an excuse.

Outside the *epikrateia*, relations with neighbouring states varied: for example, Enna kept aloof (in 261 the Carthaginians took it by treachery), while not far to its west the small but strong city of Myttistratum was stoutly loyal to Carthage until a third Roman siege in 258 crushed it. Cephaloedium on the north coast was another ally until captured by the Romans in 254. Even Acragas became friendly. Sosistratus is not heard of again and Pyrrhus' failed campaigns had left the city uncomfortably exposed. With the return of peace and with Syracuse preoccupied over other matters, the Acragantines grew friendly enough to ally with Carthage in 264 when it made the novel and fateful decision to ally with Syracuse against the Mamertines – and by implication against the Mamertines' new friend, Rome. The contemporary historian Philinus of Acragas, cited by Polybius, claimed that Carthage's dominance in Sicily in 264 stretched almost as far east as Echetla, only about 90km inland from Syracuse.[9]

After Pyrrhus' exit, Carthage's war with Syracuse came to a stop. Formally it did not, but instead of confronting Carthaginian forces wherever these now were, the Syracusan army stationed at a place called Mergane – possibly a misspelling in Polybius' text for Megara (Hyblaea) on the coast 20km north of Syracuse – had a falling-out with the authorities in Syracuse, whose leader was one Leptines (maybe descended from the family of the old tyrants?). These may have been a faction recently installed by Pyrrhus after he liquidated Thoenon. The soldiers elected two of their own to take command: an unknown named Artemidorus (who is never heard of again) and Hiero, son of Hierocles, a young aristocrat whose family claimed descent from Gelon, and who had earned military distinction under Pyrrhus. The likeliest reason for discord was lack of pay, a constant issue between cities and their soldiers, especially when the soldiers were mercenaries as those serving Syracuse seem to have been. Hiero was able to avert civil strife and conciliate all sides, partly through a marriage-alliance with Leptines. Then he was elected Syracuse's general, probably the year after Pyrrhus sailed.

The war was not formally over. In 275 or 274, a fellow-Syracusan, the poet Theocritus, sought Hiero's patronage with an effusive *Idyll* that praised patrons of old and portrayed Hiero 'girding himself for the fight, a horsehair plume waving on his helm', and preparing for battle with the already shuddering 'Phoenicians who dwell on Libya's headland under the setting sun', to free Sicily from its enemies and revive its war-ravaged lands. Before long, though, Theocritus was offering equally heartfelt praises to Egypt's Ptolemy II and his sister-queen Arsinoe. Instead of donning the war helmet, Hiero had let peace return.[10]

The last war-action by Carthage in or around Sicily had been the sea-fight with Pyrrhus in the straits. Even if formal peace was not concluded later, tacit consensus for it can be inferred. A decade later, the Carthaginian commander in Sicily could even proffer Hiero diplomatic congratulations – specious though these were – for a victory over the Mamertines. After 276,

Syracuse still held sizeable territory, even if less than in Agathocles' day, to judge from its peace with Rome in 263. This would leave Hiero ruling Leontini and Acrae to the north, Helorus and Notum to the south and Tauromenium as an enclave beyond Catana. He probably took Tauromenium from the Mamertines of Messana in the early 260s, and Catana became a Syracusan ally before 263, for the Romans took it that year while they advanced on Syracuse. From 276–63, therefore, Syracuse dominated a large block of eastern Sicily and saw no need for further confrontation with Carthage. Between them, the two states were masters, direct and indirect, of most of the island.

There was one important exception. Both Carthage and Syracuse shared a post-Pyrrhus problem: the Mamertines of Messana. These now ranged even more widely than before, raiding Carthaginian territory as well as Greek, and undeterred by Rome's long-delayed suppression of their rogue colleagues at Rhegium in 270. It may have been the restoration of Rhegium to the exiled Rhegines that encouraged Hiero, probably a year later, to don his war helmet against the Mamertines (many Messanian exiles lived at Syracuse and some served in his army). Instead, the Mamertines defeated him at the River Cyamosorus near Centuripa. Polybius, reflecting a source like Timaeus (still alive though very elderly, and able to take his history down to 264), offered an upbeat verdict on the defeat: by having most of the losses fall on his fractious and unreliable mercenaries – he left them to be slaughtered while he took his citizen troops home – Hiero made his regime secure.

The victors of course strengthened their grip on north-eastern Sicily, although details are lacking. In 265, they had mercenaries of their own holding not only Mylae nearby (as they may have done from much earlier) but a place called Ameselum between Centuripa and Agyrium – though not either of these two – and a lengthy stretch of the north coast as far as Halaesa, only 15km or so east of Cephaloedium. In 265, Hiero, at the head of citizen soldiers as well as more reliable (probably better-paid) mercenaries, opened a new offensive. In that year and the early part of 264, he overran most of the Mamertines' territories, taking towns and winning over their garrisons, with a climax beside the small River Longanus a few kilometres south of Mylae. The Campanians were catastrophically defeated. Hiero, now or earlier acclaimed 'king' by his men, moved up to lay siege to the survivors in Messana.

Carthage was watching all these events closely. It was at this moment that its general in Sicily, Hannibal – who 'happened to be moored at the island of Lipara', wrote Diodorus, with warships and troops – sailed over to offer the king his congratulations and propose himself as honest broker to bring the surviving Mamertines to terms. Hiero trusted him and waited. Instead, Hannibal put a small garrison into Messana: a symbolic, not practical, protection, enough to prompt the Syracusan to retire home rather than start yet another Punic war.[11]

Carthage's motive in saving the Mamertines is obvious, and Hiero need not have been as naive as Diodorus claimed. Carthage acted not from affection for the freebooters but, as in Agathocles' time, to thwart Syracuse, whose strength was reviving under an able new leader. Hiero's victorious campaigns looked, and probably were, intended to make Syracuse the hegemon of all eastern Sicily. If that was achieved, moreover, there would be every possibility of Hiero drawing Acragas, Enna and other central and western cities into his orbit, a standing danger to the *epikrateia*.

Almost at once the situation changed unexpectedly. The Mamertines had also appealed for aid to Rome, stressing their Campanian origin and thus their kinship with Italy's new hegemon. The Romans had long traded with, but never before intervened in, Sicily. This time they decided to intervene. Perhaps they feared Punic expansion, as Polybius, nearly all other ancient writers and most modern scholars believe, even though Carthage had long ceased to expand in Sicily or elsewhere. Or it may be that Syracuse's revival and expansion were seen as a menace, real or potential, to Rome's newly imposed mastery over southern Italy, and Hiero as an expansionist successor to Dionysius I and Agathocles. Syracuse's wealth was a further attraction: Polybius stressed how ordinary Romans were eager for the rewards a war would bring. Despite hesitations among senators, the decision was taken by a vote of the Roman *populus* (people) to send military help to the Mamertines.

This decision led to others. Over the last four decades, the Carthaginians, like the Siceliots, had watched the Italian peninsula and its varied states and peoples become a powerful military alliance directed by Rome. They were determined to keep it out of Sicily. So were Syracuse and Acragas; both preferred to share Sicily with Carthage, however difficult and sometimes hostile a neighbour, than the new ruler of Italy.

When a new Carthaginian general, another Hanno, arrived at Lilybaeum with a new army in summer 264, he found not only Acragas ready to be an ally but Hiero too. For the first time in history, Carthage and Syracuse became formal allies, aiming to crush the Mamertines and deter the Romans from crossing the straits. The alliance quickly failed. A Roman consul and army did cross, to defeat first Hiero and then Hanno outside Messana. Hiero found himself confronting Rome on his own, and in 263 agreed to terms that ended forever Syracuse's role (though not its self-image) as a major power. The Carthaginians, hesitant at first, were then forced in their turn to wage war with their old treaty-partners from Italy. Carthage's long and chequered history of wars with the Greeks of Sicily was over.[12]

Chapter 10

Carthage at War in Africa and Spain

1. Libya: subjects and rebels

The early Carthaginians' volatile relationship with their Libyan neighbours has already been described. The story that the local king wanted to marry their queen Elissa/Dido, and was forestalled only by her suicide, was a romantic fancy reflecting Carthage's dealings and difficulties with those communities. For several centuries she paid, or was supposed to pay, a yearly tribute for the ground on which the city stood. She was strong enough, probably in Malchus' time, to stop paying (see Chapter 4); but after his fall, the Libyans reasserted themselves, though Justin's curt report offers no details. As suggested earlier, it may have occurred because the city was weakened in some way – by a plague or political infighting – or was involved elsewhere and so lacked local strength to resist pressure. The communities between the lower Bagradas region and the Zaghouan range must have been able to combine their forces (as they and other Libyans did more than once in later centuries) to apply that pressure, and the restored payment-regime lasted for some more decades.

Then in the mid-fifth century, the increasingly prosperous republic reversed the relationship. 'The Africans were forced to release the Carthaginians from the tribute for the foundation of the city,' wrote Justin. As usual, no details are supplied, but if Justin can be trusted there were no great battles. This is the third item in a west-to-east list of African wars, and only the first two are reported in more warlike terms. The first states that the Carthaginians 'made war on the Mauri', the second that they 'fought against the Numidians' – an improbably wide range of conflicts (especially with the nearest Mauri living 1,400km away).

Another item occurs in the *Prologues* (the brief résumés) of the books of Trogus' *Histories*. These sometimes add a detail or two not in Justin, and one *Prologue* mentions fifth-century Carthaginian campaigns in Africa by a leader whose transmitted name, 'Rubellus Annorus', is plainly a copyist's blunder. 'Sabellus Hanno', the generally accepted nineteenth-century emendation, is just as hard to defend: 'Sabellus' was an old Latin term for someone from the Sabine hill-country north of Rome, a seriously unlikely connection for a fifth-century Carthaginian. Still, this warrior Hanno himself may be genuine, perhaps one of the Magonid family; he may even have been Hanno 'king of the Carthaginians' of *Periplus* fame, whose maritime expedition is best dated to the first half of the same century. If Carthage's activities in the far west, illustrated by that Hanno's colonies and by Punic trading posts like Chullu and Tipasa on the Algerian coast, irritated local Numidians and Mauretanians into intermittent hostilities, keeping these at bay or forcibly pacifying them might count as successes worth recording, just as turning the tables on the Libyans would.[1]

By the end of the fifth century, many Libyan communities were under Carthage's rule. As suggested earlier, it had probably imposed mastery on at least the fertile lands between the lower Bagradas River and the Zaghouan mountains: these were regions that forces from the city could readily reach within a few days, whenever it became necessary to compel obedience. Whatever cohesion these communities had earlier had broken up. The Libyans' small towns, villages and rural cantons continued to be self-governing, but now it was they who had to pay tribute to Carthage – in money or produce, or both – and furnish it with Libyan troops on demand.

This was the usual structure of imperialism in the ancient world. The contemporary Athenian empire around the Aegean Sea functioned in the same way, and reacted to defiance in the same way, with punishing armed force. Like the Athenians again and like the Roman Republic, especially from the fourth century on, the Carthaginians developed the practice of sending out citizens from time to time to settle in places in the hinterland (see Chapter 2 §4). Aristotle opined that this was to prevent political strife and enrich the settlers, which implies that these were poorer citizens with social grievances. The measure was rather like Athens' device, contemporary again, of despatching selected citizens as landholders (*klerouchoi*) to places around the Aegean that Athens controlled.[2]

What the Libyans felt about having to receive and coexist with these uninvited settlers is not recorded, nor how loyal to Carthage the settlers' descendants felt after a couple of generations. Settlers may have been one source of the bitterness among Libyans that caused the great rebellion in 396. Another was Himilco's secret pact with Dionysius to evacuate the Carthaginian citizen soldiers to Africa while leaving behind the rest of his sick and defeated army, most of it being Libyan troops.

A concerted uprising followed. The campaigns in Sicily under Hannibal the Magonid and Himilco ten years earlier must have brought home numbers of discharged Libyan fighters who could form the core of a rebel army. Certainly a large force assembled fast, and it grew larger as slaves flocked to join it. These must have been slaves working on estates and maybe in small towns in Carthage's own territory, the *chora*, which probably extended to Cape Bon by now.

Although the rebel army, even with these extra recruits, cannot have been 200,000 strong – Diodorus no doubt drew this estimate from Ephorus or Timaeus with their penchant for huge figures – it must have been sizeable. As Agathocles would do ninety years later, the rebels seized Tunes to cut Carthage off by land. For a time the city stood in dread of capture before timely measures averted disaster. To appease the Sicilians' patron deities Demeter and Persephone, whose shrines Himilco had destroyed, their cult was ceremonially initiated at Carthage with resident Greeks as priests. A more mundane but equally effective policy was to wait out the blockade while making secret contact with some Libyan leaders. Carthage could bring in supplies by sea (from Sardinia, wrote Diodorus); but the thousands of rebels around Tunes found it hard to keep themselves fed as time passed with the enemy refusing to yield or offer battle.

Eventually they began to quarrel among themselves until some leaders – bought by Punic money, according to Diodorus – took their contingents home. Once that exodus began, the rebels did not last long at Tunes. Hungry and dispirited, and it seems without any attacks from Carthage, they gave up and scattered to their homes. There may have been more to their failure than this – the plague that Himilco's men brought back in 396 could have spread to the massed encampment around Tunes, for instance – but no fuller details are recorded, nor how the Carthaginians acted after the rebellion. Some concessions may have been made, for Mago a few years later (in 392) felt it safe to recruit Libyans as well as Sardinians and Campanians for his new army. All the same, his Sicilian campaign that year was carefully defensive and ended with him offering Dionysius terms (see Chapter 6 §3): it may be that he was unwilling to take risks with troops whose obedience, should the risks go wrong, he could not rely on.

Plague returned to Carthage only a decade-and-a-half later, not long after it re-established Hipponium in southern Italy. It was so devastating to the city that both the Libyans and also the Sardinians under Punic hegemony broke out in revolt. Some extra details in Diodorus (like names and actions) would have been welcome, but he preferred penning pictures of city-wide terrors and recurring panic attacks, with citizens rushing out of their houses sword in hand to fight other citizens, hallucinating that these were invaders. These (if genuine) look like fever-induced delusions; otherwise they were conjured up by fertile Greek imaginations. Just as unsatisfyingly, we are told that 'by appeasing heaven through sacrifices' the Carthaginians 'swiftly' repressed the rebellions. Maybe this happened swiftly in Sardinia (if so, that rising cannot have been widespread), but at home neither the epidemic nor the rebellion stopped soon. As noted earlier, Dionysius of Syracuse was encouraged to renew war in 368 because he judged Carthage weakened by both.

How this episode ended is entirely ignored in our surviving sources. All that can be said is that fifty years later, Agathocles counted on Libyans' resentment of Punic rule to help his invasion. We may surmise that the Carthaginians had begun to pressure their subjects again before 378 with heavier taxes (or new ones), more requisitions and forced levies – for instance, to make up for losses inflicted on their state, economy and society by the returned plague.

After crushing them, Carthage may have used the opportunity to widen its reach further into Libya. The Trogus *Prologue* summarizing the later decades of Dionysius I's rule adds a mention of 'the campaigns which Hanno the Great [*Anno magnus*] waged in Africa': campaigns which Justin's *Epitome* omits. This was the first of two Hannos whom a few ancient writers – but not Diodorus, Polybius or Livy – called 'the Great' for reasons unclear (the other lived over 100 years later). As shown earlier, he was probably Hanno the enemy and destroyer of 'Suniatus' and afterwards the victim of his own tyrannic ambitions. A reasonable surmise is that Hanno put down the Libyan rebellion in his African campaigns and then pressed forward into regions previously free of Carthaginian interference, perhaps on the pretext that they had helped the rebels.

Some idea of the areas that Carthage controlled after the rebellion can be inferred from the Greek campaigns in inland Libya in 309–08. Agathocles seems to have advanced into the region of the middle Bagradas River, and Eumachus later on into Thugga's uplands, south of that area, and then beyond to the north coast and Hippo Regius (Anaba). Thugga and its environs, over 120km to Carthage's south-west, were populous and fertile territories, which could have attracted an ambitious and revenue-hungry Carthage half a century earlier.

Also productive and attractive were the regions to Thugga's south: the *pagus Thuscae* (so called in Roman times) around Zama Regia and Mactar, and to its east the *pagus Gunzuzi*. *Pagus*, 'rural district', was the Roman equivalent of the Punic *'rṣt, ereset*, as inscriptions show. At some date – the mid-fourth century would be a reasonable surmise again – Libya's mountainous northern regions too, the Khroumerie between the Bagradas valley and the north coast, with their valuable mines and forests, came under Carthage's dominance; and with them the fertile 'Great Plains', the Roman name for the broad lands around the upper Bagradas with Bulla Regia (near Jendouba) at their centre.[3]

The Libyan peoples remained discontented, even if Carthage's hegemony was not always as exploitative as it could be in times of stress, and even though Libyan soldiers continued to be essential to Punic armies. Agathocles had won some, maybe much, Libyan support. Yet Libyans were cautious about switching from the devil they knew to a new one, especially one ruthless and keen for plunder. The Libyan Aelymas soon turned against him, and Agathocles' Libyan allies in his final campaign, deliberately or not, managed to bring near-destruction on what was left of his army.

How the Carthaginians treated the defectors once the invasion ended is not on record. They may have made an effort to conciliate them – for a time. Libyan troops continued serving in Punic armies, and when the Romans in 256 repeated Agathocles' feat of invading Africa, no Libyans are reported changing sides, even though the new invaders, like the old, won early victories in the field and made themselves temporarily masters of the territory around Carthage. Instead, it was raiding parties from Numidia who took the opportunity to range through the Libyan countryside, inflicting even more damage (Polybius wrote) than the Romans did and driving the terrified inhabitants to seek refuge in Carthage.

The Carthaginians repaid these ravages after ridding themselves of the Romans in 255. A counter-offensive under a general named Hamilcar captured and crucified their leaders, and exacted 1,000 silver talents and 20,000 head of cattle from the offending communities. Who these were is, as usual, not specified. They may well have included the Massyli, one of eastern Numidia's major peoples, whose chief town was Cirta (Constantine) on cliffs high above the River Ampsaga (Oued Rhumel) 450km from Carthage. If so, Hamilcar's reprisals perhaps hit them more lightly than others, for a decade-and-a-half later the Massyli, though at first willing to help the new rebellion against Carthage, then had a change of heart. Without that change, the greatest of all Libyan rebellions would have brought Carthage to almost certain ruin.[4]

2. The Truceless War: origins and outbreak

Waging the First Punic War, the longest in its history, imposed stresses on Carthage greater than any in its past. The *epikrateia* was repeatedly invaded, its cities and allies were captured or – like Syracuse and Segesta – defected one after another, and after 250 BC all of it was lost except for Drepana (now a fortress as well as a harbour) and Lilybaeum; and these were under close siege. Over twenty-three years, Carthage's armies and fleets were regularly defeated in and around Sicily, and Carthage itself was placed for a time in mortal danger by the Roman invasion of 256–55. Even afterwards, Roman fleets inflicted raids on the Libyan coasts. Carthage regained strength after each disaster, but the damage in lives – to it and its subjects and allies – and to finances climbed.

The Carthaginians took various steps to cope with the financial stresses. One was to extend their territorial dominion in Libya still further, a drive led by a new general named Hanno. In a few later sources, including Appian, he is given the nickname 'the Great'; the reason is unknown, but it recalls the fourth-century Hanno 'the Great' who may perhaps have been an ancestor. In the mid-240s, Hanno captured Theveste, an independent city (given a Greek name, Hecatompylus, by Polybius and Diodorus; today Tébessa in Algeria) in fertile high country 300km south-west of Carthage. He treated the city kindly and his soldiers, Diodorus reported, were lavishly entertained by the residents. Even so, he required supposedly 3,000 hostages from the city, a figure so large it may be a copyist's error for 300. The region now came under Carthage's dominance. So too, if not earlier, did the broad plains and uplands further north-east around Sicca (El Kef), 190km west of Carthage. This territory was also under its control by 241.[5]

However amiably Hanno treated Theveste, we need not doubt that this and similarly acquired areas came under the same vassal-regimen as coastal and central Libya: paying tribute, produce and levies to Carthage. As the war wore on, this regimen worsened. Polybius' description of its ruthlessness is vivid. Libyan farmers were forced to hand over half of each year's produce, money taxes on townsmen were doubled and defaulters – even local aristocrats – were arrested. Of the various officials responsible for extracting Libyan goods and money, the most successful, lauded and therefore politically powerful was Hanno.[6]

A third, even more risky war measure was to pare back the war-effort. After two disastrous naval defeats in 249, the Romans gave up operations at sea entirely, to concentrate on besieging Lilybaeum and Drepana. This – extraordinarily for Carthage of all states – encouraged their opponents to leave the sea too. The victorious commanders of 249 retired or were dropped, the navy's warships – the large and costly quinqueremes that all Mediterranean naval powers now used as capital ships – were mostly laid up in dock and all energy went into sustaining the besieged port cities and keeping a small field army in being.

The general entrusted with this severely restricted, essentially defensive strategy was a new Hamilcar (not, it seems, the one who had chastised the Numidians after 255). His speed, boldness and enterprise as a general would earn him the nickname 'Barca' – in Phoenician-Punic *baraq*, 'thunderbolt' – but over six years in command, from 247–41, he could do nothing beyond sending ships to raid the Italian coasts and using his army to harass the Romans from improvised mountain strongholds. His first was near Panormus, his second in the deserted town of Eryx, where he was jammed between the Romans besieging Drepana below him and a body of Gallic deserters in Roman pay on the height above. In the final few years down to 241, Hamilcar and his second-in-command Gisco could not even pay their men. The home authorities, despite the revenues and supplies wrung from Libya and from Hanno's conquests, failed to send any money and left it to Hamilcar to promise the troops that all would be well in time.[7]

Then the war abruptly ended. A newly built Roman fleet arrived in Sicilian waters during the summer of 242, cutting off all supply to Lilybaeum and Drepana. The Carthaginians could not build a new fleet in time. It was the old fleet, laden with supplies and soldiers for the besieged ports, that sailed out in March 241, to be intercepted in rough weather and shattered on 10 March near Levanzo, one of the small island group called the Aegates (Egadi) outside Drepana. The admiral returned home to be crucified, while Hamilcar was given full powers to negotiate peace terms.

Inevitably, the terms included surrendering Carthage's last two footholds in Sicily. It was the end of the *epikrateia*, and the end of two-and-a-half centuries of wars against Syracuse – now Rome's chastened ally under the cautious King Hiero II – and the other Siceliot states. These shared, together with Sicily's native and Phoenician communities, the distinction of becoming the very first province of a nascent Roman empire: an unforeseeable outcome to what had begun in 264 as yet another insular three-way quarrel between Syracuse, Messana and Carthage.

The peace also required Carthage to pay to Rome 1,000 talents in reparations at once, and after that 220 a year for ten years; to hand back all its Roman and Italian captives; and to pay ransoms for the troops in Sicily (as though they were captives too) as well as for Carthaginian, but probably not Libyan or foreign, prisoners in Roman hands. As soon as the treaty was ratified, Hamilcar resigned his generalship in disgust, leaving Gisco to organize his army's return to Carthage.

This marked the start of fresh trouble. The army from Sicily was rather more than 20,000 strong: apart from its Carthaginian leaders, it consisted of Libyan veterans and western Mediterranean mercenaries, including many from Campania. The *sufetes* and *adirim*, wrestling with the republic's battered finances and the heavy initial reparations, put off paying the men their large arrears – several years' worth – and made it clear that Carthage was in no mind to meet any added promises that Hamilcar might have given. Another reason for hesitating may have been the army that Hanno the Great had recently commanded in Libya. It had not been disbanded (it reappears in ensuing events), must have been stationed somewhere nearby and might well expect the same benefits as any given to the veterans from Sicily – meaning added costs.

Quartered in the city, the veterans grew more and more restless and aggrieved, finally impelling the city authorities to send them well away into the countryside; in fact to Sicca, and along with them the families and goods they had left at Carthage during the war. Hanno soon arrived at Sicca to negotiate settling what they were owed, but in seeking to haggle their claims down succeeded only in exasperating them. The entire army marched back to the coast to encamp around Tunes: in other words, to set up a land blockade of Carthage as the rebels in 396 had done, then Agathocles in 310 and the invading Romans fifteen years before 241.

The present move, though, was not a war measure but a form of industrial action, putting pressure on the Carthaginians to deal with the men's claims. Now at last their employers did negotiate in earnest, this time through Gisco (Hamilcar Barca stood aloof), and this time conceding virtually everything the veterans demanded. But cracks had begun to appear among the claimants, dividing those willing to accept the terms from others who judged it more in their interest to foment an open break.

The leaders of the dissident faction were a Libyan named Mathos, a Campanian slave-runaway (so Polybius described him) called Spendius and Autaritus, the captain of a large Gallic mercenary contingent. When Gisco and his escort brought the payment money from the city to Tunes, the three dissident chiefs staged an army coup to take over command, seized the money chests and their old commander Gisco, and opened hostilities. Messengers sent out across Libya quickly stirred up a general revolt, probably over the winter of 241 and early spring 240.

The bitter war that followed lasted three years and four months, in Polybius' calculation. How far it spread is hard to estimate, as neither Polybius' fairly lengthy account of it nor the few excerpts surviving from

Diodorus mention many place names; even the chronology of events is debated. Though often termed the Mercenaries' War, it was really the last great Libyan revolt against Carthage, and was fought with such savagery by both sides that Polybius gave it a better name: the Truceless War.[8]

Mathos, acknowledged as leader of the revolt, could before long add 70,000 Libyan volunteers to his original forces, enabling him to lay siege to both Utica and Hippou Acra, Carthage's loyal Phoenician sister-cities, while maintaining the blockade of Carthage. The Libyan communities donated plentiful funds too, which in turn attracted swarms of foreign traders – Italians and Romans among them – to do business with the rebel forces, no doubt supplying arms, equipment and other munitions if they could elude Carthage's naval patrols.

The Carthaginians' first response to these challenges was ineffective. Hanno took his field army, probably of no great size, to hold Utica against its besiegers, but a series of indecisive clashes in early 240 made little impact on these and none on the other rebel operations. In Carthage, though, fresh forces were being readied with citizen recruits, newly hired mercenaries and even deserters from the rebels. These were put under the command of Hamilcar Barca, re-elected general, who then sortied from the city with about 10,000 troops and seventy war elephants in the summer of 240.

Polybius viewed Hamilcar as a rival to Hanno from the start, but the events that followed suggest that in fact they collaborated in their strategies. On marching out from Carthage, Hamilcar was able to defeat two rebel divisions near the mouth of the Bagradas: one that was guarding the river-crossing from Carthage to Utica and the other, under Spendius, that had been besieging Utica but rushed south to join the battle. This victory seems to have ended the siege of Utica. Since Carthage was in no danger – partly because Mathos had taken charge of besieging Hippou Acra and partly because her own defences and maritime food supplies were safe – Hamilcar's next move was to swing westward through the Libyan hinterland, winning back some communities (we are not told which) and attacking others. Perhaps intentionally, he drew Spendius and the Gaul Autaritus in pursuit with 8,000 men. Hanno apparently remained in the neighbourhood of Utica and Carthage, perhaps pinning down the rebel forces at Tunes.

Hamilcar's strategy was risky and after a time nearly brought disaster. His pursuers finally caught up with him as he camped on a small plain surrounded by mountains, maybe in the upland country near Thugga or somewhere further east close to the Zaghouan range. Rather than attacking at once, they took their station on the mountains, to be reinforced there by a newly recruited division of Libyans (or one sent by Mathos from the coast) and a body of Numidian cavalry led by a young Massylian prince whom Polybius called Naravas. This seems to have been the only Numidian force that responded to rebel calls to join the war. Spendius' and Autaritus' likely plan was to keep Hamilcar surrounded until his men mutinied or starved. It was upended when Naravas suddenly changed sides.

Late second-century BC inscriptions in Punic from Mactar and Thugga, cities by then part of the much-expanded Numidian kingdom and governed by princes of the royal house, attest a Nrwt as an ancestor living about a century earlier. This more or less certainly was Naravas. His family had old links with Carthage, while he himself (according to Polybius) much admired Hamilcar. If so, we might ask why he had brought troops to help Hamilcar's foes. There is no obvious answer. As suggested earlier, maybe lingering resentment against the earlier Hamilcar's campaigning in Numidia had spurred the Massyli to accept the rebels' calls – or, more cynically, had made them think it an opportune moment for fresh raids – but Naravas then had a change of mind. Or perhaps he intended from the start to join Hamilcar but had to pretend the opposite en route, to avoid attack by rebel Libyans in the region.

Naravas' bold defection, vividly told by Polybius, was so crucial that the general promised on the spot to make him his son-in-law. When the frustrated rebels then came down to fight, they were totally routed: Hamilcar made skilful use of his war elephants and Naravas' cavalry proved decisive. Most of the enemy army was destroyed – 10,000 killed and 4,000 captured – though its generals escaped to rejoin Mathos. Rather than pursue them, Hamilcar enrolled the captives in his own army and with his new Numidian lieutenant continued to range through Libya, offering generous terms to repentant rebels. Hanno apparently continued to keep watch over the enemy at Tunes and to protect Utica; but Mathos' siege (or blockade) of Hippou Acra went on.

Amid all this, Carthage lost its other island territory, Sardinia. The mercenaries stationed there (the numbers are unknown) mutinied on the example of the veterans from Sicily, murdered their Carthaginian fellow-soldiers, then won over a new mercenary force that the Carthaginians sent over against them. It is noteworthy that despite being cut off from all their land revenues, the Carthaginians could yet afford to recruit and fit out new mercenaries. They had to offer attractive terms of service to secure these, even though both their finances and military fortunes were badly stressed, yet it is likely that the chief choices available were mercenaries much like the mutineers. The commander sent to Sardinia, another Hanno, probably knew his task would be perilous. He paid for it by suffering crucifixion at the hands of the mutineers, who went on to massacre all the Carthaginians they could find in the island.

Important help to Carthage, though, was coming in from overseas. Hiero of Syracuse was anxious to show that his city still counted, and so from the start he complied readily with every request sent to him – we can surmise produce, military equipment, even perhaps soldiers (though no Greek soldiers appear in accounts of the war) and money. Polybius saw this as sage calculation: to keep his own state secure, Hiero reckoned that Carthage had to survive in order to balance Rome.

By now the Romans too were ready to assist their beleaguered ex-enemies. The early rush of merchants from Italy doing business with the rebels had slowed or stopped, after the Carthaginians arrested and jailed no fewer than 500 of them. An angry protest from Rome ensured that these were quickly freed, and then the Romans responded handsomely. Remaining Carthaginian prisoners of war were released ransom-free (2,743 in all, according to two later writers), merchants were forbidden to deal with the rebels and encouraged to trade with Carthage, and other Carthaginian requests were quickly and amicably met. One may have been to suspend the yearly 220 talents in reparations. If Appian and Cassius Dio are right, Rome also suspended the peace treaty's ban against Carthage recruiting mercenaries from Italy (in effect from Campania).

Two equally important Roman acts occurred later, this time of forbearance. Sometime in 239, both Sardinia's rebel mercenaries and Carthage's sister-city Utica appealed to Rome, offering to put themselves in Rome's hands. Utica had begun to despair of Carthage's prospects against the rebels, while the mercenaries in Sardinia were coming under pressure from aroused and hostile native peoples. The Romans rejected both.[9]

3. Horrors of the Truceless War

Despite Hamilcar's (rather slow) progress inland and the help from Syracuse and Rome, Carthage's overall situation did not improve much over late 240 and into 239. The rebel blockade from Tunes held firm, Hippou Acra if not Utica stayed besieged and the rebel leaders reacted to Hamilcar's reported successes by sadistically torturing to death the Carthaginians in their hands, starting with their old commander Gisco, and promising the same to every future captured Carthaginian. Hamilcar's misguided reaction was to jettison conciliation, at any rate toward captured rebels, and borrow an unpleasant practice from the Macedonian warlords in the Greek East: he dealt with captives by having his elephants trample them to death.

Predictably enough, he soon found his operations imperilled. Polybius's narrative is thin on details, but evidently resistance hardened; perhaps some places that had previously submitted now also rebelled again. Continued conciliation might have worked better. Hamilcar grew so alarmed that he sent word to Hanno (wherever that general was) to join forces with him: and Hanno came. This might mean that Hamilcar now ranked as Hanno's superior, but even if so, Hanno's years of sole and successful command in Libya, and maybe his political standing at home, gave him a mind of his own. When the two did combine forces, a furious quarrel erupted and military operations came to a near-standstill.

The most likely reason for quarrelling – unless it was purely personal antagonism – was that Hanno and Hamilcar disagreed over how to carry on operations. One point of discord could have been whether to treat prisoners and communities humanely as before; another, whether to leave the interior of Libya behind and move directly against Tunes. Neither man was willing to give way, even though their dissension was blatantly against the interests of the republic they both served.

Those interests were going from bad to worse. The city was now relying on a major shipment of grain and other supplies from the Emporia region: the fertile lands south of Byzacium and along the coast of the Lesser Syrtis gulf as far as Lepcis. It must have been high summer, a season open to unpredictable weather; in 255 and 253, Roman fleets had been almost annihilated by summer gales off the coast of Sicily, and a supply fleet for Scipio Africanus' army outside Utica would be storm-wrecked near Cape Bon in mid-203. The same fate struck Carthage's desperately awaited provision fleet in 239.

Help came from Hiero and Rome, averting starvation at least at Carthage. By contrast, hard-pressed Utica and Hippou Acra may have missed out on both this relief and any other. They had begun to despair of both Carthage's prospects and their own: Utica, as mentioned above, had contacted Rome offering to put itself in Roman hands but had been turned down. The two cities now switched allegiance, and marked their turnaround – in Polybius' view, their betrayal – by slaughtering the 500 Carthaginian soldiers stationed in each and flinging the bodies over the walls, clearly to prove to their new friends that they could match them in brutality.[10]

The immediate effect of this defection was that the rebel leaders could concentrate their forces at Tunes, save perhaps for some left to protect the two cities. This added to the danger facing Carthage, or would have, had Mathos and his colleagues taken more imaginative measures. They did turn the blockade into a siege, which must mean trying to mount (or undermine) Carthage's walls and to prevent seaborne supplies going in. But there is no mention of rebel siege engines or warships, and their efforts got nowhere. They did send off forces inland, of unknown strength, to watch Hamilcar and Hanno, for according to Polybius that duo's dissension not only lost 'many opportunities' against the rebels but exposed the Carthaginian forces to 'many' from the enemy. Yet little seems to have happened except manoeuvres and skirmishes. Whatever small opportunities the rebels did exploit, the greater opportunity of decisively striking at the impasse-ridden Carthaginian forces was forfeited.

Things began to change once the deadlock between Hanno and Hamilcar was resolved. In unusual fashion, instead of the magistrates and senate at Carthage solving it they passed the decision to the troops. The only precedent – not a very similar one – would have been in 381 or 380, when the defeated Punic army in Sicily had chosen the dead Mago's son in his place (see Chapter 6 §4). To allow the fighting men to decide who should lead them in the fighting was arguably a sound step, at least in principle, although with a risk that the vote-loser's men might desert. Probably only the Carthaginian officers and men were authorized to choose, not the mercenaries, loyalist Libyans and ex-rebel deserters serving alongside them (who may have been more numerous). The troops chose Hamilcar over his unenterprising colleague. Hanno was then replaced by a general sent from Carthage named Hannibal, who plainly acted under Hamilcar's authority.[11]

Hamilcar, Hannibal and Naravas (Polybius' narrative stresses the young Numidian's importance) followed Hamilcar's revised strategy: to cut off supplies and any reinforcements to the rebels at Tunes. To do so they 'ranged over the countryside', which suggests that their forces acted in two divisions – or less probably in three – around the routes to Tunes and its neighbourhood. With Tunes edged on its inland side by hills, valleys and the Sebhket Sijoumi salt lake, firmly blockading the rebels' position was feasible. If based, for instance, at the little town of Thuburbo Minus (Tébourba) 35km to the west on the lower Bagradas, troops could block access from that region and the Khroumerie mountains. Another force, at

Uthina for example or between Uthina and the coast south of Tunes, would make it painful for enemies to move up from Byzacium or southern districts like the *pagus Gunzuzi*.

The rebels besieging Carthage thus started to suffer more than the besieged. It is likely that these events lasted some months, from summer 239 to early in the next year – two-and-a-half years into the 'truceless war' – with winter weather making it still harder to maintain food supply. Even so, over these months a number of fresh recruits may still have got past Hamilcar's patrols, for when another rebel sortie occurred its generals were Spendius, Autaritus and with them 'Zarzas the Libyan, leading the men under his command'. Not mentioned previously, Zarzas seems to have brought in a recent contingent; he may have been a Libyan territorial 'king', like Aelymas in Agathocles' time.

This happened after Mathos and Spendius, the rebel chiefs, decided to give up the siege of Carthage and instead launch the sortie. Just what giving up the siege meant, in practice, is not clear. Mathos and much of the army stayed at Tunes, so raising the siege apparently meant just to pull back from Carthage's walls. Then Spendius and his fellow-generals led out 50,000 men (Polybius' figure) to shadow Hamilcar in the countryside. Who kept watch on Mathos, apart from the garrison of Carthage, is not mentioned, but possibly there were now enough troops in the city to make it dangerous for him to move either against its walls or to send reinforcements to the rebels in the field.

Polybius' narrative does not say, but it implies, that Hamilcar had to reunite his forces to deal with the new challenge. Instead of seeking battle, the rebels kept to high ground, as in Spendius' and Autaritus' previous sortie, because they feared his elephants and now Naravas too. As before, their strategy was to try to box him in by occupying hills and blocking passes. The Roman general Fabius Cunctator ('the delayer') would follow a similar strategy in Italy twenty years later against Hamilcar's son Hannibal. This led to 'serial actions', in Polybius' words – skirmishes, no doubt – in which Hamilcar would turn the tables and trap and destroy enemy troops, and also to large-scale combats where he ambushed or took by surprise even larger forces. Every prisoner was, as usual, thrown under his elephants.

With Polybius as uninterested in Libyan place-names as in the war's chronology, we do not know where this military duelling took place or how long it lasted. The manoeuvres and clashes between the field armies are not likely to have occurred north of the Bagradas amid the wild mountains and less populous valleys of the Khroumerie, but rather over the plains and hills between the Bagradas and the chain of heights that stretch south-west from Jebel Bou Kornine on the coast and then Zaghouan into southern Libya. The campaign must have been more ponderous than Polybius' description might suggest, if Spendius and his colleagues did have up to 50,000 men, and they even had slaves accompanying them. By its end, moreover, they had also collected an unknown number of prisoners. These imply that they had won some successes too – ignored by Polybius.

Events climaxed sometime in mid-238. Hamilcar executed an especially bold move that trapped the entire rebel army, now reduced to 40,000 troops, at a site named The Saw 'because of its similarity to the implement so called' (in Greek, *Prion*). This must have been a mountain or a ridge with a serrated crest, but where it lay is not mentioned (it has been much debated). Polybius' only extra detail is that the position was on terrain that favoured Hamilcar and not the rebels. This must mean that they were encamped on level ground beside The Saw, something they had avoided when stalking him because of his war elephants. Their retinue of slaves and prisoners might even be a clue that by this stage they were seeking to get away from fruitless collisions with him, and instead to establish themselves in a stronghold or strongholds – in upland Libya near Numidia, perhaps, or on the Byzacium coast – that would compel the Carthaginians to divide up their own resources in a war that had become a draining struggle of attrition.

Hamilcar's sudden arrival at The Saw took Spendius, Autaritus and Zarzas by surprise and they were immediately in trouble. Their camp was edged by a ditch and palisade which they had probably put up in proper military fashion – less probably, Hamilcar himself now put up these barricades and the rebels simply watched – but the ditch and palisade reinforced the trap. The rebels dared not try to break out while the elephants and Naravas' cavalry kept guard, yet the mountain ridge clearly offered no escape path either. Clearly the site was well-watered, for it was not thirst but hunger that wore the men down. Watched by the implacable Carthaginians, they hung on in the despairing hope that Mathos would come and rescue them. Once food ran out, after several days or some weeks, the camp sank into scenes of horror. The starving men slaughtered first their prisoners, then their own slaves, and ate them.

In the end, and inevitably, they capitulated. The three generals and their seven senior officers were allowed to see Hamilcar for terms. These were surprisingly, and suspiciously, moderate: he would choose ten men from their army and let the rest go unarmed. As soon as Spendius and the others assented, Hamilcar declared that they were the chosen, a piece of semi-chicanery, yet one that the rebel leaders surely realized was the point of the proviso. According to Polybius, their troops, learning of the ten's arrest, suspected betrayal and 'rushed to arms', then Hamilcar fell on them with all his forces and slaughtered the entire army. This was betrayal indeed by the Carthaginian general (not that Polybius would admit it), who made no effort to let the rebel rank and file know what had been agreed but did make ruthless use of their alarm and confusion. Now all that remained was to deal with Mathos.[12]

4. Carthage's victory

Dealing with Mathos proved harder than Hamilcar and Carthage probably foresaw. Nor did Hamilcar handle the task skilfully. After winning, or forcing, obedience from 'most of the cities' in Libya, he marched for Tunes in September or October 238. There he divided his army, sending Hannibal around to the heights on Tunes' northern side – the area of the Parc du Belvédère most likely – while taking station himself to the south of the town, probably on and around the hill of today's Cimetière du Djellaz (as Adherbal seemingly did against Agathocles in 307). Both positions looked down on Tunes and the sea. There was no question of offering terms. Instead, Hamilcar had Spendius and the other arrested chiefs crucified outside Tunes' northern fortifications: their death agonies were in plain view of their comrades.

The flaw in this blockade of Tunes was that the blockaders' positions were not just 8km apart but had a watchful and wrathful Mathos in between. Within a day or two he struck at Hannibal, whose camp was less strictly organized than Hamilcar's. The camp was overrun, many of its occupants killed or captured, and the rest fled. The captives included Hannibal himself. In a grisly tribute to Spendius, Mathos had the Carthaginian general viciously tortured beneath the dead rebel's cross, then nailed him alive to it in Spendius' place. Around the dead chief's corpse, Mathos executed thirty 'highly distinguished' Carthaginian prisoners, some or all probably taken in the attack.[13]

Hamilcar could not intervene in time. Bereft of up to half his forces, he abandoned his own position to march hurriedly first west and then north, skirting Tunes and the line of hills beyond until he reached the mouth of the Bagradas 20–30km away. The troops who had fled from Hannibal's camp may have rallied to him (they could not look for mercy from the rebels), but, more importantly, Mathos failed to give chase.

This gave the *adirim* and magistrates in Carthage a crucial opportunity. They appointed a thirty-man commission of senators to go out to Hamilcar, taking with them Hanno the Great and all remaining citizens available to bear arms, with the task of convincing the two men to co-operate once more.

Polybius, over-anxious to end the story, cut its remaining details to a minimum. We are not told the new soldiers' numbers or the commissioners' arguments and pleas. But success on every score followed. From now on Hanno and Hamilcar collaborated fully, with Hanno perhaps commanding the city troops but co-ordinating all tactics with his colleague. Nor is the immediate aftermath of their reconciliation properly reported. Very abruptly, Mathos is next found operating in Byzacium around Leptis (today's Lamta). This means that not only did he evacuate Tunes, but the remaining troops were able to march no less than 200km cross-country, seemingly in good order and with minimal harassment. Polybius' source or sources must have given at least an outline of how it happened, but he chose silence.

Around Leptis and 'some of the other cities' (another vague phrase) there followed a series of clashes – all of them defeats for Mathos – until both sides resolved on a final battle. Both 'called all their allies to the battle and gathered together the garrisons from the cities'. The only rebel-held cities still likely in rebel hands were Hippou Acra and Utica, but how the rebel garrisons there could manage to find their way past Carthage down to Byzacium is not at all obvious. Maybe some of the Libyan centres in and near Byzacium were also still in revolt and these counted as Mathos' last remaining allies. Any others are hard to surmise, unless Mathos had contacts among some Numidian peoples (Naravas' Massyli were only one of many) and hoped for unlikely help; Carthage did make war on supposedly rebel Numidians a couple of years later. The 'allies' called in by Hamilcar and Hanno might be Naravas and his cavalrymen, if they had been active elsewhere (Naravas no longer earns mention in Polybius after The Saw), but again this is a guess. Polybius' summary phrasing might actually be nothing more than a literary cliché to bring on the conflict's final and decisive battle, which is then summarized in equally conventional terms.

The battle, fought around the turn of the year 238–37, destroyed most of the remaining rebel army. Its survivors fled 'to a certain city' and soon surrendered, but Mathos was taken prisoner in the fighting. Hamilcar and Hanno left him at Carthage while they marched, one against Hippou Acra and the other against Utica. The two cities quickly capitulated. After three years and four months, the Truceless War was over.[14]

What terms were given to Utica and Hippou Acra we are again not told. On a reasonable surmise, the leaders (and other members?) of the pro-rebel faction in each city were put to death but the rest of the population was spared. Relatively mild treatment is suggested by the fact that, three decades later, neither city chose to defect to the invading Romans and Utica put up with a long siege by Scipio's army rather than give in.

Similarly calculated mildness was probably shown to most Libyans as well, now that peace had returned. Like the Libyphoenicians on the coast, they too stayed loyal during the sixteen years of Hannibal's War – even when Scipio roamed their land with fire and sword – and the core of Hannibal's invasion army in Italy was made up of his Libyan troops as well as their Iberian comrades. Indeed, even in the last years of Carthage a century later, the city, though besieged and blockaded by a new generation of vengeful Romans, could still count on some Libyan cities and peoples nearly to the end. Any more than usually intelligent treatment of Carthage's indispensable neighbours and vassals can be credited to its new leader Hamilcar Barca, whose plans for reviving the city's prosperity and power could only benefit from a reliable African base.

Polybius' story of the Truceless War ends with a vivid and bleak tableau. At Carthage, 'the young men', probably young aristocrats or selected young soldiers, led Mathos and other captives in a celebratory procession through the city and 'inflicted every torment' upon them, no doubt until they died. It was unpleasantly like the savage treatment that the Syracusans had meted out to the Hamilcar they had captured in 309, but Hamilcar Barca needed no past precedents for cruelty.

The Carthaginians gave Hamilcar, not Hanno, the credit for victory. He was from now on the effective leader of the city and the state, even though it seems his only formal position was the generalship. An unusually hostile excerpt from Diodorus' *History*, this time not based on Polybius, depicts him as putting together a faction of 'the basest men' and using it to gain power and wealth. Diodorus' source ignored Hamilcar's Carthaginian son-in-law Hasdrubal, who in Appian appears as a popular and powerful politician. The two men were able to build a political following strong enough to make the family's dominance at home and abroad equal to the Magonid ascendancy of centuries before; especially as, again like the Magonid era, it was buttressed by military triumphs and the wealth from these. Hanno, by contrast, retreated into resentful, long-lived but futile opposition.

By the start of 237 BC, Hamilcar was already making plans for post-war Carthage to repair the ravages of the Truceless War and the loss of the Sicilian *epikrateia* and Sardinia. One immediate need was to take back Sardinia, now purged of the mutineer mercenaries by the warlike islanders themselves. An expedition began to be readied for the task, probably from the time Mathos abandoned Tunes, but it was not to be led by Hamilcar. He had a bigger project, to make Carthage the hegemon of distant, rich and populous southern Spain.

This Spanish enterprise suddenly became urgent. Out of the blue, Roman envoys arrived to denounce the preparations for the Sardinian expedition as really intended for attacking Italy. Transparently bogus though the charge was, Carthage's denials and protests merely led to further hostile allegations. Then Rome sent a declaration of war. The Carthaginians were in no condition to fight a second Roman war, or even to haggle over the new demands. They gave up all claim to Sardinia, which in due course became Rome's second province along with Corsica, and paid a second indemnity: 1,200 talents in one lump sum.

The reasons for this abrupt reversal of Rome's previously friendly attitude were and are debated. Polybius himself could not explain the act, but condemned it outright: 'all would agree that the Carthaginians were compelled against all justice, because of the opportunity, to abandon Sardinia and pay over the stated amount of money.' Modern views vary: the Romans had belatedly woken up to the attractions of Sardinia; they viewed the island as ceded to them in 241 and chose now to take it over; they held that both Carthage and the mutineer mercenaries had legally forfeited possession and so they could annex it; or they seized it because they were driven by growing expansionist ambitions, or feared that the Carthaginians would use Sardinia as a base for invading Italy (more or less the Romans' own claim at the time).

Less stressed in these theories is the new indemnity, a quite separate item, yet an indemnity larger than the down payment in 241. It suggests that the Romans sought to drain from Carthage money resources which (they thought) it might use for a new war, with a disciplined army led by Hamilcar, launched from Sardinia as well as Libya: not an attack on Italy but to recover its Sicilian *epikrateia*. Carthage and Hamilcar had quite other plans, but the Romans did not know that.[15]

5. Barcid Carthage's Spanish empire

The rape of Sardinia made the invasion of Spain yet more essential. With his veteran army, and taking with him his son-in-law Hasdrubal as deputy (*trierarchos* in Polybius) and also his 9-year-old son Hannibal (as Hannibal would recall forty years later), he landed at Gades in mid-237 to create a new *epikrateia* in southern Spain, one that would replace, on a greater scale, that lost in Sicily.

The old Phoenician colonies along the Spanish south coast, east and west of the Strait of Gibraltar, had never been under even mild Carthaginian hegemony (even if Polybius and other Greeks thought they had). Pompeius Trogus did find a tale somewhere about the Gaditanes in their early days earning aid from Carthage against hostile Spanish neighbours, then being unjustly annexed to the Punic empire: a scenario with no evidence to support it. But of course the Carthaginians traded with southern Spain and beyond from early on, and as time went by they tried to keep competitors out. For instance, their second treaty with Rome, probably made in 348, forbade Romans to 'maraud, trade, or found a city' beyond 'Mastia of the Tarseians', a town later built over by New Carthage, modern Cartagena.[16]

Southern Spain had fertile territories and abundant resources of iron, lead, silver and even gold. Hamilcar's campaigns, recorded only scantily in medieval extracts from Diodorus' later books and a few remarks in Appian and others, pitted him first against the 'Tartessians' – a traditional name for the dwellers of south-western Spain, especially those in the Río Tinto region north of Gades and the lands to its east along the lower Baetis River (the Guadalquivir) – and other peoples including 'Celts'. These must have been Celtiberians from further north, enlisted as mercenaries by the southerners or themselves alarmed enough by Hamilcar to join in fighting him. The combined forces, led by a ruler named Istolatius and his unnamed brother, much outnumbered their opponents, but were defeated. The two leaders were among those slain, but Hamilcar took 3,000 of the rest – Celtiberians most likely – into his own service, a standard technique when professional troops fought wars. He had done the same after his first victory in Libya, just as Hiero of Syracuse had hired mercenaries who surrendered Mamertine strongholds to him.[17]

His next recorded armed struggle was probably further east, in the regions along the middle Baetis, full of fortified towns and other strongpoints. The coalition ranged against him there was led by an Iberian lord named Indortes at the head of supposedly 50,000 men. Indortes' soldiers, though, were unenthusiastic or unreliable: before battle began he retreated, at least with those who were still loyal, to 'a certain hilltop'. When Hamilcar put the position under siege, Indortes and his men tried to escape by night; most were slaughtered or captured. One captive was Indortes himself, whom Hamilcar treated with practised cruelty, blinding him, inflicting further tortures and finally crucifying him. He then freed the 10,000 other captives. These acts were obviously calculated to convey a message: the Carthaginian was a fearsome foe, but would be a fair friend to the peoples of Spain.

Polybius, echoed by Diodorus, stressed that Hamilcar's progress across southern Spain combined diplomacy with warfare. Cities and peoples became allies; others who resisted were defeated and subjected. The scrappy surviving accounts mention only one allied people, the Orissi north of the upper Baetis valley and across the Sierra Morena mountains, and these only because in winter 229/28 they turned against him. Until then, though, Hamilcar's continuing success in Spain made Carthage wealthy and without doubt made Hamilcar himself and his faction wealthy too. Even Carthage's Libyan subjects, who provided most of his soldiers, may have benefited from the plunder of Spain. 'With horses, arms, men, and money he enriched all Africa,' declared his biographer Nepos.

Hamilcar also had wider concerns. Early on he had to send his son-in-law Hasdrubal home to lead forces against rebellious Numidians. Hasdrubal defeated them in a bloody battle, spent some time settling affairs in the region – those not enslaved were made to pay tribute, though this may have lapsed over time – and then went back to Spain. There, sometime in the 230s, Hamilcar founded a new city called Acra Leuce (White Fort) 'from the position of the place'. It may have been the predecessor of Alicante in south-eastern Spain, a city dominated by a grey-white citadel (though another view puts it north of the Baetis). This was Carthage's first overseas foundation since Lilybaeum 150 years before, and a sign of its commitment to the new *epikrateia* in Spain.[18]

In winter 229/28, Hamilcar was besieging a place that Diodorus' excerpt calls 'the city of Helice', when the king of the Orissi arrived with his men, ostensibly to help. The only known 'Helice' was Ilici (modern Elche, famous for the ornate bust of a fourth-century BC Iberian woman aristocrat) near Alicante; but evidence in Livy on Roman operations in southern Spain fifteen years later suggests that Diodorus' Helice – more likely a fortress on a key route – lay probably in the rugged uplands between the south-eastern coast and the upper Baetis valley to its west. Now that this coastal region, over 600km from Gades, was under control (whether or not Acra Leuce stood there), the next stage was to pacify the uplands beyond.

'Helice' cannot have been a large place; Hamilcar sent away most of his forces, including his elephants, to winter at Acra Leuce, but stayed with the rest to complete the operation. Then the Orissi turned on him. They may have feared that they were next on his list should he pacify the mountain lands. His troops were routed and his own sons Hannibal and a young Hasdrubal, and their companions, were in danger. To draw the enemy away, Hamilcar rode off along a different path. Then as his pursuers neared, he leapt on horseback into a raging river.

His son-in-law, the older Hasdrubal, was on campaign elsewhere with an elephant corps of his own (over 100, Diodorus claimed). He marched to Acra Leuce and then over the mountains into Orissan territory, killing everyone he judged responsible for Hamilcar's disaster and subduing the area. As had happened after Mago's death in Sicily in 381/80, his army – probably again meaning its Carthaginians – chose him to take command, an election confirmed at Carthage. Like his father-in-law, Hasdrubal was in practice Carthage's supreme general, though neither of them – nor Hannibal later – is termed *strategos autokrator* by our sources.

Those sources are even thinner on Hasdrubal's years as leader than on Hamilcar's, but Polybius praised him for 'intelligently and sensibly handling his authority' and for enlarging Carthage's Spanish territories 'not so much through actions of war as through his friendliness with the rulers'. Actions of war certainly occurred: early on he had an army of 50,000 foot and 6,000 horse (much of it probably inherited from Hamilcar) and by the end had enlarged it to 60,000 and 8,000 respectively, if Diodorus' figures can be trusted. There was an elephant corps numbering 200, again if Diodorus can be believed. In 224, Hasdrubal appointed his brother-in-law Hannibal to command the cavalry, a role that brought out the young man's valour, judgement and charismatic leadership, and which points to a fair amount of warfare across the growing province.

At the same time, Hasdrubal did cultivate peace and good government within Punic Spain. As one token of goodwill, he married the daughter of a regional lord. Hannibal also took a Spanish aristocrat as his wife, a lady from the wealthy city of Castulo near the upper Baetis. Hasdrubal, after his marriage, was, according to Diodorus, acclaimed *strategos autokrator* 'by the whole Iberian people': this seems a Greek interpretation of Iberians declaring personal loyalty to him, an Iberian and Gallic warrior-custom and (if it did happen) another token of goodwill.

In his eight years in Spain, Hasdrubal took Punic dominance as far north as the middle course of the River Tagus, even if the rule may have been light outside the Baetis valley and its surrounding uplands. Soon after taking control he followed his father-in-law's example by founding a new city at the Iberian town of Mastia, again on the south-east coast. He named it *Qart-hadasht* after their homeland: New Carthage, as the Romans would call it, may even have been a project of Hamilcar's which he did not live to launch. It could have been at a grand gathering to mark the foundation, or dedication, of the city that Hasdrubal received the declarations of loyalty that Diodorus rephrased into an acclamation of 'general with supreme powers'.[19]

New Carthage's defensible position, sizeable harbour, fertile countryside and nearness to rich silver mines qualified it to be the capital of the new *epikrateia*. Hasdrubal emphasized this by putting up a grandiose governor's palace on one of its four hills. The name was not a declaration of independence from his homeland, as there were other Carthages in the Mediterranean, some disguised by the equivalent Greek name Neapolis, and Polybius' term for New Carthage was *Kaine Polis*, with the same meaning. It was a proclamation to Spanish natives and the outer world that the Carthaginian state, now resting on two great capitals, had metamorphosed into a land empire on two continents.

Greek and Roman observers from the Second Punic War onwards saw this metamorphosis as a project for renewing war with Rome. Hasdrubal's and Hannibal's Roman contemporary Fabius Pictor, author of the first literary history of Rome (in Greek), claimed that Hasdrubal had made himself independent of Carthage and the war project was a megalomania of his, which he passed on to Hannibal. It was not shared by the Barcids' home city, Fabius insisted: Hannibal dragged it, unwilling, into his Roman war. Strikingly, Hamilcar Barca did not figure in his accusation. Nor, it seems, did Cato the Censor, their contemporary, blame Hamilcar; as mentioned earlier, he ranked Hamilcar with Pericles and Themistocles as statesmen, hardly a compliment to pay to an alleged bitter enemy. But before long – certainly by the time Polybius began his own *Histories* – most Greeks and Romans had come to judge Hamilcar the true author of the vengeance project, an opinion challenged only in recent times.[20]

The all but certain reality is that the Barcid leaders sought a Spanish empire to restore Carthage's prosperity and power, and in a region as far away from the Romans as physically feasible. They even let the once-great Punic navy shrink into near-insignificance: Barcid policy was territorial and military. When in 225 the Romans for their own reasons offered Hasdrubal a pact that effectively conceded him the right to expand across most of Spain, so long as he stopped at the River Ebro in the north-east, he readily agreed. The Romans, anxious about a massive looming war with the Gauls of northern Italy, wanted to be free of concern elsewhere. Once the pact was made, they paid no further attention to Spain or Hasdrubal. They changed their attitude only when Hannibal later did exactly what the Ebro pact permitted him to do.

Hasdrubal met his end in late 221 on the knife of an embittered liegeman of a Spanish lord he had executed. Hannibal was at once acclaimed general in the same way his brother-in-law had been (and Hamilcar before them): first by the army in the province, then by the citizens at Carthage. He promptly moved into war-mode, attacking and subduing a people called the Olcades who dwelt somewhere near the upper reaches of the Tagus and had wealth to be plundered. A quick success and booty would impress his troops and the citizens at home, constituencies which as a new and young leader he needed to cultivate.

In the next year, 220, he launched a more ambitious military operation, far more ambitious than any of his father's or Hasdrubal's. Crossing the middle Tagus, he marched through the lands of the powerful Carpetani, in the southern half of the Meseta Central, to make war on the Vaccaei beyond. These lived on the broad wheat-growing plains around the middle Duero River, their territory more than 300km from the middle Tagus. But their wealth, and the military renown of so daring a venture, were again what counted. Hannibal took their chief cities, Hermandica (Salamanca) and – with effort – Arbocala (Toro on the Duero), then turned for home, laden with loot.

Predictably, the aggression aroused many of the central Iberian peoples. The Carpetani, warriors escaped from Hermandica and refugee Olcades – 100,000 soldiers in all, by Polybius' no doubt exaggerated estimate – combined to attack the Carthaginian army when it reached the Tagus. Unwisely, they let Hannibal cross the river first. Like Timoleon at the Crimisus, this allowed him to strike them when their forces divided, some fording the river as he deployed on the farther bank, the rest waiting their turn to cross. His forty elephants and the cavalry made havoc of the warriors who reached his side or were still in the stream; then the whole Punic army recrossed to the northern bank to rout the rest, before marching safely back to New Carthage.

Hannibal's spectacular and profitable victories showed what he was capable of. Polybius noted that henceforth 'none of the peoples below the Ebro River ventured readily to oppose them [the Carthaginians]', except a small but prosperous east-coast city, Saguntum, which had friendly ties with Rome. As pointed out above, the pact with Hasdrubal, though technically a personal accord between him and Rome, allowed Carthaginian military power to extend to the Ebro. As Carthage's now firmly accepted leader, what Hannibal's actions might have been had a new Roman war not broken out can only be guessed. Spain between the Tagus and Duero had been shown the potential of Punic power but had not been brought under Punic hegemony; equally so the peninsula's Atlantic west beyond the Tagus, and the mountains and steep valleys of Asturias and Galicia, which (Hannibal would have been delighted to discover) were full of untouched quantities of gold. After that, the coastlands of Algeria and Morocco, one day to thrive under Roman rule, could have been a vigorous challenge for an empire-building Carthaginian leader.

Instead, when he returned with his army to New Carthage in autumn 220, he found envoys from Rome waiting to see him. They demanded, very firmly, that he respect his brother-in-law's pact and also that he not molest Saguntum, even though that city stood nearly 200km south of the Ebro. In their abrupt démarche, Hannibal saw Rome opening a new assault on Carthage's territorial possessions and its renewed prosperity. His and his countrymen's response was defiance. From now until its catastrophic annihilation three-quarters of a century later, Carthage in war and peace would focus on Rome.

Conclusion

Carthage's three centuries of non-Roman wars were fought by a state assertively self-confident but capable of prudence. The Carthaginians acted vigorously and, where diplomacy failed, by force to check what they saw as threats, from the war against the Phocaeans of Alalia to the menace of Pyrrhus. Yet for long periods they were content to practise coexistence – peaceful, friendly or wary – with neighbours: with their Libyan neighbours down to the middle of the fifth century BC, with the Greeks of Sicily after 480 until 409, then again with them over several stretches of time in the fourth century and into the third.

With the notable exceptions of the aggressive Magonid offensives in 480 and 409–05, Carthage's position in Sicily was essentially to maintain the *status quo*: hold the *epikrateia*, cultivate the native Sicilians in the central regions and keep a careful watch on the Siceliot city-states whose energies – when not employed in warring on one another, their default position – often turned against it. After the fifth century and down to 264, most of the wars in the island were started by Sicily's Greeks. Dionysius the elder twice did so, in 398 and then in his old age in 368. The most calamitous of all Carthage's Sicilian wars was launched by the opportunist *par excellence* Agathocles in 311. He in his old age, too, was preparing another clash when he died.

The wars the Carthaginians started were fewer. In 383 it was Dionysius' attempts to subvert the *epikrateia* that brought them to act pre-emptively. Later, the allure of capitalizing on Siceliot dissensions so as to widen their island hegemony did prompt them into fresh wars: in 344 after the Greeks had spent a decade on self-inflicted strife and upheaval, and again sixty-five years later after the Greeks had devoted another decade to even more vicious infighting. These wars were preceded by years in which the Carthaginians kept aloof from Greek turmoils. Before Agathocles' aggression against the *epikrateia* in 311 they had even spent several years, through their then general Hamilcar, mediating (with varying lack of success) between that tyrant and his enemies and victims, both domestic and external.

Plato, fretting in the 350s that Greek Sicily might be mastered by 'the Phoenicians', was lamenting the self-destructive feuds ravaging the Siceliots – not revealing contemporary Carthage's policies, ambitions or interests. In the same way, when later Greeks and Romans claimed that Rome feared Punic designs on Italy in 264, because (allegedly) Carthage was steadily expanding its power over the western Mediterranean, they were simply echoing post-war Roman justifications. Every territory Carthage held in 264 it had held since the sixth century, and in 264 it was Syracuse that was expanding; and, arguably, Rome.

It is no less significant that during most of the Sicilian wars the Carthaginians had Greek allies and friends. Hamilcar the Magonid was, wrote Herodotus, incited to wage war by Terillus, the ex-tyrant of Himera, and Rhegium's ruler Anaxilaus, not to mention by Acragas' enemy Selinus. Near the end of the same century, and in the midst of vigorous renewed conflict with Syracuse, the Carthaginians thought it politic to make a friendship treaty with Athens.

Their fourth-century friendships were particularly complicated. In 379 or 378, the Carthaginians supported exiled foes of Dionysius I in refounding Hipponium which he had razed. Timoleon found Messana allied with Carthage in 344, and so was the then-tyrant of Syracuse itself, Hicetas. Carthage rescued Messana (briefly) from Agathocles' grasp in 314, saved Acragas from him two years later and then collaborated for a few years (not very effectively) with the Syracusan exiles against him and his generals. Friendships and enmities were turned on their heads again four decades later after a new actor, the Roman Republic, set foot on the scene. The old foes Carthage, Acragas and Syracuse joined forces to chase them out, but it was too late.

Carthage's relations with the Greek world were in fact not typically warlike. Trade, diplomacy, social ties and religious borrowings were plentiful. Hamilcar the Magonid was not the sole Carthaginian to enjoy guest-friendships with Sicilian and Italian Greeks – 'Synalus', the general in Sicily and friend of Syracuse's reformer Dion, was another. Nor was Hamilcar the sole citizen to have a Greek parent. Arcesilaus, the one-time friend of Agathocles and then the slayer of his son, stayed on in Carthage and it seems took a Carthaginian wife. Nearly a century later, their grandsons Hippocrates and Epicydes – at once Carthaginians and Syracusans – served with Hannibal in Italy and then were sent by him to play a decisive role in the affairs of Syracuse and Sicily during the Second Punic War.

Conclusion   189

There were in fact always Greeks at Carthage, coming as merchants or even living in the city. So when it became necessary to appease Demeter and Kore in 396 because of the plague that Himilco's men had brought back, the authorities appointed 'the most distinguished Greeks residing among them' to assist in the new rites. Carthaginians in turn travelled and lived overseas. In 398, the Syracusans enthusiastically approved Dionysius' proposal for a new war and then went on to loot 'Phoenician' possessions in the city and vessels in the harbour, 'for many Carthaginians resided in Syracuse and owned property'. The same things (and worse) happened to Carthaginians in other Siceliot cities. All this came less than a decade since the previous war had ended. Paradoxically, the events show how Carthaginians and Greeks could coexist and interact when they were not in arms against each other or incited to arms by ambitious dynasts.

In the other Mediterranean islands and in Africa, too, Carthaginians' outreach was relatively limited. They were satisfied with ruling Sardinia's productive south-west and a few other centres, leaving the mountainous rest to the natives. Corsica had one or two outposts for trade purposes, and the small seaports dotting the lengthy coastlands of Numidia and eastern Mauretania did the same service. These places never formed bridgeheads for expansion. Carthage's Libyan territories, even at their broadest in the later third century, were fairly compact – about the size of Sicily – but gave it the revenues and manpower which made its overseas ventures possible. When the Barcid generals began a new expansionist programme in the 230s and 220s, it was in distant Spain and driven partly by their city's anxieties about Rome.

The Carthaginians' successes in their non-Roman wars were substantial yet limited. They controlled wide sea and land dominions and held them against powerful challengers. Their greatest success was the Magonid-led Sicilian war of 409–05, which brought them hegemony over most of the island for some years. Afterwards, by contrast, successes were short-lived and every conflict ended with Carthaginian rule limited again to Sicily's western third.

Carthage had more lasting success in Africa, where for centuries it faced only disunited peoples, small kingdoms and chiefdoms; only after 201 did Masinissa's unified Numidia became a danger. The Carthaginians put down every Libyan rebellion, and were expanding their hegemony inland as late as the 240s despite their ongoing war with Rome. Similarly, but on a scale dwarfing the advances in Libya, a vigorous expansionist policy after the Truceless War was put into action in Spain. Spectacular victories and conquests were won; by 219, three-quarters of the country was under Carthage's control or influence. Had its new leader Hannibal avoided a new clash with Rome, all Spain might have been brought under Carthaginian hegemony in a few more years. The effects of that would have changed Mediterranean history.

Carthage might have fared better in its non-Roman wars had most Carthaginian generals been rather better. From Malchus onward they were usually competent, but few were outstanding – perhaps only the reformer Mago who followed Malchus, his namesake the long-serving commander in Sicily from 396–83 and Hamilcar Barca. A few proved hopeless or culpable (or both), like Himilco the Magonid, whose hapless siege of Syracuse ended in plague and flight in 396, and the Mago who fifty years later left his ally Hicetas in Syracuse in the lurch when Timoleon's small army neared, not to mention the coup-maker Bomilcar's feebleness or treachery in confrontation with the invader Agathocles. Well-prepared expeditions often met disaster too: Hamilcar's in 480 partly thanks to his negligence, those in 406 and 396 due to plague, the expedition of 342 through simple tactical mismanagement at the Crimisus, and Hamilcar's attempted surprise of Syracuse in 309, which turned into a Syracusan surprise of him.

It is certainly remarkable that the Carthaginian elite, which so far as we know always monopolized the military and naval high commands, were largely amateurish in military and naval operations. One reason may be that, compared to Roman aristocratic leaders in the same centuries, they were indeed amateurs. The Roman Republic was more often at war than at peace (a twelve-year gap in its mid-second-century wars greatly worried its leaders, according to their contemporary Polybius). On all the evidence, Carthage enjoyed – presumably the right word – long periods of peace at home and abroad. Worth notice is how, even though some forces (mainly local) seem to have been always available in the *epikrateia*, every time it undertook a major Sicilian war it had to organize suitable armaments in Africa and send them over. In 397 this gave Dionysius a head start, in 311 – and despite all his provocations – Agathocles.

Particular families might have lengthy traditions of leadership in war, like the Magonids and later the Barcids, but that was not the same as generations of aristocrats undergoing sustained practice in warfare. We may note that when the Romans invaded Africa in 256–55, the Carthaginians – despite putting three generals into the field, all of whom failed – finally overcame the enemy by appointing a Spartan mercenary officer, Xanthippus, as effective commander-in-chief.

The non-Roman wars were fought very largely on land. The conflict that climaxed at Alalia around 540 was in fact the only primarily naval one until the First Punic War. Operations in Libya, Sardinia and Spain were purely on land (the Barcids even allowed the Punic navy to dwindle). Although fleets are recorded acting independently from time to time – for instance fighting the Syracusan navy in 396 and 368, deterring Agathocles from Acragas in 311 and rather futilely blockading Syracuse's harbours every so often – they chiefly functioned to support land operations, like the expedition in 480 and most of the later wars with Syracuse. Combined operations, with naval and land forces acting together against an objective, are not often heard of. There was one in 396 to recapture Motya, another in 344 to help Hicetas against Timoleon and later the great combined sieges of Syracuse in 310–09 and 278. Every one of them failed, sometimes miserably.

Carthage's prowess at sea was in fact less accomplished than usually assumed by either ancients or moderns. For lengthy periods, it did not fight naval wars even if it kept up naval patrols around Libya's coasts. The potential naval operations along Italy's coasts which its two early treaties with Rome envisaged were, it seems, theoretical: none is recorded in practice. Although Greeks and Romans did tend to view Carthage – retrospectively – as the western Mediterranean's great naval power, when wars came its fleets seldom had unmatched superiority over their rivals. Nor did a sea battle decide any of its non-Roman wars, unlike the Battle of the Aegates in 241 which lost it the first war against Rome and, with it, western Sicily.

Alalia, Carthage's first recorded naval battle, was actually a defeat, if with a silver lining. In its wars with Syracuse, naval honours were more or less even. In 397, for instance, a lightning raid by ten ships on Syracuse's harbours did plenty of damage to merchant shipping. But when the main fleet tried soon after to prevent Dionysius from assailing Motya, it was driven away: not by battle but by archers and shore-based artillery. A year later, the fleet first defeated Dionysius' fleet off Catana, then was obliterated by a counterblow a few weeks later at Syracuse.

Carelessness or miscalculation continued to be costly at sea. In August 310, while the Punic fleet was blockading Syracuse (or trying to), Agathocles managed to sail away to Africa. He came back three years later to smash the small flotilla that was still hopefully patrolling; and smashed it so thoroughly that the Carthaginians gave up any further effort at blockade and were soon ready for peace. Thirty years later, their attempts to interfere with Pyrrhus by sea were even feebler. Despite the squadron sent to hold the Strait of Messina against him, he crossed from Italy without trouble. Carthage's admiral had also begun a new blockade of Syracuse with 100 warships, yet could deploy only seventy by the time Pyrrhus neared (the rest were away 'on some necessary tasks', Diodorus vaguely explained). Discouraged, both this fleet and the Punic army on land left the scene. It was not much compensation that on the king's inglorious return trip to Italy in 276, a Carthaginian fleet mauled (or according to Appian, virtually destroyed) his.[1]

In warfare and strategy, Carthage's enduring priority was operations by armies on land. Not one known military or political leader was a merchant, and only one, or maybe two, were seafarers: Hanno of the *Periplus* and (if he was a leader) the Himilco who in the same period voyaged to the Cassiterides islands. The ruling elite were landed grandees, like the fourth-century's Hanno the Great with his country estate and supposed 20,000 slaves, or Hannibal the Barcid, who owned a wealthy country estate in Byzacium. No surprise either that the lengthiest known work by a Carthaginian author was Mago's famous twenty-eight-book encyclopedia on estate mangement; and Mago was a retired general.[2]

Even the greatest Carthaginian aristocrats no doubt had commercial and financial interests, investments and intermediaries through whom they could sell their estates' produce and put their funds to use. They probably had kinsmen who were merchants and seafarers themselves. Nonetheless, when from time to time they went to war, land warfare and leadership took prime place. The supreme command in major campaigns was held by the general of the army, the *rab mahanet*, and the admiral (in Greek the *trierarchos*) was always his deputy. With greater emphasis on warfare at sea, Carthage might have enjoyed greater success in its 'other' wars: it might even have faced the Romans in 264 BC as ruler of all Sicily. That too would have changed history.

Abbreviations and Reading List

Abbreviations et al

CAH^2: *The Cambridge Ancient History*, 2nd edition (Cambridge: Cambridge University Press)

cf.: (*confer*, Latin) compare

DCPP: *Dictionnaire des Civilisations Phénicienne et Punique*, ed. E. Lipiski *et al.* (Tournai: Brepols, 1992)

FGrH: F. Jacoby, *Die Fragmente der Griechischen Historiker*: revised edn, *Brill's New Jacoby*, ed. I. Worthington (Leiden: Brill, 2007 [ongoing])

ed(s)., edn: editor(s), edited (by), edition

HAAN: S. Gsell, *Histoire Ancienne de l'Afrique du Nord*, 8 vols (Paris: Hachette, 1913–28)

NH = Pliny the Elder, *Natural History*

NP = *Brill's New Pauly*, ed. Hubert Cancik *et al.* (Leiden: Brill, 1996, and updates via Brill Reference Online)

OCD^4: *The Oxford Classical Dictionary*, 4th edn, ed. S. Hornblower and A. Spawforth (Oxford: Oxford University Press, 2012)

RE: *Real-Encyclopädie der Klassischen Altertumswissenschaft*, ed. G. Pauly and P. Wissowa *et al.*

SEG^3 = *Supplementum Epigraphicum Graecum*, 3rd edn, ed. W. Dittenberger (Leipzig: 1915)

StV 2 = H. Bengtson, *Staatsverträge des Altertums* 2 (see below)

StV 3 = Schmitt, *Staatsverträge des Altertums* 3 (see below)

s.v.: *sub verbo*; under the entry (in encyclopaedia)

tr.: translated (by), translation, translator

UP: University Press

vol.: volume

Reading List

Ameling, W., *Karthago. Studien zu Militär, Staat und Gesellschaft* (München: C.H. Beck, 1993)

Ameling, W., 'The rise of Carthage to 264', Chapter 3, in Hoyos (2011), pp.39–57
Ameling, W., 'Carthage', in P.F. Bang and W. Scheidel (eds), *The Oxford Handbook of the State in the Ancient Near East and Mediterranean* (Oxford: Oxford UP, 2013), pp.361–83
Asheri, D., 'Carthaginians and Greeks', Chapter 9, in CAH^2 vol.4, ed. J. Boardman *et al.*, *Persia, Greece and the Western Mediterranean, c.525–479 BC* (1988), pp.739–90
Aubet, M.E., *The Phoenicians and the West: Politics, Colonies, and Trade*, 2nd edn, tr. Mary Turton (Cambridge: Cambridge UP, 2001)
Aubet, M.E., *Tiro y las Colonias fenicias del Occidente*, 3rd edn (Barcelona: Ediciones Bellaterra, 2009)
Bengtson, H. (ed.), *Die Staatsverträge des Altertums: Die Verträge der griechisch-römischen Welt von 700 bis 338 v. Chr.*, vol.2. 2nd edn (München: C.H. Beck, 1975)
Bickerman, E.J., *Chronology of the Ancient World* (London: Thames and Hudson, 1968)
Bicknell, P.J., 'The date of Timoleon's crossing to Italy and the comet of 361 BC', *Classical Quarterly* 34 (1984), 130–34
Caven, B., *Dionysius I: War-lord of Sicily* (New Haven and London: Yale UP, 1990)
Champion, J., *The Tyrants of Syracuse: War in Ancient Sicily*, vol.1, *480–367 BC* (Barnsley: Pen & Sword, 2010)
Champion, J., *The Tyrants of Syracuse: War in Ancient Sicily*, vol.2, *367–211 BC* (Barnsley: Pen & Sword, 2012)
Compernolle, R. van., 'La clause territoriale du traité de 306/5 conclu entre Agathokles de Syracuse et Carthage', *Revue belge de philologie et d'histoire* 32 (1954), 395–421
Consolo Langher, S.N., [1992a] 'Agatocle in Africa. Aree operative e implicazioni politiche fino alla pace del 306 a.C.', *Messana* 13 (1992), 19–77
Consolo Langher, S.N., [1992b] z'Eknomos e la valle dell'Himera nelle vicende storiche tra VII e IV secolo a.C. fino ad Agatocle', *Archivio Storico Messinese* 60 [Messina, Italy] (1992), 5–56
Consolo Langher, S.N., 'Greci e indigeni nella *Libye*: le spedizioni di Eumaco a nord-ovest di Cartagine', in M. Khanoussi *et al.* (eds), *L'Africa Romana* 15, 3 vols, (Roma: Carocci Editore, 2004), vol.1, pp.343–54
Cornell, T.J., *The Beginnings of Rome: Italy and Rome from the Bronze Age to the Punic Wars (c.1000–264 BC)* (London and New York: Routledge, 1995)

Culican, W., 'Phoenicia and Phoenician colonization', chapter 32, in *CAH*² vol.3, part 2 (1992), pp.461–546

Curry, A., 'The weapon that changed history', *Archaeology* 65 (2012), 32–37

De Angelis, F., *Archaic and Classical Greek Sicily: a Social and Economic History* (Oxford: OUP, 2016)

De Sensi Sestito, G., *Gerone II: un Monarca ellenistico in Sicilia* (Palermo: Editrice Sophia, 1977)

De Souza, P., 'Naval forces', in N. Sekunda and P. De Souza, chapter 11 ('Military forces'), in *The Cambridge History of Greek and Roman Warfare*, ed. P. Sabin *et al.* (Cambridge: CUP, 2007), vol.1, 325–67

De Vido, S., 'La Sicilia nel IV secolo: dai Dionisi a Agatocle', in *Storia d'Europa e del Mediterraneo. IV. Grecia e Mediterraneo. Dall'età delle guerre Persiane all'Ellenismo*, ed. M. Giangiulio (Roma: 2008), pp.337–70

De Vido, S., *Le Guerre di Sicilia* (Roma: Carocci Editore, 2014)

Devillers, O. and Krings, V., 'Carthage et la Sardaigne. Le livre XIX des *Histoires philippiques* de Justin', *L'Africa Romana* 12 (1998), 1,263–77

DeVincenzo, S., 'Zwischen Griechen und Karthagern. Beitrag zur punischen Identität Selinunts im Kontext der Expansionspolitik Karthagos auf Sizilien', *Mediterraneo Antico* 17.1 (2014), 235–68

Dittenberger, W., *Sylloge Inscriptionum Graecarum*, 3rd edn (Leipzig: 1915)

Docter, R.F.; Niemeyer, H.G. *et al.*, 'Radiocarbon dates of animal bones in the earliest levels of Carthage', in *Oriente e Occidente: metodi e discipline a confronto* (Pisa: Istituti Editorial e Poligrafici Internazionali, 2005), 557–75

Dommelen, P. van., *On Colonial Grounds: a Comparative Study of Colonialism and Rural Settlement in First Millennium BC West Central Sardinia* (Leiden: Faculty of Archaeology, University of Leiden, 1998)

D'Oriano, R. and Sanciu, A., 'Phoenician and Punic Sardinia and the Etruscans', in Turfa (2013), 231–43

Fantasia, U., 'Entella, Etna, Galaria. Greci e non Greci in Sicilia fra Dionisio I e Timoleonte', in *Quarte Giornate Internazionali di Studi sull'Area Elima (Erice, 1–4 dicembre 2000)*, ed. A. Corretti (Pisa: Scuola Normale di Pisa, 2003), 467–95

Fornara, C.W., ed. and tr., *Archaic Times to the End of the Peloponnesian War* (Translated Documents of Greece and Rome, vol.1, 2nd edn) (Cambridge: Cambridge UP, 1983)

Gass, E., 'Syntaktische Notizen zur Inschrift eines in Karthago gefundenen Goldmedaillons (KAI 73)', *Die Welt des Orients* 34 (2004), 54–63

Geus, K., *Prosopographie der literarisch bezeugten Karthager* (Orientalia Lovanensia Analecta, Studia Phoenicia 13) (Leuven: Peeters, 1994)

Gozalbes Cravioto, E., 'Los inicios del ejercito cartaginés (siglo VI a.C.)', *Aquila Legionis: Cuadernos de Estudios sobre el Ejército Romano* [Salamanca] 20 (2017), 9–30

Gran-Aymerich, J., 'Etruria marittima: Massalia and Gaul, Carthage and Iberia', in Turfa (2013), 319–48

Gsell, S., *Histoire ancienne de l'Afrique du nord*, 8 vols (Paris: Hachette, 1914–24)

Günther, L.M., 'Die karthagische Aristokratie und ihre Überseepolitik im 6. und 5. Jh. v. Chr.', *KLIO* 75 (1993), 76–84 (shorter version: 'L'aristocratie des grands négociants à Carthage et sa politique d'outre-mer aux VIe et Ve siècles av. J.-C.', in *Actes du III Congrès international des Études phéniciennes et puniques*, ed. M.H. Fantar and M. Ghaki [Tunis: 1995], vol.1, 128–32

Günther, L.M., 'Timoleons "Kolonisationsprogramm" und die massenhaften Einbürgerungen im spätklassischen Sizilien', in Günther, L.M. (ed.), *Migration und Bürgerrecht in der hellenistischen Welt* (Wiesbaden: 2012), 9–19

Hammond, N.G.L., *A History of Greece to 322 BC* (Oxford: Clarendon Press, 1986 [first edn, 1959])

Hammond, N.G.L., 'The expedition of Xerxes', in *CAH* 4[2] (1988), 518–91

Harris, W.V., *War and Imperialism in the Roman Republic, 327–70 BC* (Oxford: OUP, 1979)

Hoyos, B.D., 'The rise of Hiero II: chronology and campaigns 275–264 BC', *Antichthon* 19 (1985), 32–56

Hoyos, B.D., *Unplanned Wars: the Origins of the First and Second Punic Wars* (Berlin and New York: W. de Gruyter, 1998)

Hoyos, D., 'Towards a chronology of the "Truceless War", 241–237 BC', *Rheinisches Museum für Philologie* 143 (2000), 369–80

Hoyos, D., 'Hannibal's Olcades', *Habis* (Universidad de Sevilla) 33 (2002), 131–40

Hoyos, D., *Hannibal's Dynasty: Power and Politics in the Western Mediterranean 247–183 BC* (London: Routledge, 2003)

Hoyos, D., *Truceless War: Carthage's Fight for Survival, 241 to 237 BC* (Leiden and Boston: Brill, 2007)

Hoyos, D., *The Carthaginians* (Peoples of the Ancient World) (London and New York: Routledge, 2010)

Hoyos, D. (ed.), *A Companion to the Punic Wars* (Malden and Oxford: Wiley-Blackwell, 2011)

Hoyos, D., *Mastering the West: Rome and Carthage at War* (Oxford: OUP, 2015)
Huss, W., *Geschichte der Karthager* (München: C.H. Beck, 1985)
Kaufman, B., 'Political economy of Carthage', in *Bridging Times and Spaces*, ed. P.S. Avetisyan and Y.H. Grekyan (Oxford: Archaeopress, 2017)
Krahmalkov, C.R., 'The foundation of Carthage, 814 BC. The Douïmès pendant inscription', *Journal of Semitic Studies* 26 (1981), 177–91
Krahmalkov, C.R., *Phoenician-Punic Dictionary* (Leeuven: Peeters, 2000)
Krings, V. (ed.), *La Civilisation phénicienne et punique: Manuel de recherche* (Leiden: Brill, 1995)
Krings, V., *Carthage et les Grecs, c.580–480 av. J.-C.: textes et histoire* (Brill: Leiden, 1998)
Lancel, S., *Carthage: a History*, tr. by A. Nevill (London: Batsford, 1995). Original edition: Lancel, S., *Carthage* (Paris: Fayard, 1992)
Lazenby, J.F., *The First Punic War: a Military History* (London: UCL Press, 1996)
Lewis, D.M., 'Sicily, 413–368 BC', Chapter 5, in *CAH* 6^2 (1992), 120–55
Lipiński, E., et al. (eds), *Dictionnaire de la Civilisation phénicienne et punique* (Turnhout: Brepols, 1992)
Littman, R.J., 'The plague at Syracuse: 396 BC', *Mnemosyne* 37 (1984), 110–16
Loreto, L., *La Grande Insurrezione Libica contro Cartagine del 241–237 a.C.: una Storia Politica e Militare* (Rome: École française de Rome, 1995)
Loreto, L., *La Grande Strategia di Roma nell'Età della Prima Guerra Punica (ca. 273–ca. 229 a.C.): L'inizio di un paradosso* (Napoli: Jovene Editore, 2007)
Maraoui Telmini, B., Docter, R., Bechtold, B., Chelbi, F. and van de Put, W., 'Defining Punic Carthage', in Quinn and Vella (2014), 113–47
Medas, S., 'Les équipages des flottes militaires de Carthage', pp.79–106, in G. Pisano (ed.), *Phoenicians and Carthaginians in the Western Mediterranean. Studia Punica* 12 (Roma: Università degli Studi di Roma 'Tor Vergata', 1999)
Meister, K., 'Agathocles', chapter 10 in CAH^2 7, Part 1, *The Hellenistic World* (Cambridge: CUP, 1984), 384–411
Miles, R., *Carthage Must be Destroyed: the Rise and Fall of an Ancient Mediterranean Civilization* (London: Allen Lane, 2010)
Molthagen, J., 'Der Weg in den Ersten Punischen Krieg', *Chiron* 5 (1975), 89–127

Murray, W.M., *The Age of Titans: the Rise and Fall of the Great Hellenistic Navies* (Oxford: Oxford UP, 2012)

Orsingher, A., 'Understanding tophets: a short introduction', *The Ancient Near East Today*, vol.6.2 (2018), at http://www.asor.org/anetoday/2018/02/Understanding-Tophets-Short

Peters, S. (ed.), *Hannibal ad Portas: Macht und Reichtum Karthagos* (Stuttgart: Theiss Verlag, 2004)

Petschenig, M. (ed.), *Notitia Provinciarum et Civitatum Africae*, in *Corpus Scriptorum Ecclesiasticorum* vol.7 (Vienna: C. Gerold, 1881)

Picard, G.C. and Picard, C., *Daily Life in Carthage at the Time of Hannibal*, tr. A.E. Foster (London: George Allen and Unwin, 1961)

Picard, G.C. and Picard, C., *The Life and Death of Carthage* (London: Sidgwick and Jackson, 1968) [= New York: Taplinger, 1969] (cited as Picard, 1968)

Picard, G.C., 'Carthage from the battle at Himera to Agathocles' invasion (480–308 BC)', chapter 9*a* in *CAH* 6^2 (1992), 361–80

Pilkington, N., 'A note on Nora and the Nora stone', *Bulletin of the American Schools of Oriental Research*, No. 365 (2012), 45–51

Pittau, M., 'Gli Etruschi e Cartagine: i documenti epigrafici', in *L'Africa Romana: Atti dell'XI convegno di studio. Cartagine, 15–18 dicembre 1994* (ed. M. Khanoussi *et al.*) Università degli Studi di Sassari: Ozieri, 1996), 1,657–74

Quinn, J.C., 'The Syrtes between east and west', in A. Dowler and E. R. Galvin (eds), *Money, Trade and Trade Routes in Pre-Islamic North Africa* (London: The British Museum Press, 2011), 11–20

Quinn, J.C. and Vella, N.C. (eds), *The Punic Mediterranean: Identities and Identification from Phoenician Settlement to Roman Rule* (British School at Rome Studies) (Cambridge: Cambridge UP, 2014)

Raffone, L., 'Per una lettura di *P. Oxy.* XXIV 2399 sulla campagna d'Africa di Agatocle e la situazione politica di Siracusa', in *Minima Epigraphica et Papyrologica* [Università di Catanzaro 'Magna Graecia'] 4 (2001), 209–28

Reeve, C.D.C., ed. and tr., *Politics: A New Translation, with Introduction and Notes* (Indianapolis, IN: Hackett Publishing Co., 2017)

Rhodes, P.J. and Osborne, R. (eds), *Greek Historical Inscriptions, 404–323 BC* (Oxford: Oxford UP, 2004)

Richardson, J.H., 'Rome's treaties with Carthage: jigsaw or variant traditions?', in C. Deroux (ed.), *Studies in Latin Literature and Roman History* Vol. 14 (Brussels: Éditions Latomus, 2008), 84–94

Roller, D.W., *Through the Pillars of Hercules: Greco-Roman Exploration of the Atlantic* (London and New York: Routledge, 2006)

Rose, A.B., *A Case Study of Six Montefortino Helmets from the Battle of the Egadi Islands (241 BC)*, M.A. thesis (M.A. in Maritime Studies), East Carolina University. Downloaded 2/11/2017 at http://thescholarship.ecu.edu/bitstream/handle/10342/6176/ROSE-MASTERSTHESIS-2017.pdf?sequence=1

Salimbetti, A. and D'Amato, R., *The Carthaginians 6th–2nd Century BC* (Oxford and New York: Osprey, 2014)

Sanders, L.J., 'Punic politics in the fifth century BC', *Historia* 37 (1988), 72–89

Schmitt, H.H., *Die Staatsverträge des Altertums: Die Verträge der griechisch-römischen Welt von 338 bis 200 v. Chr.*, vol.3 (München: C.H. Beck, 1969)

Schmitz, P., 'The name "Agrigentum" in a Punic inscription (CIS I 5510.10)', *Journal of Near Eastern Studies* 53 (1994), 1–13

Schmitz, P., 'The Phoenician text from the Etruscan sanctuary at Pyrgi', *Journal of the American Oriental Society* 115 (1995), 559–75

Serrati, J., 'Neptune's altars: the treaties between Rome and Carthage (509–226 BC)', *Classical Quarterly* 56 (2006), 113–34

Shapiro, H.A., 'Demeter and Persephone in western Greece: migrations of myth and cult', in M.J. Bennett, A.J. Paul and B.M. White (eds), *Magna Graecia: Greek Art from South Italy and Sicily* (New York and Manchester: Cleveland Museum of Art and Hudson Hills Press, 2002), 82–97

Sjöqvist, E., 'A portrait head from Morgantina', *American Journal of Archaeology* 66 (1962), 319–22 and Plate 86

Stylianou, P.J., *A Historical Commentary on Diodorus Siculus Book 15* (Oxford: Clarendon Press, 1998)

Talbert, R.J.A.. *Timoleon and the Revival of Greek Sicily 344–317 BC* (Cambridge: Cambridge UP, 1974)

Tillyard, H.J.W., *Agathocles* (Cambridge: CUP, 1908)

Trifirò, M.S., 'La battaglia di Himera (480 a. C.) nelle interpretazioni storiografiche antiche e nelle moderne riletture di G. Grote ed E. A. Freeman', *Anabases: Traditions et réceptions d l'Antiquité* 20 (2014), 11–31 (http://journals.openedition.org/anabases/4779)

Tronchetti, C., 'Sardaigne', in Krings (1995), 712–42

Trundle, M., *Greek Mercenaries: From the Late Archaic Period to Alexander* (London and New York: Routledge, 2004)

Trundle, M., 'The Carthaginian navy: questions and assumptions', in G. Fagan and M. Trundle (eds), *New Perspectives on Ancient Warfare* (Leiden and Boston: Brill, 2010), 253–87

Turfa, J.M. (ed.), *The Etruscan World* (London and New York: Routledge, 2013)

Tusa, S. and Royal, J., 'The landscape of the naval battle at the Egadi islands (241 BC)', *Journal of Roman Archaeology* 25 (2012), 7–48

Vacanti, C., *Guerra per la Sicilia e Guerra della Sicilia. Il Ruolo delle Città Siciliane nel Primo Conflitto Romano-Punico* (Napoli: Jovene Editore, 2012)

Warmington, B.H., *Carthage* (Harmondsworth: Penguin Books, 1964)

Whittaker, C.R., 'Carthaginian imperialism in the fifth and fourth centuries', in *Imperialism in the Ancient World*, ed. by P.D.A. Garnsey and C.J. Whittaker (Cambridge: Cambridge UP, 1978), 59–90

Endnotes

Chapter 1: Sources of knowledge

1. Hanno's *Periplus*: E. Lipiński, *Itineraria Phoenicia* (Studia Phoenicia XVIII: Leuven, 2004), 435–76.
2. Greek inscriptions: Chapter 5 §3, Chapter 6 §3. Parian Marble, or Parian Chronicle: *FGrH* 239; the text with English translation is now accessible at http://www.ashmolean.museum/ash/faqs/q004/.
3. Archaeology and history of Carthage: Lancel, 1995; Hoyos, 2010; Miles, 2010.
4. Mago's farming encyclopedia: Lancel, 1995, 273–79; K. Ruffing, *NP* s.v. Mago (12).
5. 'They are bitter': Plutarch, *Moralia: Precepts of Statecraft* 799 D-E. Cato on Hamilcar Barca: Plutarch, Cato the Elder 8.

Chapter 2: Carthage: city and state

1. Timaeus in Dionysius of Halicarnassus, *Roman Antiquities* 1.74.1; other ancient datings for Rome ranged from 753–27. Carthage's foundation story: Culican, 1992, 490–95; Hoyos, 2010, 6–12; Ameling, 2011 and 2013. Yadomilk: Krahmalkov, 1981; Gass, 2004. Livy's Bitias: so Servius, in his fourth-century AD commentary on the *Aeneid*, Book 1, line 738.
2. The ceremonial bronze panoply from Ksour es-Saf near Sousse: Peters, 2004, 33.
3. Carthaginians 'the most powerful people of Europe': Diodorus 14.41.2. Delegates to Delphi: Diodorus 19.2.3 (just before the birth of Agathocles the tyrant). Hippocrates and Epicydes: Polybius 7.2.3–4; Livy 24.6.2–3.
4. Carthage's political system: Aristotle, *Politics* 2.1273a–b, 1293b, 1316a; Polybius 6.51, tr. R. Waterfield (Oxford World's Classics, 2010); Appian, *Libyca* 68.304–05; Picard, 1968, 56–61, 80–86, 143–46; Huss, 1985, 458–74; Ameling, 1993, 67–117, 155–81; Lancel, 1995, 110–20; Hoyos, 2010, 20–38; Kaufman, 2017. Magonids as kings: Diodorus 13.43.5, 14.56.5; taken literally by (e.g.) Picard, 1968, 80–86, 100–04, 125, 128;

Picard, 1992, 367–68, 370; Lancel, 1992, 111–14; Ameling, 1993, 64–97. Magonid inscription: below, Chapter 5 §3.
5. West African barter: Herodotus 4.169 (Loeb translation). Similar bartering in the same region was reported by the medieval Arabic geographer Yaqut al-Hawari, around AD 1200 (Picard, 1961, 233).
6. *Vicus Africus*: Varro, *de Lingua Latina* 5.159 – supposedly it was named from Carthaginian war-hostages, but see R.E.A. Palmer, *Rome and Carthage at Peace* (Wiesbaden, 1997), 73–79. Aristotle on states' agreements: *Politics* 1280a. 'Nobas': P. Harding (ed.), *From the End of the Peloponnesian War to the Battle of Ipsus* (Cambridge, 1985), no.48.
7. Pol. 1.71.1 (Carthage's food and goods supplies); Aristotle, *Politics* 2.1273b (citizens sent out to the cities). Hannabaal (priestess), Gry and Hannobaal: Krahmalkov, 2000, 200; Hoyos, 2010, 96, 67–68. Slaves: Justin 21.4 (Hanno's); Polybius 1.29, Zonaras 8.12 (liberated in 256 BC); Appian, Libyca 15.61 (in 204) and 9.35 (slaves purchased in Second Punic War). Population in 149: Strabo 17.3.15. Carthaginian names: Geus, 1994, is the standard guide to all those mentioned in historical and literary records.
8. On Libyphoenicians, Punic Libya: H. Ben Younès in Krings, 1995, 796–827; G. Hiesel in Peters, 2004, 60–69. Muttines: Hoyos, 2015, 163–64, 223. He and his four sons, all with Roman names, are commemorated in a later list of sponsors at Delphi: *SEG*[3], no.585 (190/89 BC).

Chapter 3: Fleets and armies

1. Carthaginian warships: Connolly, 1981, 271–72; Medas, 1999; De Souza, 2007. Aegates rams: Curry, 2012; Tusa and Royal, 2012. The total number of recovered rams, mostly Roman, is sixteen (as of August 2018).
2. Early Carthaginian armies as powerful aristocrats' private militias: Ameling, 1993, 64–75, 94–96; and 2013, 365–67; Günther, 1993. A citizen non-professional militia: Gozalbes Cravioto, 2017. Mercenaries: Polybius 6.52; Diodorus 5.38.
3. Carthaginian armies: P. Connolly, *Hannibal and the Enemies of Rome* (London, 1978), 34–47; G. Brizzi, 'L'armée et la guerre', in Krings, 1995, 303–15; A. Goldsworthy, *The Punic Wars* (London, 2000), 30–36; Hoyos, 2010, 149–63; Salimbetti and D'Amato, 2014. Goblets and drinking cups: Diodorus 13.88.3, 16.81.1.
4. The plate armour (panoply) from near Sousse: Peters, 2004, 33.

5. Daily pay for fifth-century soldier and servant: Thucydides 3.17, 7.27; Trundle, 2004, 92–95. Carthage's high rates of pay: Diodorus 14.47.3, 16.81.4. Cavalry and light-armed pay in Hellenistic Mediterranean: *Inscriptiones Graecae*² vol.4 part 1, no.68, 9.1.3; Hoyos, 2007, 28 n.4. Abandoned mercenaries: Diodorus 5.11; Zonaras 8.16 (epitomizing Cassius Dio).
6. Appian, Libyca 95.446–51; Lancel, 1995, 415–19 (slightly modifying Appian's details). The Greek 'foot' roughly matched the modern 12in (30cm) version, though there was more than one foot-measurement (e.g., F.N. Price et al., 'Measures of length (1)', *Oxford Classical Dictionary*, 4th edn [Oxford 2012]).

Chapter 4: Early wars: Malchus to 'King' Hamilcar

1. Malchus: Justin 18.7; Orosius 4.6.6–9. Varied views on him: (e.g.) Picard, 1968, 56–59; Huss, 1985, 59–60, 62–63, 71; Lancel, 1995, 111–13; Geus, 1994, 196–98; Krings, 1998, 33–92; Hoyos, 2010, 46–48, 55–57, 101–02, 124–30. Malchus-like examples include Constantine the Great invading Italy from Gaul in AD 312, the future Byzantine emperor Heraclius sailing from Carthage to Constantinople in 610 and William the Conqueror seizing England in 1066. Historical records at Carthage: Hoyos, 2010, 105–08.
2. Justin 19.1.1–5 (Carthage's rent to Libyans); Ovid, *Tristia* 3.10, *Ex Ponto* 1.2 (Tomi's barbaric neighbours).
3. Thucydides 1.13.6 (Phocaean victory c.600 BC), 6.2.5–6 (Greeks settling in Sicily push Phoenicians and others west). Greeks in western Sicily c.580: Diodorus 5.9. Phalaris at Himera: Aristotle, *Rhetoric* 2.20, 1393b. On Carthage's early power-projection, (e.g.) Asheri, 1988, 748–53; P. Barceló, 'Zur karthagischen Überseepolitik in vi. und v. Jahrhundert v. Chr.', *Gymnasium* 96 (1989), 13–37; Günther, 1993; Aubet, 2001, 226–30 (= Aubet, 2009, 241–44).
4. Malchus' defeat in Sardinia supposedly may be commemorated by a large number of sculpted stone 'giants' (originally several dozen) set up at Mont'e Prama in north-west Sardinia (Salimbetti and D'Amato, 2014, 53); this is still very much a minority view. Alalia: Herodotus 1.165–67; Krings, 1998, 93–160. Alalia is sometimes dated around 535 even though Herodotus' account points to around 540.
5. From tyranny to aristocracy at Carthage: Aristotle, *Politics* 5.1316a – but the item may be someone else's intrusion; earlier Aristotle wrote

that Carthage had never suffered tyranny (*Pol.* 2.1272b; cf. Reeve, 2017, 343, 345). Malchus' coup-story: Krings, 1998, 76–92; cf. Lancel, 1995, 111–12; Devillers and Krings, 1998 (viewing Justin 18.7.1–19.1.9 as largely Greek literary embroidery); van Dommelen, 1998, 115–25. More favourable views: Ameling, 1993, 73–80; Hoyos, 2010, 124–28.

6. Justin 19.1 (Magonids, Leonidas, Darius); Krings (1998, 184–88) sees 'Leonidas' as simply a literary emblem for Greek Sicily's wars with Carthage. Hamilcar as 'son of Hanno': Herodotus 7.165. Saphon was an epithet of the god Baal (*DCPP* 60) and may be the god whom Herodotus called Poseidon, Greece's sea-god (7.167; Huss, 1985, 522), or may be Melqart (Bonnet and Lipiński, *DCPP* 358; cf. A. Cadotte, 'Neptune africain', Phoenix 56, 2002, 330–47). Himilco: Justin 19.2.7–3.11. Human sacrifice banned: so Theophrastus claimed (c. 300 BC) according to the Scholiast (ancient commentator) on Pindar, Pythians 2.3; Plutarch (c. AD 100) credited Gelon with banning child-sacrifices (*Delays of Divine Vengeance* 6; *Sayings of Kings and Commanders*, p.175).

7. Punic-Roman treaty of 509: Polybius 3.22–23; F.W. Walbank, *A Historical Commentary on Polybius* 1 (Oxford, 1957), 337–45; Huss, 1985, 86–92; Ameling, 1993, 130–33, 141–54; Cornell, 1995, 210–15; Serrati, 2006, 113–18 (over-optimistically seeing a 'wealth' of benefits for Rome); Richardson, 2008 (doubts all the source-traditions); B. Scardigli in Hoyos, 2011, 28–38.

8. Aristotle on mutual-benefit treaties: *Politics* 3.9, 1280a, tr. Reeve, 2017. Pyrgi tablets: Cornell, 1995, 213–15; Schmitz, 1995; Pittau, 1996, 1,657–66. Flourishing sixth-century Punic-Etruscan trade: Gran-Aymerich 2013.

9. Changes at Sardinian sites c. 500 BC: Tronchetti, 1995, 728–30; P. Bernardini in Peters, 2004, 147–48; van Dommelen and Gómez Bellard, 2008, 8–9; D'Oriano and Sanciu, 2013; A. Roppa, 'Identifying Punic Sardinia', in Quinn and Vella, 2014, 257–82. Carales and Neapolis: van Dommelen, 1998, 124–25, 158 n.12.

10. Dorieus and followers in Sicily: Herodotus 5.46–48; Diodorus 4.23.3; Pausanias, *Description of Greece* 3.16.4–5.

11. Malchus' and Magonids' policies: Whittaker, 1978, 59–65, 71; Hans, 1983, 105–07; Asheri, 1988, 748–53, 770–75; Ameling, 1993, 15–65; Champion, 2010, 26–45. Carthage's Sicilian *epikrateia*: Hans, 1983, 119–53; De Vido, 2014, 144–46. *epikratein* means 'to rule' or 'dominate'. Selinus' cavalry in 480: Diodorus 11.21.4. Greek cities taxed by Carthage: 13.114.1. Theodorus' supposed speech in 396: 14.65–69;

Caven, 1990, 3, 5, 115–16; Champion, 2010, 236 n.12; DeVido, 100–01. (Note Diodorus' opinion of speeches in historical works: 20.1.1–2.2.) Officer, probably a *boetharchos*, in fourth-century *epikrateia*: Chapter 7 §1.
12. Envoys at Syracuse: Herodotus 7.157–62. Krings, 1998, 312–13, thinks the disputed ports were in Africa, but this is much less likely. Terillus and Hamilcar: 7.165. Himera and Salamis on same day: 7.166; Aristotle, Poetics 23, 1459a (whereas Diodorus 11.24.1 has it simultaneous with Thermopylae, a couple of months earlier); Trifirò, 2014. Orders from Xerxes: Diodorus 11.1.4; Scholiast on Pindar, Pythians 1.146b, citing the historian Ephorus (*FGrH* 70 F186). Ephorus may have been Diodorus' source too.
13. Hamilcar's contingents: Herodotus 7.165; Diodorus 11.1.5, 11.20.2, 13.59.5, 13.94.5. Xerxes' army: Herodotus: 7.60 and 184–85 (two million as European contingents came in); Hammond, 1988, 532–36.
14. The campaign of Himera: Herodotus 7.165–67; Diodorus 11.20–26.

Chapter 5: The Revenge of Hannibal the Magonid

1. Treaty of 480: Diodorus 11.26.2. Damarete's coinage: 11.26.3 – but the fine 'Damareteion' coins are to be dated to the 460s (e.g., H.B. Mattingly, *From Coins to History: Selected Numismatic Studies* [Ann Arbor, 2004], 2–15). Gelon's enfranchised mercenaries: 11.72.3. The 'Motya youth': J.K. Papadopoulos, 'The Motya youth: Apollo Karneios, art, and tyranny in the Greek West', *The Art Bulletin* 96:4 (2014), 395–423; favouring an idealized Gelon and suggesting that in 409 the Carthaginians looted it from Himera or Acragas. Hamilcar's cult honours: Herodotus 7.167 (though disbelieved by Geus, 1994, 39).
2. Segesta vs Selinus (?) in 454: Diodorus 11.86.2 pits Segesta against Lilybaeum, but the latter (a Carthaginian creation) did not exist before 396; the battle-site, the River Mazara just east and north of Selinus, was Selinus' border (*NP* s.v. Mazara; Hans, 1983, 10–11, 163–64). *Inscriptiones Graecae* vol.14, no.268, a damaged mid-fifth century inscription from Selinus, thanks numerous gods for a victory over unnamed foes (Fornara, 1983, no.91; Huss, 1985, 102 n.30; R. Meiggs and D. Lewis, *A Selection of Greek Historical Inscriptions to the End of the Fifth Century BC*, revised edn [Oxford, 1989], 82–83): maybe over the Selinuntines. Carthaginians and Etruscans humbled: Pindar, Pythians 1.70–80. Ducetius: Asheri, 1992, 161–65. Prosperity and magnificence of fifth-century Syracuse and Acragas: ibid., 165–70.

3. Carthage after 500 BC: Picard, 1992; Maraoui Telmini et al., 2014, especially 118–31, 142–47. Acragas' olive exports to Carthage, and unbelievable wealth: Diodorus 13.81.4–84.6. Hermocrates' remark: Thucydides 6.34.2.
4. Justin on African wars: 19.2.3–4. Court of 'one hundred judges': 19.2.5–6. Summary of Carthage's Sicilian wars of 409–396: Trogus, *Prologue* 19. The One Hundred and Four: Aristotle, Politics 2.1272b, 1273a: dated to 396 by Huss, 1985, 464; similarly Hoyos, 2010, 133–34. Supposed struggle from 480 on between Magonid kings and Carthaginian aristocracy: Sanders, 1988. Gisco's Selinus exile proof of good relations between it and Carthage: Hans, 1983, 40; Geus, 1994, 31 n.157 (who [159] wants to exile Gisco's brother Hamilcar too).
5. Segesta and Halicyae allied with Athens: Fornara, 1983, no.81. Other possible dates are 458/57 and 454/53 (Bengtson, 1975, no.139), but if so the treaties must have been purely ceremonial; there was no question of Athens intervening so far west in the mid-fifth century.
6. Hannibal the Magonid in 410: Diodorus 13.43.5–6. His old age: 13.80.1. Expeditions of 480 and 409–05 as private Magonid enterprises though funded by the state: Sanders, 1988; Günther, 1993; Ameling, 2013, 365–67. Alcibiades on conquering Carthage: Thucydides 6.15.2, 90.2. Athenian overtures to Carthage in 415: 6.88.6.
7. Hannibal's forces in 409: Xenophon, *Hellenica* 1.1.37 (Geus, 1994, 67 is happy with his figure); Diodorus 13.54.5 (Ephorus' and Timaeus' figures), 59.6 (40,000 plus locals), 60.3 (80,000); Caven, 1990, 31–32 (50,000–60,000); Stylianou, 1998, 61–64; Champion, 2010, 137 (40,000-plus at the start). Greeks in the army (perhaps Selinuntine exiles): Diodorus 13.58.1. Selinus' casualties: 13.57.6, 58.3. Fall of Himera: 13.62.1–4. Three months' campaign: Xenophon, ibid.
8. Diodorus 13.59.3, 79.8; Cicero, Against Verres 2.2.86 (Himera's survivors allowed back). Hermocrates: Diodorus 13.63, 13.75.2–9. Syracusan embassy: 13.79.8.
9. Punic forces in 406: Xenophon, *Hellenica* 1.5.15 (with the trireme total); Diodorus 13.80.5. Carthage's treaty with Athens: Fornara, 1983, no.166 (= Bengtson, 1975, no.208).
10. The inscription later set up to record the campaign (below, n.13) mentions that they went via a place called 'lš (Halish?), usually interpreted as Halaesa. If so, not the important Halaesa founded only in 403 and on the mid-north coast, but one of the many others noted by

Diodorus (14.16.2). 'Iš, though, may not refer to a 'Halaesa' at all; the meaning of the word is disputed.
11. Alleged intent of subduing all Sicily: Diodorus 13.80.1. Syracusan naval victory: 80.5–7. Himilco's human and animal sacrifices: 86.3.
12. Dionysius' rise to power: Caven, 1990, 50–58; Lewis, 1992. Age and character: Cicero, *Tusculan Disputations* 5.20.57. Gela and Camarina in 405: Diodorus 13.108.2–112.2. Treaty of 405: 13.114.1.
13. *Corpus Inscriptionum Semiticarum* vol.1, 5510.7b–11a, translated by Schmitz 1994 (amending the views of C.R. Krahmalkov, 'A Carthaginian report of the battle of Agrigentum 406 B.C.', *Rivista di Studi Fenici* 2 [1974], 171–77). The interpretation turns on what '*grgnt* in the inscription means; Huss, 1985, 117 n.63, rejects (like some other scholars) that it refers to Acragas at all.

Chapter 6: Carthage against Dionysius the Great

1. Dionysius' regime: De Vido, 2004, 337–40, 349–52. Diodorus 14.46.1–2 (Carthaginian commerce with Greek Sicily reviving); 14.9.9 (Campanians seize Entella). Campanians in fourth-century Sicily: Fantasia, 2003. Entella's site is Rocca d'Entella, high above the Belice Sinistro River where this has been dammed to form the reservoir Lago Garcia.
2. Diodorus 14.41–42 (enthusiastic description of the navy-building); Pliny the Elder, *NH* 7.208 (Aristotle on the quadrireme). Dionysius' two (?) quinqueremes: Diodorus 14.44.7, 100.5. Doubts about these inventions: Lewis, 1992, 141 n.90. Hellenistic warships generally: Murray, 2012.
3. Huss, 1985, 127 n.29, prefers seeing the small cavalry total as a sign of how unfriendly Syracuse's horse-riding elite were to the tyrant; but in this period, including before Dionysius came on the scene, other reported Syracusan cavalry forces were no greater.
4. Diodorus 14.46.1–4 (pillage and massacre of Carthaginians in Siceliot cities), 46.5, 47.1–2 (Dionysius declares war).
5. Motya campaign: 14.47.4–53.5; Polyaenus, *Stratagems* 5.2.6 (confused account of Dionysius extricating his fleet). For similar fighting in narrow streets and high buildings during the final days of Carthage itself in 146: Appian, *Libyca* 128.610–130.621.
6. Caven, 1990, 105, estimates about 50,000 troops from Africa, beefed up with local troops though not as many as Timaeus claimed. He dates

(107) Himilco's crossing to late summer, spreading the ensuing events over 396 and 395 (like Hammond, 1986, 476–77) – although there is no sign of this in Diodorus.
7. Temple of Demeter and Kore in Achradina: Diodorus 14.63.1, 70.4; Shapiro, 2002, 87–90. Pharacidas: Diodorus 14.63.4, 70.1–3, 72.1; Polyaenus, *Stratagems* 2.11. Pharax: Xenophon, *Hellenica* 3.2.12–14; Anonymous, *Hellenica Oxyrhynchia* (a surviving but fragmentary contemporary account of Greek events of 397–96) VII.1; Diodorus 14.79.4–5. Both the same man: Caven, 1990, 115–18; Lewis, 1992, 142 n.93.
8. Smallpox and Himilco's plague: Littman, 1984; F. Fenner et al., *Smallpox and its Eradication* (World Health Organization, 1988), chapter 5: 'The history of smallpox and its spread around the world', 209–44, on pp.214–15. Half the army died: Diodorus 14.76.2, '150,000' (so this is from Ephorus). Hiero II's trick (around 269 BC): Polybius 1.9.4–6.
9. Himilco's fate: Diodorus 14.76.3–4; Justin 19.3.1–11 (imagining that this Himilco was 'king' Hamilcar's successor in Sicily in 480).
10. Athens' decree: Rhodes and Osborne, 2004, 48–51 no.10.
11. Mago, Himilco's successor: Geus, 1994, 175–77 (who sees him as a Magonid). Warfare in 393: Diodorus 14.90.2–91.1. Troops in 392 'carefully equipped': 95.1.
12. Campaign of 392 and treaty: 14.95.1–96.4; StV 2, no.233. Alternative view of campaign: Caven, 1990, 129–30.
13. Dionysius in southern Italy: Caven, 124–46.
14. Dionysius' Adriatic and Tyrrhenian doings: Diodorus 15.13.1–4, 14.1–4; Justin 20.1.1–3, 5.1–2; Strabo 5.1.4 (horse-breeders); 5.2.8 (Corsica raid); Polyaenus 5.2.21 (Pyrgi loot); Caven, 1990, 124–53. Philistus' exile: Diodorus (15.7.4) claimed that he was recalled along with Leptines, but this confuses Dionysius I with his son Dionysius II who did recall the by then aged exile around 356 (Nepos, *Dion* 3.2; Plutarch, *Dion* 11.4 and 7; *FrGH* no. 556, T5a–d, with F. Pownall's commentary).
15. Greek cities under Carthage's rule defected to Dionysius: Caven, 1990, 192. Sican and maybe Elymian cities: Huss, 1985, 137–38. Causes and outbreak of the new war: Diodorus 15.15.1–3. 'Thucydides trap': Thucydides 1.23.6, 33.3, 88.1; modern formulation by G.T. Allison of Harvard (see, e.g., https://thediplomat.com/2015/05/the-real-thucydides-trap/).
16. Diodorus' account abbreviated: Caven, 1990, 186–88.

17. The war is very variedly dated by moderns: e.g., 383–82 (Hans, 1983, 68–71), 383–c. 374 (Huss, 1985, 136–40), 377–76 (Caven, 1990, 186–90), 382–74 (Lewis, 1992, 148–49), 383–c. 378 (Stylianou, 1998, 200–02; Champion, 2010, 213); c. 382–75 (K. Meister, *NP* Dionysius I [1]). Justin's résumé (20.5.1–6) is not supported by Cicero's notion that Dionysius sacked Locri's revered temple of Persephone (*On the Nature of the Gods* 3.83), for that shrine was untouched down the centuries until Pyrrhus of Epirus looted it in 276 (Diodorus 27.4.2–3; Appian, *Samnite Wars* 12.4–6; Cassius Dio, fr. 48). Aelian's Dionysius attacking Thurii: *Varia Historia* 12.61; generally believed – e.g., by Hans, 1983, 294 n.25; Huss, 1985, 140 n.43; Hammond, 1986, 480; Caven, 1990, 193–94; Champion, 2010, 214. Another Aelian tale has Dionysius poison his own mother and let Leptines die in a sea battle (*VH* 13.45) – a confused scramble of the stories that he poisoned his Locrian mother-in-law (Plutarch, *Dion* 3.3) and Leptines was killed at Cronium in Sicily (Diodorus 15.17.1). Croton and Rhegium captured in the same campaign: Livy 24.3.8 (Croton captured); Dionysius of Halicarnassus 20.7.3 (both captured), with Dionysius adding that the tyrant held them for twelve years – but this can apply only to Croton and including Rhegium must be a slip.
18. Mago vs Dionysius: Diodorus 15.15. Himilco son of Mago: Polyaenus 5.10.5. Mago may have had Carthaginian senators as officers, as Roman armies did (eighty or so were slain at Cannae in 216: Livy 22.49.17) and as Hannibal did in 216 (Polybius 7.9.1, 4), and these might be the spokesmen – but they had no authority to make treaties. Diodorus' archontes as the magistrates in self-governing *epikrateia* cities: Whittaker, 1978, 297–98 n.9.
19. The 'admiral' stratagem: Polyaenus 6.16.1. Both Diodorus' and Polyaenus' stratagems disbelieved, Punic army slipped away by night to the coast for winter, war renewed under Himilco the next year: thus Caven, 1990, 197–98 – doubting that Dionysius could really have trapped a Punic army on a waterless hill in Sicily because it looks like an invented doublet of what he had once done to an Italiot army near Caulonia (Diodorus 14.105.1–2) – even though the outcomes were very different.
20. Himilco's supposed ruse at Cronium: Polyaenus 5.10.5. A fourth-century BC coin stamped 'Kronia', found on Pizzo Cannita, a peak 13km east of Palermo, might suggest that such a town stood on the coastal plain below (www.coinarchives.com/a/results.php?results=100&search=kronia; cf. Huss, 1985, 139; Lewis, 1992, 149). 'Kronia', though, can refer to

cult festivals of the god Cronus, popular in Sicily and – both there and elsewhere – celebrated on mountains (G. Baudy, *NP* Kronos, part D).

21. 'Manly' Carthaginians and peace terms: Diodorus 15.17.5. Halycus: Hans, 1983, 122–23, 229 n.36 argues that the Platani's ancient name was the Lycus (so too Huss, 1985, 166 n.91; Stylianou, 1998, 207; De Vincenzo, 2014, 235–40), and that Halycus was another name for the Himeras (now Salso) near Gela. Against this: Talbert, 1974, 83 n.1. In fact no second name for the Himeras is attested; the 'Lycus' at Heraclea Minoa in a contemporary, Heracleides Lembos (fr. 29 in C. Müller, *Fragmenta Historicorum Graecorum* 2 [1853], 220–21), is fairly certainly a copyist's mistake. In any case, the name problem does not clarify Acragas' territory between 406 and 381/80. That Dionysius' Sicilian territory after the treaty extended 'up to 17,500 square kilometres' (De Angelis, 2016, 126; cf. his p.109 map 9) assumes that he did control the Sicels and Sicans as well as all the Siceliot cities.

22. Hipponium restored: Diodorus 15.24.1. Croton: Dionysius of Halicarnassus 20.7.3 (n.17 above). The idea that it fell to the tyrant as late as 379 and broke free when he died in 367 ignores that Dionysius of Halicarnassus paired its capture with Rhegium's. Planned wall: Strabo 6.1.10; Pliny, *NH* 3.95; N. Biffi, *L'Italia di Strabone: Testo, traduzione e commento dei libri V e VI della Geografia* (Genova, 1988), 318. Dionysius' dealings with Sparta and Athens after 374: Caven, 1990, 202–06. Friendship, citizenship and alliance with Athens: Bengtson, *StV* 2, no.280; Rhodes and Osborne, 2004, 160–68 nos.33–34.

23. Diodorus 15.24.2, 73.1.3 (plague and rebellions); Trogus, *Prologue* 20; Justin 20.5.11–13 (Hanno and Suniatus); E. Lipiński in *DCPP*, 430 (Suniatus); Geus, 1994, 106–07 (Hanno), 202 (Suniatus).

24. Dionysius' last war and death: Diodorus 15.73–74; Justin (previous n.); Caven, 1992, 206–10. Peace in 366 or 365: Plato, *Letter* 7.338a (*Letters* 7 and 8 are judged genuine by scholars); Diodorus 16.5.2 (technically under the year 359/58, but in a general summary of Dionysius II's reign); Plutarch, Dion 6.5, 14.4–7.

Chapter 7: Carthage against Timoleon

1. Hanno's sedition: Justin 21.4, copied almost verbatim by Orosius 4.6.16–20, who adds that it happened in the time of Philip of Macedon, Alexander the Great's father (thus after 359 BC) – a detail he could have inferred from Justin.

2. Lunar eclipse: Plutarch, *Dion* 24.1. On 19 September 357: <en.wikipedia.org/wiki/List_of_4th-century_BCE_lunar_eclipses>; the heliacal rising of Arcturus soon after fits this (*Dion* 25.6; Bickerman, 1968, 119 col.1). The sailing is dated to August by (e.g.) Westlake, 1992, 699; Champion, 2012, 15. Synalus: Plutarch, Dion 25.12–26.3; Diodorus 16.9.4 (calling him Paralus, perhaps a text error); Geus, 1994, 202–03. *Boetharchos*: Polybius 1.79.2; Appian, *Libyca* 68.306; D. Hoyos, *Truceless War: Carthage's Fight for Survival 241 to 237 BC* (Leiden and Boston, 2007), 155–56 n.3.
3. Dion and aftermath: Westlake, 1992, 698–710; De Vido, 2014, 52–70. Plato's fears: *Letter* 8, 353a, 353e; echoed by Plutarch, *Timoleon* 17.2.
4. Mago: Talbert, 1974, 79–81, 90–91; Geus, 1994, 177–79. Hanno (Geus, 108) is mistakenly termed the overall commander by Diodorus 16.67.2.
5. Diodorus 16.66–68; Plutarch, *Timoleon* 7.1–13.2. Diodorus spreads out over three years the events from the appointment of Timoleon down to the younger Dionysius' departure from Syracuse – thus from 345/44 (the archonship, summer to summer, of Archias at Athens) to 343/42 (Pythodotus' archonship). This is generally accepted as implausible (e.g., Talbert, 1974, 47–49). Huss prefers dating Timoleon's journey from Greece to 345 rather than Diodorus' 344 (1985, 156–57); but Bicknell, 1984, 130–33, holds that night-time sky phenomena seen on his crossing to Italy (Diodorus 16.66.3; Plutarch, *Timoleon* 8.5–9.1) were probably the Lyrid meteor shower which Han Chinese records show occurred during March in ancient times; Bicknell even suggests it happened precisely before dawn on 21 March 344.
6. Galaria: Fantasia, 2003, 472–74. Corinthian reinforcements: Plutarch, *Timoleon* 16.3–4, 19.2–20.1; Diodorus 16.69.4. Plentiful mercenaries available: Talbert, 1974, 56–58, citing Isocrates, *Oration* 5.96, 120–21.
7. Diodorus 16.68.7–11, 69.3–6, 70.1–4; Plutarch, *Timoleon* 10.6–13, 16–20. Event sequences: detailed discussion by Talbert, 1974, 97–110 (unsure about both); Westlake, 1992, 710–12 and 710 n.1.
8. Dionysius' fall and departure: in 343 BC according to Diodorus (16.70.1) and an anonymous (third century AD) compiler of event-dates from 355/54 to 316/15 bc (*Oxyrhynchus Papyri* vol.1, no.12). But Diodorus' chronology is confused as just shown, and the Oxyrhynchus chronographer gets other items wrong (for a start, he has Dion murdered in 355/54 not at Callippus' instigation but by Dionysius II, who had gone into his first exile the year before). That the departing

ex-tyrant spent some time at Catana admiring Timoleon is Westlake's notion (1992, 711).

9. Talbert, 1974, 48–49, sees the Corinthian reinforcements setting out only in spring 343, and Mago arriving at Syracuse in the same season. But it is not at all likely that Timoleon's operations in Sicily began in 344 and dragged on over the winter, with the reinforcements not able to arrive until the following spring (despite also Westlake, 1992, 711). Neither Diodorus nor Plutarch hint at so leisurely a sequence. The reinforcements were organized as soon as news of Adranum reached Corinth (Diodorus 16.69.4; Plutarch 16.3; note 6 above), so could have sailed in May; though they stayed at Thurii for the length of their hosts' campaign against Bruttian neighbours, this need not have lasted more than six to ten weeks; then they could have reached Timoleon by late August or early September 344.

10. Plutarch's story does not imply that the upbraided mercenaries were Hicetas' alone (contra G.T. Griffiths, *The Mercenaries of the Hellenistic World* [Cambridge, 1935], 209), since they were upbraided for being in Carthaginian pay. 'Fifty days': Plutarch, *Timoleon* 16.2; unconvincingly rejected as impossible by Talbert, 47–48 (he prefers Diodorus' account); Champion, 2012, 48–49, follows Talbert without discussion.

11. Mago's deficiencies: Warmington, 1964, 121–22; Talbert, 1974, 81, 91. Sent to repress rebellion: Hans, 1983, 74–75. Recalled against Hanno the Great: thus originally A. Holm, *Geschichte Siciliens im Alterthum* (Leipzig, 1874), 2.203; against this, (e.g.) Talbert, 80–81; Geus, 1994, 179 n.1,056. Collusion between Hicetas and Timoleon: Holm, 203–04; H.W. Westlake, *Timoleon and his Relations with Tyrants* (Manchester, 1952), 33–35; Talbert, 92–93.

12. Claiming minimal casualties was far from unique. In 368, a Spartan victory in Greece supposedly cost no Spartan lives and was nicknamed 'the tearless battle' (Xenophon, *Hellenica* 7.1.31–32; Plutarch, *Agesilaus* 33.3). The Roman proconsul Sulla's victory in 86 BC over the Pontic army of Mithridates VI, at Chaeroneia in Greece, cost him (he said) just fourteen men – and two of them returned towards evening: Plutarch, *Sulla* 19.4; Appian, *Mithridatica* 45.174 (fifteen men). Another Roman proconsul, Lucullus, admitted to losing five dead and 100 wounded in defeating the Armenian king Tigranes' huge army in 69 BC (Plutarch, *Lucullus* 28.6).

13. Mago's suicide: Plutarch, *Timoleon* 22.8. Hans, 1983, 76–77, not very persuasively sees Mago remaining in western Sicily during the Greek raids that followed, then being recalled home.
14. Timoleon's activities between 344 and 341: Diodorus 16.70.4–6, 72.2–73.2; Plutarch 22.1–24.4. Talbert, 1974, 44, implausibly dates the second Carthaginian expedition to the year after Timoleon took Syracuse.
15. Timoleon encouraging Greek immigrants: Diodorus 16.83.5; Plutarch 22.4–24.1, 35.1–3; Günther, 2012 (judges the desolation of Sicily exaggerated). Timoleon and Hicetas: Plutarch 24.1 ('compelled Hicetas' etc.); contrast Diodorus 16.72.1–4; Talbert, 1974, 92–94 (suggesting some such – ultimately meaningless – agreement between Timoleon and Hicetas later).
16. Corinthians raid the *epikrateia*: Diodorus 16.73.1–3 (including Timoleon's actions); Plutarch 24.4 (Timoleon not mentioned).
17. Carthage's alleged aim in 341: Plutarch, *Timoleon* 25.1–2. Crush Syracuse and its allies, perhaps attack Syracuse: Hans, 1983, 75–77. Simply re-establish control of *epikrateia*: Talbert, 1973, 82; Huss, 1985, 163; Westlake, 1992, 713. Size of expedition: Diodorus 16.73.3 ('managing the war ignobly'); Plutarch 25.1; Polyaenus 5.12.3. Sacred Corps: Diodorus 16.80.4.
18. Timoleon's army: Diodorus 16.78.2; Plutarch 25.4–5. Desertions: Diodorus 78.3; Plutarch 25.5. Deinarchus and Demaretus may have reinforced Timoleon: so too Talbert, 60. The shortest, and perhaps least hilly, route to Acragas was probably via Leontini, then west and southwest (past modern Caltagirone) down to the south coast close to Gela and after that along the coast, a total of just about 210km. Battle site: Talbert, 1974, 69–75 (discussing various views); Westlake, 1992, 713 n.19.
19. Thargelion month: Plutarch, *Timoleon* 27.1 (close to solstice), *Camillus* 19.4 (specifies 24th Thargelion). Dionysius of Halicarnassus implies that Thargelion, a thirty-day month, ended on the ninth day before the summer solstice (*Roman Antiquities* 1.63.1); as this occurs between 20 and 22 June, the 24th of Thargelion should be between 5 and 7 June.
20. The battle: Diodorus 16.79.5–80.5; Plutarch, *Timoleon* 27–29; Nepos, *Timoleon* 2.4 (one sentence). Victory inscription at Corinth: J.H. Kent in *Hesperia* 21 (1952), 9–18; Talbert, 76–77.
21. Gisco's gesture: Polyaenus 5.11. Picard, 1968, 160, supposes without evidence that the Egypt-inspired (?) performance was a standard victory ritual at Carthage.

22. 'Just as they previously had been': Diodorus 19.71.7; the clause is not in Plutarch.

Chapter 8: Carthage against Agathocles

1. Alexander threatens Carthage: Quintus Curtius, *Alexander* 4.2.10, 4.4.18, 10.1.17. Tyrian refugees taken to Carthage: Diodorus 17.41.2, 46.4; Curtius 4.3.20. Hamilcar the secret agent: Frontinus, *Stratagems* 1.2.3; Justin 21.6; Orosius 4.6.21–22; Geus 1994, 42–43. Punicized Selinus: DeVincenzo, 2014.
2. Immigrants to Sicily: Diodorus 16.82.5 (50,000 to Syracuse, 10,000 to Agyrium his home town); Plutarch, *Timoleon* 23.6 (60,000, citing Timoleon's contemporary Athanis). Siceliot revival: Westlake, 1992, 719–20; De Vido, 2008, 357; Günther, 2012 (restrained view of size and impact); de Angelis, 2016, 123–24, 129–32, 217–19 ('grossly exaggerated' yet real), 303–04. Timoleon's reputation: Cicero, *ad Familiares* 5.12.7; Nepos, *Timoleon* 1.1; Talbert, 1974, 39–43. Polybius 200 years later sneered at what he achieved (*Histories* 12.25), but that was because Polybius detested his uncritical admirer Timaeus.
3. Agathocles' early career and coup: Diodorus 19.1.5–9.7 (narrating everything under the year 317, implausibly; Parian Marble, B12 (319/18), B14 (316/15); Justin 22.1–2; Polyaenus 5.3; Meister, 1984, 384–90. A possible portrait-bust of Agathocles: Sjöqvist, 1962.
4. Agathocles' attacks on Messana: Diodorus 19.65.1–6 (under 315). Treaty of 313: 19.71.7; StV 3, no. 424 (both dating it 314); Huss 1985, 181–2.
5. Hamilcar's dilemma: so too Hans, 1983, 81. Censure: Diodorus 19.72.7; Justin 22.3.1–7. Hans, 82–83, 202 n.111 (following others), thinks that a rival faction, an 'action party', now took over.
6. Diodorus puts Hamilcar's settlement in archon-year 314/13 (19.66.1, 71.7); has nothing about Sicily in 313/12; then gives Agathocles' takeover of Messana, thwarted attempt on Acragas, and the Carthaginian encampment on Mount Ecnomus all in 312/11 (19.77.1, 102.1–104.5). The new Carthaginian expedition under Hamilcar son of Gisco is reported for 311/10 (19.105.1, 106.1–110.5); then in Diodorus' next Book but with no stated time-break in the narrative, Agathocles' sailing to Africa (20.3.1–5.5), and this is datable to August 310 because of the accompanying eclipse of the sun. (But see also note 10 below, on the year.) As a result, Hamilcar's expedition is dated to 311 by some

(e.g., Meister, 1984, 392–93; Consolo Langher, 1992b, 41–42 n.76) and to 310 by others (Huss, 1985, 183; Geus, 1994, 45).
7. Diodorus 19.104.3–4 (Athenian archon-year 312/11: 19.77.1), 106.1–108.2 (archon-year 311/10: 105.1).
8. Hamilcar also brought along 200 Etruscan '*zeugippai*' (19.106.2), a unique word which – Liddell-Scott-Jones' Greek Lexicon suggests – is a copyist's error for *zeugitai*, 'yoked teams' (farm animals). But what this would mean in military contexts is unknown. Perhaps two-man chariot teams (so too Huss, 1985, 184), but Etruscan armies of the time are not noted for chariots. In any case these fighters do not reappear. Agathocles loses twenty ships: Diodorus 19.107.2.
9. Agathocles' preparations for Africa: Diodorus 20.3.2–4.8; Justin 22.4.1–5. Agathocles' calculations: 20.3.3. Punic warships moored or beached outside the harbours (Diodorus 20.32.3), perhaps in the coves just to the south at the Plemmyrion headland.
10. Himeras battle dated to 311: Picard, 1968, 168; Hans, 1983, 101; Meister, 1984, 392–93; Hoyos, 2010, 173; Miles, 2010, 149; Champion, 2012, 90. To June or July 310: O. Meltzer, *Geschichte der Karthager* 1 (Berlin, 1879), 363–64, 523–34; van Compernolle, 1954, 413 n.2; Huss, 1985, 183; Geus, 1994, 45. The actual day of the Dog Star (its heliacal rising) is in late July, but Diodorus' time-phrase is broad: 'the season being around [the time of] the Dog' (19.109.5; similarly Compernolle).
11. Army and crews: Diodorus 20.11.1–2. Ships' bronze beaks: 20.15.1–2.
12. Another grain shipment, rather less successful, is mentioned in 309: 20.32.3–5.
13. Megalepolis and Leukos Tynes: Diodorus 20.8.2–7; *Oxyrhynchus Papyri* vol.24, no.2,399; Huss, 1980, 63–68 (prefers Maxula); Raffone, 2001, 216–21. The fifth-century AD 'Meglapolitanus' (sic) bishop is in the same group-list as those of Curubis, Clupea, Ziqua (Korba, Kelibia, Zaghouan) and Thimida (near Oudna), all on the peninsula or in the district between there and Carthage; Uthina is not listed as such even though it was a bishopric and important (Petschenig, 1881, 117–19 [list]; W. Huss, *NP* 'Uthina'). Consolo Langher, 1992a, 33–36, sees Megalepolis as Curubis (Korba) on the east coast of the peninsula, with Leukos Tynes nearby.
14. Bomilcar's connections: Justin 22.7.10.
15. The battle: Diodorus 20.10–13; Justin 22.6.6–7. Battle site: Huss, 1985, 187 n.81, and Consolo Langher, 1992a, 36–37 (Belvédère area). Battle

of Ad Decimum: Procopius, *History of the Wars* 3.18–19. Agathocles' two ships: Diodorus 20.16.3–6.

16. Child-sacrifice and other rituals in 310: Diodorus 20.14. On this much-debated topic, (e.g.) Aubet, 2001, 243–56 (= 2009, 258–66); Hoyos, 2010, 100–05, 229–30 n.57; M.M. McCarty in *Religion in the Roman Empire* 3 (2017), 393–428; J.H. Schwartz et al., *Antiquity* 91 (2017), 442–54; Orsingher, 2018. The foreign child in 406: Diodorus 13.80.1. Battle-captives put to death by fire: 20.65.1–2.
17. Diodorus 20.17.3–5; accepted by Champion, 2012, 107. Zaghouan range visible but story doubted: Gsell, *HAAN* 3.36 and n.4; Huss, 1985, 189 n.95 (also sceptical).
18. Agathocles's eastern campaign: Diodorus 20.17. Aspis: Strabo 17.3.16; Tillyard, 1908, 126–27; N. Biffi, *L'Africa di Strabone: Libro XVII della Geografia* (Modugno, 1999), 410–11. Ophellas in 309: Diodorus 20.40.
19. *Oxyrhynchus Pap.* 2,399, column 1 (my tr.); Huss, 1980, 63–64 (text); Raffone, 2001, 209–12 (text and Italian translation), suggesting (226–27) that the author was none other than Antander.
20. Diodorus 20.16.1 (with pun on Antander's name – *Antandros* was *anandros*, 'not a man'); *Oxyrhynchus Pap.* 2,399, columns 2–3; Huss, 1980, 64–71; Berger, 1988; Raffone, 2001, 221–23. Hamilcar's new campaign: Diodorus 20.29.2–30.2.
21. The number 50,000 in Greek, '5 myriads', might conceivably suffer a later copying corruption later to '12 myriads' (that is, from E' *myriades* to IB' *myriades*). The exiles' army was growing: by 306, after years of war in alliance with Acragas against Syracuse, Deinocrates had 23,000 men in arms (Diodorus 20.79.2) and a year later 28,000 (20.89.2).
22. A different, less plausible version is Cicero's (*On Divination* 1.50): Hamilcar dreamed the prophecy, then next day his own soldiers and the allied Greeks fell to blows in camp, prompting a Syracusan surprise attack in which he was captured and carried off. Tillyard (1908, 132–35) and Meister (1984, 401) reject the story of Hamilcar planning a night assault; they suppose that, marching through the Anapus River area toward the Olympieum, his army was attacked and routed. This replaces Diodorus' account with a much less convincing one – among other things, the Anapus area is fairly flat whereas Diodorus repeatedly stresses how rocky and narrow the route was.
23. Diodorus 20.33–34. The Bagradas: Consolo Langher, 1992a, 42.
24. Diodorus 20.38–39.

25. Ophellas' career: W. Heckel (ed.), *Who's Who in the Age of Alexander the Great* (Oxford and Malden, 2006), 184–85. On the ancient Syrtes coasts: Quinn, 2011. Lotus fruit eaten on the march: Theophrastus, *History of Plants* 4.3.2.
26. The tenth-century Byzantine encyclopaedia the Suda, in its entry on Ophellas' contemporary Demetrius the Besieger, states that Ptolemy I took over Cyrene (in 308) after the Isthmian Games in Greece and after Ophellas' murder in Libya (Suda, Δ 431); these biennial games were held in April or early May. That Ophellas perished near the end of 308 is implied by Diodorus (20.70.3 – Agathocles a year later abandoned the expedition around 1 November 307, supposedly on the anniversary of Ophellas' murder). This is accepted by several moderns (B. Niese, *RE* 1.753, s.v. 'Agathocles'; Meister, 1984, 397; Consolo Langher, 1992a, 43), but it would implausibly cram into 307 alone all ensuing events down to Agathocles' final flight from Africa. In 307, Ophellas' men instigated the murder of Agathocles' sons after his flight, and this may have led to belief in a false synchronism with Ophellas' murder. Tillyard (1908, 186) puts Ophellas' death in August.
27. Diodorus 20.43.1–44.6. What the coup-makers called their chief in Punic is not known – probably not the actual Greek word *tyrannos*, even though Carthaginians knew Greek; maybe a phrase like *rab rabim*, 'chief of the chiefs'? Justin (22.7.7–8) has Bomilcar intending to defect with his troops to Agathocles, but a mutiny in the tyrant's army stops him and the Carthaginians then crucify him. Bomilcar's denunciation: Justin 22.7.9–10.
28. Sicilian fighting in 308–07: Diodorus 20.56.1–57.3.
29. Eumachus' raids: 20.57.4–58.6. Efforts to identify the places mentioned: (e.g.) Huss, 1985, 197 (viewing Eumachus as ranging southward from Thugga); Consolo Langher, 1992a, 46–53, and 2004, 343–54 (westward and then along Algeria's east coast).
30. Diodorus 20.59–60. Geus too (1992, 9) sees Adherbal's goal as the Hammamet coast.
31. Battle of Tunes: 20.641–45. The text's '6,000' (64.3), though written out as *hexakischilion*, as a numeral would have been ς' while 200 (*diakosion*, written out) would have been ,ς: a copyist or Diodorus himself might have written out the wrong word.
32. Close of the war in Libya: Diodorus 20.64–70, mostly about the burning of the camps and Agathocles' treacherous flight. The more famous camp-burning occurred outside Utica in spring 203, when

Scipio Africanus got himself out of difficulties by a surprise night attack during a truce, which incinerated tens of thousands of Carthaginians and Numidians (Polybius 14.1–5; Livy 30.3–6). Arcesilaus: Justin 22.8.14; Polybius 7.2.3–4; Livy 24.6.2; Justin implies that his existing Syracusan family was afterwards killed by Agathocles.

Chapter 9: The woes of post-Agathoclean Sicily

1. Hicetas and other tyrants in the 280s: Diodorus 21.18.1–3, 22.2, 22.7.1–3; Dionysius of Halicarnassus 20.8.1.
2. Pyrrhus in the west: Hans, 1983, 85, 96–97; Huss, 1985, 207–15; Franke, 1989; Vacanti, 2012, 3–12, 38–47. His western ambitions: Plutarch, *Pyrrhus* 14 (a story perhaps made up later), 22.2. Appeals from Acragas, Syracuse and Leontini: Plutarch, 22.1 – adding the extra plea 'to help free Sicily from tyrants', surely another later addition (the appealers were all tyrants themselves).
3. Carthage's dealings with Rome and Pyrrhus: Livy, *Epitome* 13; Valerius Maximus, *Famous Deeds and Sayings* 3.7.11; Justin 18.2.1–5; Polybius 3.25.3–5 (text).
4. 'We shall be totally annihilated': Plutarch, Pyrrhus 21.9. 'Two years and four months': Diodorus 22.8.1. Expedition's forces: Appian, *Samnite Wars* 11.6.
5. 'Azonae' comes in Diodorus' list between Heracleia and Selinus (22.8.2), but no such place is known in Sicily. It looks like a copying error for Mazara: this stood, and still stands, on the south coast west of Selinus and was important enough for the Romans to capture it in 259 (Diodorus 23.9.4, calling it 'Mazarin'). Though Diodorus' list puts 'Azonae' before Selinus, this could be because 'Azonae' was taken by force whereas Selinus changed sides.
6. Plutarch's narrative has Pyrrhus capture Eryx, next clash with the Mamertines and then refuse to negotiate with the Carthaginians (*Pyrrhus* 22.4–23.2; no mention of Lilybaeum). Diodorus implies him pausing between taking Panormus and attacking Lilybaeum (22.10.5; no mention of Mamertines).
7. Pyrrhus' tyrannical behaviour: Dionysius 20.8.2–4; Plutarch, *Pyrrhus* 23.3–5; Zonaras 8.5 (from Cassius Dio). Harassment tactics: Zonaras, ibid.
8. Plutarch, Pyrrhus 24; Appian, *Samnite Wars* 12.2 – losses believed by Huss, 1985, 215 n.65; Franke, 1989, 481.

9. Echetla lay between Syracusan and Carthaginian territory according to Philinus (so Polybius 1.15.10); it stood probably at Occhiolà beside Grammichele (G. Falco, *NP* s.v.). Philinus was echoed by the travel writer Pausanias, four centuries later, who described the Carthaginians as controlling 'more than half the island' in 264 (*Description of Greece* 6.12.3).
10. Hiero's rise: *SEG*³ no.427; Theocritus, *Idyll* 16.76–100; Polybius 1.8.3–5; Justin 23.4; De Sensi Sestito, 1977, 9–30. His name is conventionally spelled in the Roman way, unlike his distant alleged ancestor Hieron I.
11. Hiero's campaigns and Carthage's rescue of Messana: Polybius 1.9.3–8; Diodorus 22.13.1–8; Hoyos, 1985 (discussing previous views).
12. Background and outbreak of the First Punic War: (e.g.) Molthagen, 1975; Harris, 1979, 111–14, 182–90; Huss, 1985, 216–20; Lazenby, 1996, 1–52; Hoyos, 1998, 17–115; Loreto, 2007, 9–43; Hoyos, 2011, 131–48.

Chapter 10: Carthage at war in Africa and Spain

1. Trogus, *Prologue* 19 ('per rubellum annorum' in all the manuscripts); F. Rühl suggested 'Sabellus', in his 1886 edition; accepted and discussed by Geus, 1994, 97, 218, 223–24. Another emendation treats 'rubellum annorum' as a distortion of three Magonids' names – Hasdrubal, Hamilcar and Hanno – but this is even harder to explain. If Trogus' Hanno was 'king' Hanno, 'rubellum' might, just possibly, be a miscopying of 'regulum', the Latin diminutive of *rex*.
2. Carthaginians sent out into Libya: Aristotle, *Politics* 2.1273b; 6.1320b; Ameling, 1993, 260–62. Klerouchoi: K.-W. Welwei, *NP* s.v.; S. Hornblower, *OCD*⁴ s.v. Cleruchy.
3. Thusca and Gunzuzi: Lancel, 1995, 259–62; Hoyos, 2010, 142–44. Picard, 1968, 76, holds that Carthage never controlled the Khroumerie, but no evidence supports this.
4. Numidian raids in 256: Polybius 1.31.2. Hamilcar's counter-offensive: Orosius 4.9.9 (probably from Livy's no longer surviving account). This Hamilcar, active in Sicily against the Romans from 261 on, cannot be the famous Hamilcar Barca who came to prominence a decade later: Geus, 1994, 46 n.246.
5. Theveste: Polybius 1.73.1; Diodorus 4.18.1, 24.10.1–2; E. Lipiński, *DCPP* 442–43 s.v. 'Tébessa'. '3,000' (Diodorus 24.10.2) as a Greek numeral would be, Γ while '300' would be T'; an early copyist might confuse the two when choosing to write the number in full.

6. Carthaginians oppress Libya in 240s: Polybius 1.72.1–5.
7. Hamilcar Barca: (e.g.) Geus, 1994, 50–58; Hoyos, 2003, 1–72; Miles, 2010, 198–222; E. MacDonald, *Hannibal: a Hellenistic Life* (New Haven and London, 2015), 43–67.
8. The sole detailed account of the Truceless War is Polybius 1.65–88; Diodorus' few surviving excerpts (25.2–8) are based on Polybius. Nepos, *Hamilcar* 2, adds a few items; episodic mentions by Appian (e.g., *Iberian Wars* 4.15–17; *Libyan Wars* 5.18–22) and in Zonaras' epitome of Cassius Dio (8.18) offer varied inaccuracies. Modern treatments include Gsell, *HAAN* 3.100–28; Huss, 1985, 252–68; Loreto, 1995; Hoyos, 2007. The chronology of the war is opaque as Polybius' time-indications are almost non-existent (Loreto, 211–13; Hoyos, 2000); the proposed time-line in Hoyos, 2007, 275–76, is followed here. Flaubert's famous novel *Salammbô* (1862) was inspired by the French historian Michelet's retelling of the war, but imagined a voluptuously orientalized Carthage and ends in a rush after the rebels' disaster at The Saw (reimagined as 'the pass of the Axe').
9. Traders arrested then freed, and Hiero's and Rome's help to Carthage: Polybius 1.83.2–11, 3.28.3; Appian, *Libyan Wars* 5.21–22, *Sicilian Wars* 2.10; Zonaras 8.17, 18. Released prisoners' total: Valerius Maximus 5.1.1; Eutropius, *Résumé of Roman History* 2.27. Sardinia mutineers' and Utica's appeals to Rome: Polybius 1.83.11.
10. Brutalities: Polybius 1.79.8–82.1. Carthaginian quarrels and losses: 82.3–11; Diodorus 25.3.2 (from Polybius).
11. Siege of Carthage, Hanno sacked: Polybius 1.82.12–14.
12. Inland campaigning and The Saw: 1.83.12–85.7.
13. Mathos destroys Hannibal: 1.86.
14. Closing events of the war: 1.87.1–88.7. 'Three years and four months', 88.7; Diodorus' four and four (24.6.1) must be another copying error, and Livy's 'five years' (21.2.1) a very loose rounding-off.
15. Rome seizes Sardinia: 1.88.8–12; also 3.10.1–3, 15.10–11, 28.1–3.
16. Justin 44.5.1–3; Polybius 3.24.4.
17. Hamilcar and Hasdrubal in Spain: Polybius 2.1.5–9, 13.1–9, 36.1–2; 3.9.6–12.7; Diodorus 25.10–12; Appian, *Iberian Wars* 5.17–6.24.
18. Acra Leuce: Diodorus 25.10.3; P. Barceló, *NP* s.v. (against Alicante); Lancel, 1995, 379 (for Alicante); Hoyos, 2003, 63–65, 248 n.12–13 (ditto).
19. Hasdrubal acclaimed by Iberians: Diodorus 25.12.1. Warriors' oath of loyalty: Caesar, *Gallic Wars* 3.22. The oath-takers, called *soldurii*,

swore not to outlive their leader if he was slain. Extent of Hasdrubal's expansion: Hoyos, 2002.
20. Cassius Dio's story (fr.48) of Roman envoys going to Hamilcar in 231, aiming to find fault with his empire-building but not succeeding, is not in any other source and is hard to believe though many do believe it: e.g., Harris, 1979, 201; Geus, 1994, 57; H. Beck, in Hoyos, 2011, 235. Disbelief: Hoyos, 1998, 147–49.

Conclusion

1. 'Some necessary tasks': Diodorus 22.8.3.
2. Carthage ruled by landed grandees: Ameling, 1993, especially chapters 6 and 9. Himilco the voyager: Geus, 1994, 157–59; Roller, 2006, 27–29; Hoyos, 2010, 54–55.

Index

Abacaenum, 78–80, 119, 124
Acestorides (Corinthian), 117
Acra Leuce (Spain; Alicante), 181–2
Acragas (Agrigentum), 2, 12, 14,
    19–20, 27, 30, 37, 39, 46–50,
    52–4, 56, 58, 61–4, 69, 82,
    87, 90, 92, 95, 108–109, 114,
    116, 118–20, 122, 140, 145–7,
    150–1, 154–7, 159, 188, 191
Acrotatus (Spartan prince), 119–20
Achradina (quarter of Syracuse),
    74, 76, 98–9, 101–102, 104
Acrae (Sicily), 100, 158
Ad Decimum (battle), 129
Adherbal (general against
    Agathocles), 141–3, 149, 176
Adherbal (Magonid), 39–40
Adirim (Carthaginian senate), 11,
    39, 55, 76, 90, 119, 121, 128,
    168, 177
Adranum, 97–101, 108
Aegates (Egadi) islands, 24, 28,
    167, 191
Aegean Sea, 11, 13, 19, 21, 35–6,
    39, 53, 56, 60, 72, 104, 162
Aelian (writer), 83–4
Aelymas (Libyan king), 132, 165, 174
Aeschrion (officer), 142
Aetna (city), 67, 97, 105, 116
Agathocles (tyrant of Syracuse
    and king), 4, 27–9, 31–2, 115,
    117–33, 135–47, 149–50, 152,
    155, 158–9, 163–5, 168, 174,
    176, 187–8, 190–1
'Agragant' (Acragas), 64
Agyris (tyrant of Agyrium),
    79–80, 95
Agyrium, 20, 77–80, 84, 95, 105,
    116, 151, 158
Alalia (Corsica), 21, 34, 36, 38, 42–3,
    81, 187, 191
Alcibiades, 56
Alexander the Great, 30, 73, 115,
    117, 135, 137, 146
Algeria, 13, 15, 18, 127, 141, 162,
    166, 185
    see also Numidia
Anaxilaus (tyrant of Rhegium), 20,
    37, 43, 46–7, 51, 188
Anapus river (Syracuse), 74, 102
Andromachus (tyrant of
    Tauromenium), 95, 97
Antander (brother of Agathocles),
    117, 125–6, 133, 135, 138,
    140, 145
Antiochus of Syracuse (historian), 4
Apollonia, 95, 105, 108, 140
Apolloniades (tyrant), 95, 105
Appian (historian), 2, 6, 9, 16, 31–2,
    128, 153, 156, 166, 171, 178,
    180, 192
Arbocala (Toro, Spain), 184

Arcesilaus (officer), 144, 188
Archagathus (son of Agathocles), 126, 135–6, 139, 141–2, 144
Aristocrats (Carthaginian), 10, 14, 16–17, 33, 39, 41, 52, 112, 115, 117, 123, 178, 192
Aristocrats (non–Carthaginian), 12, 20, 23, 46, 53, 63, 94–5, 105, 116–7, 122, 155, 157, 166, 181, 182, 190
Aristotle, 3, 6, 11–12, 14–15, 26, 39, 41, 43, 45, 68, 93, 162
Armour, 9, 27–9, 44, 68, 101, 107–108, 111
Army strengths and losses
   Carthaginian, 17, 27, 28–9, 31, 47–8, 57, 60, 71, 72, 75, 78, 85, 96, 99, 103, 107, 110–11, 118, 123, 129, 134, 138, 141, 150, 169, 182
   Other, 56, 89, 98, 156, 168–70, 174–5, 180–1, 184
   Sicilian Greek, 48–9, 59, 62–3, 69, 73–5, 79, 84, 87, 90, 97, 100, 102, 106, 108, 121–2, 125, 127, 130, 135–7, 140, 142–4, 146, 153–4, 163
Artillery, 101, 107, 191
   see also Catapult(s)
Aspis (Clupea, Kelibia), 132, 135, 139, 143–4
Assorus, 79
Astarte (Phoenician–Punic goddess), 8–9, 43, 81
Athanis (historian), 5
Athens, Athenians, 1–2, 6, 12, 14, 19, 23, 39, 44, 51, 54–7, 60, 65, 72, 74–5, 77, 89, 91, 94, 109, 118, 121–2, 132, 162, 188

Augustine, St, 6, 141
Augustus (emperor), 2, 9, 33, 35
Autaritus (rebel leader), 168–70, 174–5
Avienus (Latin poet), 13

Baal Hamon (god), 9, 17, 130
Baal Saphon (god), 17, 40, 61
Baetis river (Guadalquivir), 180–2
Bagradas river, 15, 34, 136, 142, 161–2, 164–5, 169, 173–6
Balearic islands and slingers, 26, 29, 60, 123
Barca, *see* Hamilcar ('Barca')
Barcid (family and period), 16, 183, 189–92
Belvédère, Parc du (Tunis), 129, 176
Boeotia (Greece), 14, 89
Boetharchos (regional military commander), 94, 106, 204
Bomilcar (general against Agathocles), 128–31, 136, 138–9, 141, 146–7, 190
Booty, plunder, 19, 21, 26–7, 30, 37–8, 50, 58, 65, 74, 81, 84, 92, 106, 111, 122, 125, 128, 134, 136–7, 139, 141–2, 150, 165, 181, 184
Bruttians (Italy), 21, 88, 102, 112, 117
Bulla Regia, 165
Byrsa (citadel of Carthage), 2, 7–9, 25, 31–2, 53, 64
Byzacium (region), 131, 137, 143, 172, 174–5, 177, 192

Cabala (battle), 83–4
Caere (Etruria), 38, 43, 81
Callippus (tyrant of Syracuse), 94

Camarina, 19–20, 56, 63–4, 69, 95, 116, 124, 140, 150
Campania, Campanians, 21, 26, 28, 57–8, 60–2, 67–8, 78, 90, 94–5, 97, 105, 116, 149–50, 158–9, 163, 168, 171
Cannae, 69
Cape Bon (and peninsula), 7, 15, 28, 42, 54, 126–7, 143, 163, 172
Cape Pachynus (Passaro), 63, 126
Cape Pelorias (Punto del Faro), 73
Captives, prisoners of war, 16, 30, 49, 56, 58, 61, 63–4, 85, 97, 111, 130, 135, 143, 167, 170–2, 174–8, 180–1
Carales (Sardinia), 13, 44
Carpetani (Spanish people), 184
Carthalo (son of Malchus), 33, 38–40
Casmenae (Sicily), 100
Cassius Dio (historian), 6, 31, 171
Castulo, 182
Catadas river (Meliane), 15, 142
Catana, 19, 67, 73, 79, 81, 94, 98–102, 105, 108, 124–5, 144, 151, 158, 191
Catapult(s), 24, 68, 70
Cato the Censor (Roman leader and historian), 6, 166, 183
Caulonia (Italy), 80, 84
Celtiberians, 180
Centuripa, 77, 79, 95, 105, 116, 122–3, 158
Cephaloedium, 78, 86, 140, 145, 156, 158
Cephalus (Corinthian), 105
Chariots (war), 48, 72, 96, 103, 107, 109–11, 129, 136–7, 143
Chullu (Numidia), 13, 162
Chrysas river (Dittaino), 79–80

Cimetière du Djellaz (Tunis), 143, 176
Cineas (Pyrrhus' adviser), 153
Cirta (Constantine, Algeria), 18, 165
Coins, 2, 9, 28, 45, 86
Corcyra (Corfu), 83, 88, 149
Corinth, Corinthians, 4, 19, 53, 95–6, 98–109, 111, 117
Cornelius Nepos (biographer), 4, 181
Corsica, 13–14, 21, 23–4, 26, 34, 36, 38, 47, 81, 179, 189
Crimisus (Belice, river and battle), 9, 27, 108–11, 116, 121, 184, 190
Cronium (battle), 83, 86–8, 91
Croton, 21, 80, 83–4, 88, 117
Crucifixion, 11, 33, 39, 71, 104, 138, 165, 167, 171, 176, 181
Cumae (Italy), 21, 52
Cyamosorus river, 158
Cyme (Asia Minor), 21
Cyrene, 5, 14, 60, 115, 132, 136–7, 139

Damarete (wife of Gelon), 6, 51
Daphnaeus (Syracusan general), 62–3
Darius (king of Persia), 40–1
Deinarchus (Corinthian officer), 102, 106, 108–10
Deinocrates (Syracusan leader), 118, 122, 133, 135, 140, 143–6
Delphi, 9, 52, 81, 97
Demaretus (Corinthian officer), 102, 106, 109
Demeter (goddess), 9, 74, 127, 163, 189
Demophilus (Agathocles' general), 122

Deserters, 8, 28, 30–2, 57, 61–3, 69, 106, 132, 136, 144–5, 169, 173
Dexippus (Spartan officer), 61–3
Dido (Elissa, Elishat), 7–10, 16, 33, 161
Diekplous, 1, 23–5
Diodorus (historian), 3–4, 6, 9–10, 20, 24, 29–31, 35, 37, 41, 44–5, 47–52, 54–61, 64, 67–9, 71–2, 74–7, 79, 81–7, 89–91, 94, 96–101, 104, 106–108, 110–13, 116, 118, 120–31, 133–5, 137–46, 151–2, 154, 159, 163–4, 166, 169, 178, 180–3, 192
Diognetus (Syracusan), 133
Dion (liberator), 4–5, 10, 91, 93–5, 188
Dionysius (Corinthian), 105
Dionysius I (tyrant of Syracuse), 2, 4, 9, 24–5, 45–6, 59, 62–5, 67–91, 112, 114, 117, 120, 134, 146, 150, 159, 162–4, 187–91
Dionysius II (his son), 93–5, 97–101, 103–5
Dionysius of Halicarnassus (historian), 7, 88, 156
Docks, dockyards, 8, 25, 68, 81, 90–1, 140, 151, 167
Dorieus (Spartan prince), 23, 36, 41, 44–7, 60
Drachma (Greek money unit), 30, 51
Drepana, 90–1, 168–7
Ducetius (Sicel leader), 53, 88

Ebro river, 183–5
Ebusus (Ibiza), 13, 35
Echetla, 157, 218
Eclipses, 94, 125–6

Ecnomus, Mount (near Gela), 123–4, 151
Eel-fishing (mercenaries), 102–103
Egypt, Egyptians, 9, 14, 18, 75, 112, 115, 127, 129, 132–3, 137, 157
Elephants, 19, 31, 153–4, 169–70, 172, 174–5, 181–2, 184
Elishat, *see* Dido
Elissa, *see* Dido
Elymians, 19–20, 35, 37, 44–5, 53, 56, 64, 96
Emporia (region), 172
Engyum (Sicily), 95, 105, 108
Enna, 20, 67, 77–9, 84, 97, 116, 140, 151, 154, 156, 159
Entella, 20, 68, 70–1, 88, 90, 95–7, 106, 108, 114, 150
Epaminondas (Greek general), 89
Ephorus (historian), 4–5, 29, 57, 60, 71, 163
Epicydes (Punic Syracusan), 10, 188
Epikrateia (Punic Sicily), 45–6, 53, 55, 58–60, 67–8, 70–2, 77, 79–82, 86, 88, 90–2, 94–5, 97–8, 103–104, 106, 108–109, 112, 114–19, 121–3, 126, 135, 140, 144–6, 151, 153–6, 159, 165, 167, 179, 180, 187, 190
Epipolae (Syracuse), 74, 76, 99–100, 102, 134–5
Erymnon (mercenary officer), 125, 133
Eryx (city and mountain), 20, 35–6, 41, 44, 61, 70, 72, 90, 106, 154, 167
Eshmun (deity), 2, 8, 89
Eshmunhalos (Greek 'Synalus'), 10, 94

Eshmuniaton (Greek 'Suniatus'), 89–90, 93, 164
Etna, Mount, 46, 68, 73, 77, 97
Etruria, Etruscans, 14, 21, 38, 42–3, 52, 81, 127
Eucleides (Corinthian officer), 101
Eumachus (military officer), 141–2, 164
Euryalus (Syracusan fortress), 67, 99, 102, 135

Fabius Pictor (Roman historian), 183
Fair Cape (Cape Bon or Cape Farina), 42, 53
Flaubert, Gustave, 5
Fleets
    Carthaginian, 1, 16, 23–5, 27, 29, 48–9, 58, 71–6, 78, 83, 88, 91, 98–101, 126–7, 152–3, 156, 166, 191–2
    Syracusan and others, 56, 62, 70, 75, 90, 121, 126–7, 137, 139, 149, 154–5, 167, 172
Fortifications, 8, 31, 74, 118, 124, 128, 131, 134, 176

Gades (Cádiz), 7, 13, 180–1
Galaria, 97, 122–3
Gaul(s), 4, 21, 26, 47, 83, 107, 127, 169, 183
Gela, 19–20, 37, 46, 56, 62–4, 95, 114, 116, 119–20, 123–4, 126, 140, 145, 147, 150
Gelon (tyrant of Gela and Syracuse), 6, 20, 41, 46–52, 57–8, 64, 68, 74, 81, 157
Gisco (3rd century general), 167–8, 172

Gisco (son of 'king' Hamilcar), 40, 52, 55–6, 61, 64, 95, 112–15, 117, 121–3, 138, 146
Goblets (Carthaginian officers'), 27, 62
Great Harbour (Syracuse), 70, 73–4, 76, 97, 99, 101, 122, 126, 152–3, 189, 191
Gunzuzi (*pagus*), 164, 174

Hadrumetum (Sousse, Tunisia), 9, 15, 18, 28, 131–2, 136, 142
Halaesa, 158, 206
Halicyae, 56, 70, 72, 90, 106, 154, 156
Halycus river (Platani), 87–8, 113–14, 146
Hamilcar ('Barca', Carthaginian leader), 4, 6, 10, 15, 27, 167–84
Hamilcar 'the king' (leader in 480), 6, 10, 26, 33, 37, 39–41, 43–9, 51, 52, 54–9, 72
Hamilcar (general against Agathocles), 141
Hamilcar (general in Libya), 165
Hamilcar (general in 318–314), 115, 117–22, 138, 145
Hamilcar (general in 341–340), 104, 108–109, 111
Hamilcar (son of Gisco; general in 314–309), 122–6, 128, 130, 132–5, 139, 146, 147
Hannabaal (priestess of Kore), 15
Hannibal (enemy of Rome), 4, 6, 10–11, 15–16, 27–8, 53, 69, 174, 179–80, 182, 183–5, 188, 190, 192
Hannibal (general in Sicily, in 264), 158–9

Hannibal (general in Truceless War), 173, 176
Hannibal (son of Gisco, general 410–405), 12, 55–61, 64–5, 91, 94, 162

Hanno (5th–century general; same as Hanno 'the king'?), 54, 89
Hanno (general against Agathocles), 128–30, 141–3, 149
Hanno (general in Sardinia, 240/239), 171
Hanno (general in Sicily, 264), 159–60
Hanno (general against Timoleon), 96, 100–102, 104, 106, 110
Hanno (Magonid general, 368), 83, 89–91
Hanno 'the Great' (3rd century leader), 28, 166–70, 172–3, 177–8
Hanno 'the Great' (4th century plotter), 89, 93, 95, 103, 112, 114, 128, 138, 164, 166
Hanno 'the king' (*Periplus* author; same as Hanno 'Sabellus'?), 1, 3, 10, 162, 192
Hanno (in Plautus, *Poenulus*), 5–6
Harbours, enclosed (at Carthage), 8, 25, 32
Hasdrubal (founder of New Carthage), 8, 178–9, 181–4
Hasdrubal (general in 341–340), 104, 108–12
Hasdrubal (grandson of Mago, late 6th century), 40, 52
Hecatompylus, *see* Theveste
Helice (Spain), 181
Helorus (near Syracuse), 100, 158
Heraclea (Dorieus' Sicilian foundation), 44
Heraclea Minoa, 19, 46, 61, 88, 94, 114, 120, 140, 145
Heracleides (son of Agathocles), 126, 144
Heracleides (tyrant of Leontini), 150–2
Herbessus, 67, 140
Herbita, 67, 116
Hermandica (Salamanca), 184
Hermocrates (Syracusan leader), 54, 59, 62
Herodotus, 1, 3, 6, 13, 37–8, 40–1, 44, 47–9, 188
Hicetas (tyrant of Syracuse, 3rd century), 150–1, 188, 190–91
Hicetas (tyrant of Syracuse, 4th century), 94–105, 108, 112–13
Hiero (king of Syracuse), 75, 157–60, 167, 171–2, 180
Hieron (tyrant of Syracuse and Acragas), 52, 64
Himera (city), 19–20, 37, 40, 43, 46–9, 51–3, 56–9, 64, 92, 188
see also Thermae Himeraeae
Himeras (river near Gela), 62, 123, 125, 147
Himeras (river near Panormus), 114, 146
Himilco (general against Agathocles), 142–3, 149
Himilco/Iomilkos (at Delos), 11
Himilco (Magonid leader, late 5th century), 10–12, 27, 41, 54–5, 57, 60–5, 69–78, 85–7, 89–91, 130, 134, 162–3, 189–90

Himilco (seafarer), 13, 192
Himilco (son of Mago, general against Dionysius I) 85–7, 89–91
Hipparinus (father-in-law of Dionysius I), 63, 74, 91
Hippocrates (tyrant of Gela), 46
Hippocrates (Punic Syracusan, 3rd century), 10, 188
Hippon (tyrant of Rhegium), 105, 113
Hipponium (Italy), 80, 83–4, 88–9, 163, 188
Hippo Regius (Anaba), 141, 164
Hippou Acra (Bizerte), 15, 18, 24, 35, 139, 142, 147, 169–72, 177–8

Iberia, Iberians, 26, 29–30, 47, 57, 60, 62, 71, 75, 89, 107, 178, 180–2, 184
see also Spain
Ietae (Monte Iato), 113, 154
Indemnity, 51, 87, 179
Indortes (Spanish leader), 180
Inscriptions, 1–2, 9–12, 14–17, 30, 56–7, 60, 64, 77, 111, 118, 164, 170
Isias (Corinthian officer), 102
Isocrates (Greek writer), 12
Istolatius (Spanish leader), 180
Issa (Dalmatia), 81

Jebel Bou Kornine (mountain), 128, 175
Julius Caesar, 2–3, 5, 33
Justin (epitomator of Pompeius Trogus), 4–5, 10, 16, 26, 33–5, 37–42, 44–5, 52, 54–5, 76, 83, 89, 93, 115, 117–18, 120–1, 125–6, 128–9, 138, 144, 161, 164

Khroumerie (mountains), 165, 173–4
Kore–Persephone (goddess), 9, 15, 74, 127, 163, 189
Kronia (coin–legend), 86, 209

Latomiae (Cape Bon), 127–8, 132
Leonidas (Spartan king), 5, 40–1
Leontini, 19, 55, 63–4, 67, 73, 81, 95–5, 100, 102–103, 105, 118, 124, 140, 149–52, 154, 158
Lepcis (Magna), 41, 60, 172
Leptines (Dionysius I's brother), 70–5, 81, 84, 87
Leptines (tyrant of Agyrium), 95, 105
Leptines (Agathocles' lieutenant), 140
Leptines (Syracusan leader, 3rd century), 157
Leptis (Minor; Lamta), 18, 177
Leukos Tynes (near Carthage), 127–30, 132, 143
Libya, Libyans, *passim*
Libyphoenicians, 18, 25, 27, 45, 60, 67, 78, 89, 131, 178
Liguria, Ligurians, 26, 35, 47, 107
Lilybaeum, 58, 73, 86, 90, 108, 111, 119, 122, 126, 154–5, 159, 166–7, 181
Lipara (island), 35, 73, 159
Lissus (Illyria), 81
Locri (Italy), 68, 74, 80–1, 83–4, 88, 94, 101
Longanus river, 158
Lotus fruit, 137
Lucanians, 21, 80, 84, 88, 93

Macae (African people), 41, 60
Mago (6th–century leader), 39–44
Mago (admiral in 279), 152

Mago (agricultural writer), 6, 15, 192
Mago (general against Dionysius I), 77–80, 82–90, 147, 163, 173, 182
Mago (general against Timoleon), 96–104, 107–8, 153
Malaca (Spain), 13
Malchus (Mazeus), 17, 26, 33–41, 44, 54, 93, 125, 161, 190
Mamercus/Marcus (tyrant of Catana), 94, 98–100, 105, 108, 112–13
Mamertines, 150, 152–9
Marcellus (Roman general, 3rd century), 74, 76
Masinissa (Numidian king), 10, 189
Massacres, slaughter, 54, 56, 58, 64, 68, 71, 75, 101, 118, 139, 112, 124–5, 136, 140, 143, 146, 171–2, 175–6, 180
Massilia, 1, 35–6, 53
Massyli (Numidian people), 165, 170, 177
Mastia 'of the Tarseians' (Spain), 180, 182
  see also New Carthage
Mathos (Truceless War rebel leader), 168–70, 173–9
Mauretania, Mauretanians, 54, 60, 162, 189
Mazara (Sicily), 154, 218
Megalepolis (Uthina), 127
Megara (headland outside Carthage), 7–8, 31, 138
Megara Hyblaea (Sicily), 19, 157
Mehashbim (Carthaginian officials), 12, 26
Melqart (city-god of Tyre and Carthage), 9, 17, 34, 40, 115

Menae (Minio, Sicily), 88, 100
Menon, 150
Mercenaries, 5, 20, 25–8, 30–2, 36, 44, 46, 49, 51, 57–61, 63, 67–9, 71, 73–5, 77–80, 84, 89–90, 94–6, 98, 100–3, 105–9, 112–13, 117, 121, 123, 125, 127, 132, 138–9, 142–3, 149–52, 157–8, 168–71, 173, 179–80, 191
Mercenaries' War, *see* Truceless War
Merchants,
  Carthaginian, 6, 8, 13, 15, 16, 38, 42, 70, 75, 191–2
  Others, 5, 14–16, 25, 42–3, 73, 119, 122, 124, 136–7, 171, 189
Messana, Messanians, 19–20, 43, 46, 56, 64, 67, 73, 77–8, 82, 97–9, 102, 105, 108, 113–14, 116, 119–22, 124–5, 144, 150, 152, 158–60, 167, 188
Messina, Strait of, 35, 78, 123, 126, 156, 192
Metapontum (Italy), 84, 97
Motya (Sicily), 14, 35, 44, 47, 52, 58–9, 61–2, 68–73, 82, 92, 191
Mylae, 19, 113, 119, 158
Myttistratum, 156

Naravas (Numidian prince), 10, 170, 173–5, 177
Naro (Hammam Lif), 128
Nauarchos (Greek, 'admiral'), 85–6, 121
Navy,
  Carthaginian, 15, 23–5, 36, 72, 74, 90, 96, 103, 122–3, 146, 152, 166, 169, 183, 190–1

see also fleets
Other, 42, 49, 56, 81, 83–4, 88, 90, 103, 120, 126, 140, 149, 156, 166, 183, 191
Syracusan, 68, 90, 97, 123, 134, 140, 151, 153, 191
see also fleets
Naxos (Sicily), 19, 64–5, 67, 81
Neapolis (Nabeul, Tunisia), 8, 44, 127, 131–2, 135–6, 142
Neapolis (quarter of Syracuse), 98, 102
Neon (Corinthian officer), 101–2
Nepheris (city), 142
New Carthage (Cartagena), 8, 180, 182–5
Nicodemus (tyrant), 95, 105
Notum (Sicily), 100, 158
'Nomads', see Zouphones
Nrwt, see Naravas
Numidia, Numidians, 6, 10, 18–19, 26, 29–30, 54, 60, 141, 161–2, 165, 167, 170, 173, 175, 177, 181, 189

Olcades (Spanish people), 184
Olives (Acragas), 14, 54
Olympieum, see Zeus, temple of
One Hundred and Four, the (council and court), 3, 11–12, 54–5, 104
Ophellas (Macedonian general), 115, 132, 137, 139, 142, 144, 146
Orissi (Spanish people), 181
Orosius (historian), 6, 33–4, 129
Ortygia (the Nesus, island centre of Syracuse), 67–8, 76, 94, 97–102, 104, 151, 154

Panormus, 14, 19, 35, 44, 46–8, 55, 59, 61–2, 68, 70–2, 74, 77, 84, 86–7, 91, 113–14, 119, 122, 126, 145, 150, 154, 167
Parian Marble, 2, 118
Pasiphilus (Agathocles' general), 122, 140, 144, 146
Pausanias (Greek travel writer), 45
Pay (army and navy), 2, 5, 27, 29–30, 34–5, 61, 63, 105–6, 108, 136, 144, 157, 168
Pentarchies (Carthaginian), 3, 12
Pentathlus (Greek adventurer), 35–6, 41
Penteconters (warships), 23–4, 122
Pericles, 3, 6, 183
Periplus of Hanno, 1, 10, 13, 33, 162, 192
Persephone (goddess), see Kore–Persephone
Persian empire, 23, 30, 34, 36, 38, 40, 48, 72, 96, 115
Phalaris (tyrant of Acragas), 20, 30, 37, 39, 62
his brazen bull, 20, 30
Phalarium (fortress), 123–4
Pharacidas (Spartan officer), 72, 74–6
Philinus (Acragantine historian), 157
Philistus (Syracusan politician, historian), 4, 63, 71, 75, 81, 87, 93–4, 117
Phintias (tyrant and city), 150–1
Phocaea, Phocaeans, 13, 19, 21, 23, 34, 36, 38, 81, 187
Phoenicia, Phoenicians (including western colonies), 2, 7–10, 12–14, 18–20, 33, 35–8, 41,

43–5, 47, 52, 59–60, 64, 90–1, 95, 157, 169, 180, 188–9
Phoenician (language), 2, 8, 12, 14, 33, 44, 167
Pindar, 37, 52
Plague, 9, 61–2, 64–5, 69, 78, 89–90, 92–3, 134, 161, 163–4, 189–90
Plato, 5, 81, 93–5, 188
Pliny the Elder (encyclopaedist), 13
Plunder, *see* Booty, plunder
Plutarch (biographer), 4–6, 46, 91, 94, 96, 98–110, 112–13, 116, 154–5
Poenulus (Plautus' comedy), 5–6
Polyaenus (Greek author), 6, 81, 84–7, 107, 112, 115, 124
Polybius (historian), 5–6, 11–12, 15, 25, 29, 31, 42, 157–9, 164–6, 168–84, 190
Polyxenus (Dionysius I's brother-in-law), 74
Pompeius Trogus (historian), 4, 34, 40–1, 54, 83, 89, 138, 161, 164, 180
Population, Carthaginian, 8–9, 15, 17, 36, 53, 64
Population, Roman (3rd century), 17
Priests and priestesses, Carthaginian, 3, 12, 15, 33–4, 38–9, 40, 52, 134–5, 163
Prisoners of war, *see* Captives
Ptolemy I (king of Egypt), 115, 137
Ptolemy II, 157
Pygmalion (king of Tyre), 7–8
Pyrgi (Etruria), 43, 81
Pyrrhus (king of Epirus), 5, 38, 149–58, 187, 192

Quadrireme(s), 24, 68
Qart–hadasht (Punic, 'New City'), 44, 182
Quinquereme(s), 24–5, 68, 81, 166

Rab, rabim ('chief(s)', Punic title), 11–12, 16, 64, 192
Rams (warships), 23–4, 57, 126, 133
Rebellions, revolts, 15, 25, 27, 33, 69, 76–7, 81, 89, 92, 103, 106, 162–5, 168–9, 177, 189
see also Truceless War
Rhegium, 20–1, 37, 43, 55, 67, 77–8, 80–1, 83–4, 88, 93, 97, 102, 116–17, 150, 152, 158, 188
Rio Tinto (Spain), 180
Rome, Romans, 1–12, 14–18, 21, 24–34, 37, 39, 41–3, 45, 69, 73–4, 77, 80, 83, 108, 115–16, 128, 130, 132, 141, 150, 152–62, 164–9, 171–2, 174, 178–185, 187–192

Sacking of cities, 2, 9, 21, 30, 56, 58, 62–3, 83, 91, 106, 115
Sacred Corps/Band (*hieros lochos*), 27–8, 107, 110–11, 129
Salammbô (novel), 5
Sallust (historian), 5
Samnites, 21, 127
Samos (island), 13, 23, 39
Sardinia, Sardinians, 8, 13, 17, 20–1, 26, 30, 33–4, 38–9, 42–4, 47–8, 60, 74, 78, 89, 94, 107, 149, 163–4, 170–1, 179, 189, 191
Saw, The (Prion), 175, 177
Scipio Aemilianus, 30, 32
Scipio Africanus, 10, 172, 178

Scylletium (Italy), 88
Segesta (Aegesta, Egesta), 20, 35, 38, 44–5, 52, 55, 56–8, 68, 70–2, 88, 90, 96, 106, 140, 145, 154, 156, 166
Selinus, 19–20, 30, 35, 38, 43, 45–9, 51–2, 55–9, 61, 64, 69–70, 82, 87–8, 90, 92, 114, 116, 120, 140, 145, 154, 188
Senate (Carthaginian), *see Adirim*
Shrines, *see* Temples and shrines
Sicani, Sicans, 19, 53, 57–8, 64, 72, 88
Sicca (El Kef), 166, 168
Sicels, 53, 57–8, 64, 72, 80, 88, 91, 96, 106–107, 117–20, 145–6, 156
  see also Siculi
Sicily, Sicilians, *passim*
Siculi, 19
Siege towers (*helepoleis*), siege engines, 58, 61, 68, 71, 139, 173
Sierra Morena (Spain), 181
Siliana river, 15, 141
Sirte (Gulf of), 14, 127
Six Hundred (Syracusan oligarchs), 116–18
Slaughter, *see* Massacres
Slaves, slavery, 15–17, 30, 38, 50, 58, 61, 64, 67, 70–1, 73, 76, 79–81, 91, 114, 116, 125, 127, 144–5, 163, 168, 175, 181, 192
Smallpox, 75
Solous (Soluntum), 14, 35, 70, 77–8, 88, 144
Sosistratus (tyrant of Syracuse, 3rd century), 151–6

Sostratus (Syracusan leader), 117, 120
Sosylus (Greek author), 1, 24–5
Spain, Spaniards, 7–8, 13, 15, 35–6, 51, 53, 179–83, 185, 189–91
  see also Iberia
Sparta, 1, 5, 12, 19, 23, 36, 40–2, 45, 55, 61–2, 72, 83, 88–9, 119–20, 191
Spendius (rebel leader), 168–70, 174–6
Storms, 48, 102, 110, 122–3, 137, 172
Strabo (geographer), 6, 13, 17, 18, 88, 132
Strategos, strategos autokrator 63, 112, 118–19, 182
Sufes, sufetes, 11, 15, 17, 40, 44, 52, 56, 64, 71, 82, 112, 119, 168
Suniatus, *see* Eshmuniaton
Synalus, *see* Eshmunhalos

Tagus river, 182, 184–5
Talent (Greek money unit: 6,000 drachmas), 51, 62, 73, 75, 81, 87–8, 119, 144–5, 165, 167, 171, 179
Tanit (Carthaginian goddess), 9
Tarentum, 21, 81, 84, 119, 152–3, 156
Tauromenium, 73, 77, 80, 95, 97, 101–102, 122, 124, 150, 153–4, 158
Taxes, 18, 37, 45, 54, 59, 64, 164, 166
  see also Tribute
Telemachus (Corinthian officer), 101
Temples and shrines, 1–3, 8–9, 43, 50, 51, 55, 58, 62, 71, 74–6, 81, 111, 118, 124, 134, 163
Terias river (near Catana), 151

Terillus (tyrant of Himera), 20, 37, 43, 46–8, 188
Thapsus, 15, 131–2
Thargelion (Athenian calendar month, May–June) ,109
Tharros (Sardinia), 13, 20, 38, 44
Thearidas (brother of Dionysius I), 84
Thefarie Velianas (king of Caere), 43, 81
Themistocles (Athenian leader), 6, 183
Theocritus (poet), 157
Theodorus (Syracusan), 45
Theophrastus (writer), 41
Thermae Himeraeae, 59, 61, 68, 82, 88, 114, 117, 120, 140, 145
  see also Himera
Theron (tyrant of Acragas), 46–9, 51–2, 62
Theveste (Tébessa), 166
Thoenon (tyrant of Syracuse, 3rd century), 151–2, 155, 157
Thrasius (mutineer), 108, 112
Thuburbo Minus (west of Carthage), 173
Thuburbo (south–east of Carthage), 142
Thucydides (historian), 36, 82
Thugga, 141–2, 164, 169–70
Thurii, 81, 83–4, 102, 211
Thusca (*pagus*), 164
Timaeus (historian), 4–5, 7, 57, 60, 71, 95, 133, 145, 158, 163
Timoleon (liberator), 4–5, 9, 27–8, 95–114, 116–17, 119–20, 145, 150, 153, 184, 188, 190–1
Timonides (writer), 94
Tipasa (Numidia), 13, 162
Tocae, *see* Thugga

Torture (of prisoners and enemies), 58, 70, 135, 138, 145, 176, 178, 180–1
Trade, traders, 5, 7–8, 13–14, 18, 21, 25, 35–6 42–3, 46, 53, 67, 69, 140, 159, 169, 171, 180, 188–9
Tribute, 15, 37, 45 82, 161–2, 166, 181
  see also taxes
Trierarchos (Greek, 'admiral'), 179, 192
  see also nauarchos
Trireme(s), 23–5, 48, 58, 60–3, 68, 70–1, 75–6, 81, 83, 88, 90–1, 97, 107, 122–3, 126, 140
Trogilus (Syracuse), 76
Trogus, *see* Pompeius
Truceless War, 5, 32, 130, 165, 169, 171, 174, 177–8, 190
Tunes (Tunis), 31, 127, 129–33, 133, 135–7, 141–3, 147, 163, 168–74, 176–7, 179
Tyndarion (tyrant of Tauromenium), 150, 153
Tyndaris (Tindari), 77–8, 86, 98
Tyrants, 4, 9, 20, 24, 37, 43, 45–7, 63–4, 67, 70–4, 79–83, 85–91, 94–6, 98, 101, 103–105, 113, 118, 120–2, 125–8, 131, 138, 140, 144–7, 151, 153, 157, 164, 187
Tyre, 7–9, 14, 34, 38, 115, 130

Ustica (island), 31
Uthina (Megalepolis), 127, 136, 142, 174, 215
Utica, 15, 18, 24, 35, 139, 142, 147, 169–72, 177–8, 217

Vaccaei (Spanish people), 184
Venice, Veneto, 14–15, 81

Walls, Carthage's, 8, 31–2, 53,
 130–1, 138, 143, 169, 173–4
Weapons, 27–9, 44, 68, 77, 111,
 130, 154

Xenodicus (Acragantine general),
 140
Xenophon (historian), 57, 60

Xerxes (king of Persia), 3, 41,
 47–9, 57

Zaghouan (mountain range), 34,
 131, 161–2, 170, 175
Zancle, *see* Messana
Zarzas (rebel leader), 174–5
Zeus, temple of (Syracuse),
 74–6, 134
Zouphones (Numidian people),
 136, 147